Advance Praise for *The Blood of Lambs*

"*Kamal Saleem is a courageous man. In* The Blood of Lambs, *he chronicles his incredible life as an Islamic terrorist and gives readers an inside look at the cruel world of terrorism and the threat it poses to democracy. Kamal's riveting story is a must read. Thanks, Kamal, for telling the world the truth about terrorism and your new life of faith.*"

—*LTG (Ret.) William G. Boykin,* Former Commander
of U.S. Army Special Forces and Founding Member of Delta

"*Many Americans are oblivious to the threat that exists within our own borders from radical jihadists. By highlighting some of the motivations and tactics used by our enemies, this book will serve as a clarion call for the great struggle that America will face for many years to come.*"

—*Major General Bentley Rayburn,* USAF (Ret.),
former Commandant of the Air War College

"The Blood of Lambs *is a book that all Americans who love truth and freedom should read. Using guile, patience, intimidation, and violence, Islamic fundamentalists are trying to replace the U.S. Constitution with Sharia Islamic law. Kamal is one of the few brave former terrorists telling the truths that most wish to close their eyes and ears to. I commend Kamal in his work to wake up America.*"

—*Walid Shoebat,* Former Islamic terrorist,
speaker and author of *Why I Left Jihad* and *Why We Want to Kill You*

"*Kamal Saleem was a highly trained, efficient killer—a dedicated Islamic terrorist who wanted to see America and Israel destroyed. But today, he is risking his life by telling his secrets and laying his life bare. Kamal is now a professed Christian, trying to live a normal, American life. He has grown to love his adopted country and wants to see it protected from radical Islam. You have never read a book like* The Blood of Lambs. *Kamal is one of the boldest and most courageous men that I have ever met. He has a message that you need to hear.*"

—*James Fitzgerald, Jr.,* Producer, ColdWater Media, Inc.

THE BLOOD OF LAMBS

A Former Terrorist's Memoir

of Death and Redemption

KAMAL SALEEM

WITH LYNN VINCENT

HOWARD BOOKS
A DIVISION OF SIMON & SCHUSTER

NEW YORK LONDON TORONTO SYDNEY

Our purpose at Howard Books is to:
- *Increase faith* in the hearts of growing Christians
- *Inspire holiness* in the lives of believers
- *Instill hope* in the hearts of struggling people everywhere

Because He's coming again!

 **HOWARD BOOKS**
A DIVISION OF SIMON & SCHUSTER

Published by Howard Books, a division of Simon & Schuster, Inc.
1230 Avenue of the Americas, New York, NY 10020
www.howardpublishing.com

The Blood of Lambs © 2009 Arise Enterprises, LLC

Published in association with the literary agency of Alive Communications, Inc.,
7680 Goddard Street, Suite 200, Colorado Springs, CO 80920,
www.alivecommunications.com

Library of Congress Cataloging-in-Publication Data is available.
ISBN-13: 978-1-4165-7780-5
ISBN-10:   1-4165-7780-7

10 9 8 7 6 5 4 3 2

Manufactured in the United States of America

For information regarding special discounts for bulk purchases,
please contact: Simon & Schuster Special Sales at
1-866-506-1949 or business@simonandschuster.com.

Cover design by Cherlynne Li
Interior design by Jaime Putorti
Photography/illustrations by Frank Veronsky

Many names have been changed in an effort to protect the privacy and/or ensure the
safety of individuals included in these memoirs.

You once said to me,
"God has something special planned for your future."
That something special was you, my dear wife.

When I was thirsty, you gave me drink.
When I was hungry, you fed me—
not lies
not hate
not cruelty
just love.

Your love has brought healing to that young boy who cried out
on the rooftop, in his secret place, and on the sea cliffs.
The boy who learned to love hate and dream murder is no longer.

Victoria, you are my new dreaming window.
And the boy in the man still looks out and dreams,
but now only of loving you.

Nothing can separate us.

Contents

*I came to have this new power, the "power of two"—
the Koran in one hand and the gun in the other.
One equipped me spiritually and one physically.
One spoke into my life, and one spoke into
the lives of others.*

Kamal Saleem

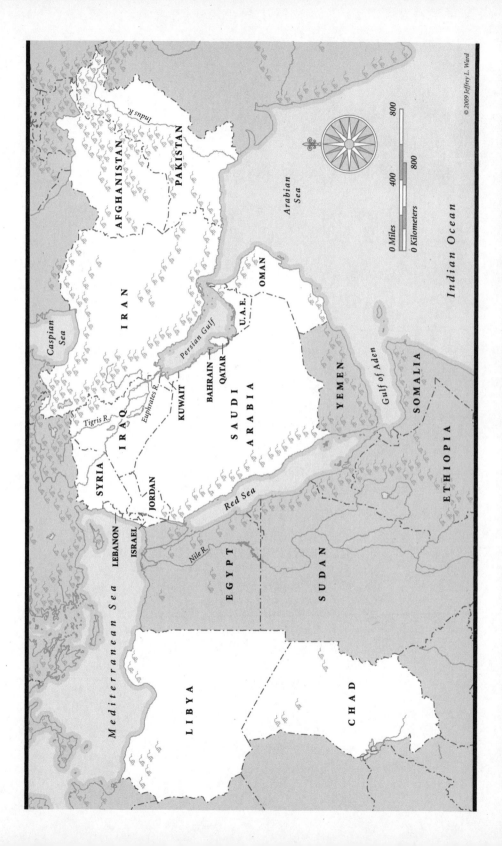

Chino, California
2007

1

Leaving the auditorium, we rolled through Southern California sunshine in a pair of black Yukons. Zakariah in the rear vehicle, me in the lead, and six 9 mm handguns between the two. People born in this country might not think weapons are necessary when returning from a speaking engagement. I know differently. When I was with the PLO, our special unit assassinated a grand imam on his way home from leading evening prayer.

Five minutes to the hotel. The security men riding with us were off-duty law enforcement and antiterrorist agents—six locals, each with a Sig Sauer or Glock concealed beneath his plain shirt or jacket. Back at the venue, Jack, our host, had introduced these men only by first name.

"Kamal, this is John," Jack said to me as we stood in a huge empty auditorium built on an oasis campus of palm and trickling fountains that reminded me of a safe house villa where I had once hidden in Spain. "He'll be heading up security for you this afternoon."

About three dozen men in plainclothes gathered loosely around me, Zakariah, and our friend Walid, waiting to be assigned their posts. Four plainclothes policemen stood in the background. An unusual amount of armed security for three civilians, but certain jihadists were growing tired of our little road show. Already Walid had been threatened dozens of times. Zak had been severely beaten twice and once almost beheaded. He had moved six times in six years—once out of the country—to protect his family from those who wished to silence him.

Blond and blue-eyed, John shook my hand with a firm grip and looked me in the eye. "While you're speaking, I'll be standing right beside you," he said, his muscled frame squaring the shoulders of his sport jacket. I guessed him to be off-duty SWAT. "If anything happens, run straight toward me. I'll get you out."

I believed him.

Now, three minutes from the hotel, John sat beside me in the Yukon's leather backseat, talking quietly over the headrest with a dark-haired agent whose large head nearly scraped the roof over the passenger seat. Outside the window to my right, I saw planned communities and business districts skating by. I wondered how Zak liked the scenery in California and whether Walid had made his plane on time. When the driver stopped at a traffic light, John's low murmuring also stopped as each agent scanned the area. But the only movement was to our left, in a small, pine-shaded park with kids on swings. Two women watched them from a park bench, laughing.

Sleeping, I thought. *Sleeping through an invasion that is already underway.*

Zak, Walid, and I had delivered our message to an audience of three thousand. People filled the overflow rooms and even sat outside on the stamped-concrete terraces, listening on loudspeakers. Zak, a Koran scholar who had once assassinated a man by flinging him from a Lebanese rooftop, explained the theology of *jihad*. Walid, a Bethlehem-born, former terrorist who was now a U.S. citizen, discussed Islamic-Jewish hatred. I told the audience how I had been recruited into the Muslim Brotherhood at age seven and how at age twenty-three I had crossed the Atlantic, on a mission to destroy America from the inside out.

All three of us had abandoned *jihad*, each for a different reason and by a different road. When we finished telling our stories, the audience rose and showered us with waterfalls of applause. For a moment, my heart was glad. But I also knew most would drive off and discuss the "3 Ex-Terrorists" over lunch or Starbucks. Then they would rejoin the national slumber, the comfortable sleep of prosperity.

They would not remember what I had told them about *Al-Anfâl*—Koran, Sura 8, "The Spoils of War"—in which Allah counsels his warriors to be patient. Or that I had told them the invaders had already breached America's borders and were spreading. Silently. Lethally. Like a cancer.

In the Yukon, we rolled again. After several blocks, the driver turned in at a hotel where Zak and I had checked in the day before. As the driver glided past the glassed lobby, I froze.

Two men standing on the sidewalk locked eyes with me. One was Middle Eastern. The other looked Pakistani. Both carried canvas tote bags—not luggage. Both men bolted through the sliding glass doors into the lobby. Inside, a half-dozen more men rose from their seats.

Instantly, my muscles tensed for battle, heart thumping, hands tingling.

The men with tote bags nodded in our direction.

John spotted them. "Code Red," he said. "That's a Code Red!"

The driver braked to a halt. On a handheld radio, John relayed the alert to the rear Yukon. I saw the two men striding rapidly out of the lobby and toward the hotel interior. Toward my room.

It had been more than twenty years since my last armed mission, but my right hand now screamed for the familiar, comforting weight of a gun.

John turned sharply to me: "Stay here. Do not leave this vehicle." Then, to the agent up front: "Let's move."

Weapons already drawn, each man chambered a 9 mm round, kicked open his door, and jumped to the pavement. Glancing behind me, I saw two more agents spill from Zak's vehicle. John and a man from the rear vehicle jogged into the lobby, holding their weapons beside their legs.

Hotel guests backed away with wide, frightened eyes. John and the other agent scanned the room and in four long strides reached the lobby desk. I could see a young woman behind it talking with him and pointing.

The other agents fanned out in the parking lot, feeling the hoods of cars, checking for recent arrivals. I watched as they read license plate numbers into their radios.

I did not like my exposed position. Looking up, I could see row after row of hotel windows with direct lines of sight to the Yukon roofs. The men had dispersed *into*, not out of, the hotel. I flashed back to Lebanon. How many times had I fired an RPG from elevation and watched a vehicle below erupt into shrapnel and flame?

This could be it.

When somebody runs from you in a war, it does not mean they are afraid of you. What preparations are they running *toward*? What button are they running to push? Who is lying in wait? In urban warfare, if you cannot take cover, sometimes the smartest move is aggression. I itched to burst out of the Yukon and join the hunt.

Head swiveling, I scanned the windows, the parking lot, the lobby. My mind whirled and I tensed, half expecting the searing whine of an incoming RPG, something that had not been seen in the streets of America. Yet.

But then, until 2001, America—my adopted country—had not seen jets used as missiles. Until 2001, she had never seen skyscrapers dissolve into avalanches. She had never seen thousands of innocent civilians murdered at once. Yet even with the horrific impact of 9/11, America did not understand what I *knew*: that the invasion was on. The enemy already lurked inside her walls, the cancer of *jihad* seething through her inner cities, her prisons, her small, sleepy towns. And while the cancer ate and ate, metastasizing in the intellectual centers, the elite stood on the ramparts screaming, "Peace! Peace!" They closed their eyes, willfully blind, accomplices in the rape of their own nation.

I knew because I had helped to cause it. I had *planned* it. I came here, funded by Islamists in the Arab countries, willing to die for this glorious invasion. To someday see blood running in American streets.

2

Twenty minutes passed before John and his agents returned to the Yukon outside the Holiday Inn. John opened the rear door, and I saw he had holstered his weapon.

"We checked the hotel, the public areas, the parking lots. No sign of them," he said. "No Middle Eastern names on the hotel register. They probably checked in under western names. We notified Chino PD, SWAT, and the FBI SAIC of suspicious activity."

SAIC. Special Agent in Charge. I knew the term well from staying off the FBI's radar in my former life.

"I called Jack," John said. "He thinks we should move you and Zak to another hotel."

I was tired from traveling, but unwilling to take chances. "Good idea."

John shut the Yukon door and walked back to the lobby to wait while the agent driving the Yukon pulled under the portico. Walking in the center of a knot of six agents, I passed through the lobby and down the first-floor corridor that ran off to the left. Now three agents moved ahead of me and three fell back.

We passed the open door of a travelers' business center on the left. Empty.

Then past a sitting room and a small gym with a glass door on the right. No one.

My room was next, on the left.

"It's open," one of the agents said, a tense whisper. "The door is open!"

Adrenaline surged through me. Sounds of cycling steel as all six agents drew their weapons and one man pushed me against the far wall. Two agents flattened themselves against the wall on each side of the door. John knelt before the door, gun raised. I felt naked and wished again for a weapon.

Hand and eye signals passed between the men. On a silent count, John rose up and kicked the door wide open.

Two agents knelt in the door frame, sweeping their weapons in a room-clearing arc. Two agents stood above.

Empty.

John crossed the carpet and checked the bathroom. He turned to us and shook his head. Nothing.

I was not so sure. My mind whirred, flipping back through what I would have done in the same situation. Rig the lamp switch with explosives? Lace the toothbrush with poison? Put a tank mine under a couch cushion?

"Touch nothing," I said.

3

John and his men listened as I quietly explained that in Fatah and the Palestinian Liberation Organization, when we missed our mark, we did not give up. Instead, we resorted to booby traps. As the security team looked on, I threw away all my toiletries, checked under my luggage for wires, stuffed in my robe and slippers, latched it, and walked out of the room.

An hour later, Zak and I were traveling across the city. The agents deposited us in a nameless hotel on the other side of Chino. Satisfied that we had not been followed, the security team swept the room and left. Now, sitting in an overstuffed chair facing the bolted door, I had time to think. I wondered if there was a Kamal, another me, among those Middle Easterners at the Holiday Inn. A man with a heart like I used to have, who would stop at nothing to fulfill his mission for Allah. A zealot whose very heart was a wick on which the flame of *jihad* burned.

If so, would I still be alive in the morning?

I stared at the back of the hotel-room door. How many had I seen since I came out from the shadows, since I revealed to my American wife my secret past, since I started speaking out against radical Islam?

Nearly thirty years before, empowered by the Muslim Brotherhood and the Palestinian Liberation Organization (PLO), I had come to America. From the Koranic teaching of my youth, I knew that by infiltrating the American education system, overrunning its universities and jails, and swarming its poor neighborhoods, my jihadist brothers and I could usher in *Umma*—one world under Islam. It would be, as Americans like to say, "a piece of cake."

I had worked odd jobs as cover only, since I was being well paid by Middle Eastern sheikhs. While on the jihadist side, I came to realize that the strength of the American people and infrastructure is also its weakness. An open society with constitutionally protected freedom of speech and religion, which prides itself on its embrace of foreign cultures, was the perfect place to teach a message of hatred in broad daylight. I was a master at reaching the poor and those who perceived themselves oppressed. I taught them that Allah cared for them. I found them jobs, mentored them, and invited them to fellowship with my jihadist brothers, who all the while never mentioned *jihad*. Once the converts were hooked, we turned them over to the imams at small "apartment mosques" to be radicalized.

Now, sitting in the hotel room, I knew I had introduced a deadly disease into an unsuspecting host. The human body does not know when a cancer is growing within. It hums happily along, seeming to function normally. Even when the immune system performs its routine protective scans, it does not recognize the cancer cell as a threat because the cell itself takes on the aspect of its neighbors, fooling the body for months and sometimes years. But over time, the cancer spreads and then becomes dominant, until finally it brings the host to the point of death.

So is radical Islam to America. Now I was speaking out against it. And apparently had become a target. Some might call it poetic: the cancer had circled back to one of its makers.

My mission could have ended today, I thought.

I thought about my wife, my children. What if they had been with me? What if there had been an attack? Should I stop? Should I stop telling America to wake up? To rise up and fight?

When I met my American wife, I was unprocessed, like the minerals in a rock. She saw something in me I did not know was there. Was it goodness? I did not think that was quite the right word. But she knew if she could chisel it out, if she could polish it, it might shine. I could not risk losing her. And yet she was the one who kept me going forward with my message.

"It's the right thing to do, Kamal," Victoria often said.

If she was not afraid, how could I be afraid? Yet I knew how deadly these people were. Their blood was darkness and they had no tears. They were not only willing to die, but *hoping* to die, to be ushered into the presence of Allah and the glorious rewards of *al-shaheed*, the martyrs.

On the clock beside the bed, red numbers flickered past. Throughout the long watch of the night, I stared at the door, certain that any moment the knob would silently turn.

Beirut, Lebanon
1963

1

It was at my mother's kitchen table, surrounded by the smells of herbed olive oils and pomegranates, that I first learned of *jihad*. Every day, my brothers and I gathered around the low table for *madrassa*, our lessons in Islam. I always tried to sit facing east, toward the window above the long marble sink where a huge tree with sweet white berries brushed against the window panes. Made of a warm, reddish wood, our table sat in the middle of the kitchen and was surrounded by *tesats*, small rugs that kept us off the cool tile. Mother sat at the head of the table and read to us from the Koran and also from the *hadith*, which records the wisdom and instruction of Allah's prophet, Muhammad.

Mother's Koran had a hard black cover etched ornately in gold and scarlet. Her grandfather had given the Book to her father, who had given it her. Even as a small boy I knew my mother and father were devout Sunni Muslims. So devout, in fact, that other Sunnis held themselves a little straighter in our family's presence. My mother never went out without her *hijab*, only her coffee-colored eyes peering above the cloth that shielded her face, which no man outside our family had ever seen. My father, respected in our mosque, earned an honest living as a blacksmith. He had learned the trade from my grandfather, a slim Turk who wore a red *fez*, walked with a limp, and cherished thick, cinnamon-laced coffee.

Each day at *madrassa*, Mother pulled her treasured Koran from a soft bag made of ivory cloth and when she opened it, the breath of its frail, aging pages floated down the table. Mother would read to us about the glory of Islam, about the good Muslims, and about what the Jews did to us. As a four-year-old boy, my favorite parts were the stories of war.

I vividly remember the day in *madrassa* when we heard the story of a merciless bandit who went about robbing caravans and killing innocent travelers. "This bandit was an evil, *evil* man," Mother said, spinning the tale as she sketched pictures of swords for us to color.

An evil bandit? She had my attention.

"One day, there was a great battle between the Jews and the sons of Islam," she went on. "The bandit decided to join the fight for the cause of Allah. He charged in on a great, black horse, sweeping his heavy sword left and right, cutting down the infidel warriors."

My eyes grew wider. I held my breath so as not to miss a word.

"The bandit fought bravely for Allah, killing several of the enemy until the sword of an infidel pierced the bandit's heart. He tumbled from his horse and died on the battlefield."

Disappointment deflated my chest. *What good is a story like that?*

I could hear children outside, shouting and playing. A breeze from the Mediterranean shimmered in the berry tree. Mother's *yaknah* simmered on the stove—green beans snapped fresh, cooked with olive oil, tomato, onion, and garlic. She would serve it cool that evening with pita bread, fresh mint, and cucumbers. My stomach rumbled.

"After the bandit died," Mother was saying in her storytelling voice, "his mother had a dream. In this dream, she saw her son sitting on the shore of an endless crystal river, surrounded by a multitude of women who were feeding him and tending to him."

I turned back toward Mother. Maybe this story was not so bad after all.

"The bandit's mother was an observant woman, obedient to her husband and to Allah and Muhammad," my mother said. "This woman knew her son was a robber and a murderer. 'How dare you be sitting here in paradise?' she scolded him. 'You don't belong here. You belong in hell!' But her son answered, 'I died for the glory of Allah and when I woke up, He welcomed me into *jannah*.' "

Paradise.

My mother swept her eyes around the kitchen table. "So you see, my sons, even the most sinful man is able to redeem himself with one drop of an infidel's blood."

2

Through one window of our flat in West Beirut, the blue Mediterranean smiled up at me, not more than two kilometers away. That was my dreaming window. From that cinderblock frame upon the world, I gazed across the rooftops where children played, old men smoked, and drying clothes flapped in the sunlight.

Even as a child, I knew the proud history of my country. My grandmother, Fatima, would tell me stories about the ancient coastal kingdoms and the peoples who used to line the shores of Lebanon, like the Phoenicians, the swarthy maritime traders in Tyre and Sidon. Although my country had been conquered many times, it was often under the siege of mighty warriors like Alexander the Great, a fact that always fired my boyhood imagination.

"Even the great King Nebuchadnezzar took thirteen years to conquer Lebanon," my grandmother once told me. I later learned that Lebanon had been annexed to Rome and conquered by France, but she always fought bravely and when beaten rose again.

To the modern ear, Beirut means war and smoking ruins. But the Beirut of my childhood was a lush jewel encircled in a green mountain embrace. Century after century, the tread of foreign feet had turned it into a seaside feast of cultures and religions. The Jews, the Christians, the Sunni and Shia Muslims, and the Druze all worshipped freely, in separate neighborhoods that melted one into another. In my neighborhood alone, I could see the imprint of many nations. Cafes sold filet mignon bordelaise, a French dish; Greek *baklava; shish tawook*, Turkish chicken on a skewer; and from America, Wimpy Burgers.

From my dreaming window I could see the hills by the seashore where my family went each spring to picnic in the fields. Mama would take scissors with her for cutting wild herbs while my brothers and I ran across the meadows flying brightly colored kites. From my window, I could also see white sailing ships sliding into port. I imagined the wealthy passengers: cream-suited gentlemen smoking fine cigars and fair-skinned ladies who smelled brazenly of musk and roses and did not cover their heads. If I passed such a woman in the streets, my mother taught me, I was to avert my eyes and hold my breath so that her sinful odor didn't spark sin of my own.

I thought about the tourists and the places they came from: Britain. Italy. Germany. France. When the cruise ships set sail again, their foghorns lowed, wooing me with an invitation. At night, as I lay awake with my brothers in our tiny living room, the salt breeze carried the sound in through my dreaming window. To me, it was the voice of the sea, vast and colossal where the moon touched the water, promising a freedom bigger than our three-room flat.

When you are a very small child, you do not know you are poor. Early on, when I had only four, and not ten, brothers and sisters, we were clean and well-fed. I did not think it was remarkable that we had only one bedroom for a family of seven, that we pulled out mattresses in the living room each night, arranged them like puzzle pieces for sleeping, and stuffed them away in a metal cabinet each morning. I did not notice that our only light was a naked bulb dangling from a wire attached to our high Lebanese ceiling, or how infrequently we ate meat, or how carefully my mother pressed the olives, sure to squeeze out every drop of oil.

I did not get to go outside in the street to play very often because Mother looked down on the "street" people and thought them of a lower class. But I loved the street kids; and the rare times she let me go out, I had the time of my life. My friends—Hisham, Marie, and my best friend Eli—and I played "Cowboys and Indians" and "Germans and Americans." The Germans and the Indians always won—our small revenge against the Americans, whom we had heard were generally a loud and dirty people.

My favorite game was "seven stones." The children broke into teams and stacked seven square stones in a tower. Each team rolled tennis balls at the tower to try and knock it over, and the team that knocked it over had to rebuild it before getting pinged out with more tennis balls. I loved that game, and a couple of times I snuck out of the house to play it while Mother was taking a nap.

That ended when I got caught. Mother beat me with a stout, knobby switch from a pomegranate tree. She used to order a stack of these from my Uncle Mahmoud every year. She kept them on a high shelf in the entry way, where we could see them every time we entered the house. The day I snuck out to play seven stones, she gave me the worst kind of beating—smacking the bottoms of my feet, each blow causing fire to light up in my brain. But my mother was fair in her judgment: if she beat one of us, she beat everyone. Her reasoning was that if one of us was doing a crime, the rest of us were thinking about doing it.

Whenever I scraped together a few *kroosh*, I gave the money to my brother and asked him to buy me comic books. Batman and Superman took me outside of *madrassa*, giving me a different window on life. I carried my treasures to my hiding place, an attic storage area above the bathroom, and escaped from the world for awhile. I also remember a book I had from Egypt about child spies, kids who knew how to decode phone numbers and who rode fast, powerful motorcycles. They were devastatingly clever: if they wanted to know someone's nationality, for example, they would watch to see which flag the person saluted.

I looked forward to the Muslim festivals, Adha and Ramadan. During Adha, people went on a pilgrimage to the mountains to make sacrifices for their sins. During Ramadan, we fasted for thirty days then celebrated like crazy for three. Before those celebrations, Mother baked all day long, kneading dough and mixing it in huge copper pots. All of us children helped, waking before sunrise to line up along the marble counter and around the low kitchen table.

"Kamal, crush these very finely," Mother would say, dumping a kilo of pistachio meats on the table before me. I loved helping in this way, the scent of nuts and dough and pastry glazes wrapping around me like a comforting blanket. Amira, my oldest sister, chopping the spinach for *fatire,* small pies. My oldest brother, Fouad, browning meats for the *sanbousick,* meat pies. Ibrahim smashing dates for *baklava*—my mother would make six different kinds.

Laughter filled our tiny kitchen during these times, the pink sun warming us through the window as it rose.

3

When I was small, I was awakened most mornings by the smoky scents of brewing Turkish coffee and my father's Italian cologne. He bought this elixir by the liter and slapped it on after showering in the chilly water that ran under Beirut from the springs of *Jabal Sunnin.* Each day, before the sun peeked over the mountains, Father left for his blacksmith shop, and all day long I looked forward to his homecoming. In the evenings, he would scoop me up in a hug, and I could smell the metal dust on his skin, the masculine scents of iron and fire.

I always loved climbing on my father's back, holding onto his big thick neck. He had a French moustache, thin, not thick, sitting just on top of his lips.

I liked to run my finger over it. "Daddy, when I grow up will I have a moustache like you?" I would ask.

Fifty times I asked him that and yet each time, he would smile and say, "Yes, my son, you will have one just like mine one day."

My father almost always arrived home after sunset, almost always carrying two leather sacks filled with fresh vegetables and grains from the market, or *souk.* One day over a family dinner in the kitchen, when I was about six years old, Father looked at me across the table where I sat between Fouad and Ibrahim.

"Kamal, would you like to go to work with me tomorrow?"

Joy surged through my heart and that night I could hardly sleep, my anticipation percolating in me as though I were going to a great feast. It was before sunrise when Mother rousted me from the couch in the living room. I could already smell the coffee and Father's cologne, and I heard ice-laced rain pelting against the windows. Mother double-dressed me, pulling Ibrahim's trousers and shirt over my pajamas. She had made for me a special hat of a shape she had seen in pictures from Tunisia. It was shaped like a ship, pointed in the front and back, wide around the middle, and trimmed in fake fur.

When I stepped outside with Father, an icy wind snapped at my ears. I could hear the ice pinging down on tin roofs. My father tried to cover us both with his good umbrella.

The blacksmith shop was in an area called Zaytoon, not far from the Mediterranean, set between an area called St. George Chalet and the Valley of the Jews. When we reached it, Father used a key to unhinge a great padlock, then rolled up the door, which rattled its way to the top.

I hurried inside out of the biting wind and into the dark place that smelled like my father. Quickly, he exchanged his street clothes for blue work pants and a khaki shirt. Right away he began building up a fire of rock coals, not wood, in two big barrels. In Father's shop, everything was manual, nothing was electric. In the middle of the wall, high up, two huge barrels created pressure, and Father used the big chain dangling from the ceiling to pump heavy air into the ovens.

I stood watching him in awe as he strode back and forth across the floor, yanking tarps off the machinery and bringing the shop to fiery life.

Soon the coals glimmered in the furnaces, sending off an orange glow. The shop radiated with dry heat and Father took his shirt off. Suddenly, I saw him in a new light. Covered in a thin sheen of sweat, his skin reflected the fire's copper glow. He was muscular, cut all over, his torso the shape of a sharp V, with wide shoulders narrowing to a trim waist and a hard belly that rippled in the shape of my mother's washboard. His arms were thicker than all of me. The heat in the room ignited the smell of his cologne, and it mixed with that of the metal. Suddenly, I realized the strength of my father and pride swelled my heart.

At that moment, he flashed me a smile; and a great warmth, far beyond the heat of any furnace, flooded through me. To me, my father was everything a man is supposed to be.

4

My father did not teach *madrassa* often, but would sit in during especially important lessons. I remember the day we learned about the seventy-two virgins. My brothers—Fouad, Ibrahim, Omer—were there and also my mother's brothers, Uncle Khalid and Uncle Shafiq. My mother sat quietly at the end of the table while Father told us a story from the *hadith* about a man who charged into a Jewish army all alone, sacrificing himself for Allah.

"The moment he died, he woke up instantly in *jannah*," Father said. "Allah presented him with seventy-two virgins, women who had never before been touched by a man. And each virgin also had seventy-two virgins attending her, and all these women belonged to the man who died as *al-shaheed*, a martyr."

Uncle Khalid winked at Fouad, who grinned widely. It seemed my oldest brother thought this was a fine arrangement. But I sat on my *tesat* and thought about it. *Seventy-two times seventy-two?* At six years old, I could not even count that high.

"Father," I said, "You only have one woman in the house, and you fight all the time. How are you going to be able to manage so many women?"

My uncles burst out laughing, and Father smiled a little sheepishly. He thought it over for a moment, then said, "The grace of Allah is sufficient."

He went on to explain that there would be no bickering or fighting in *jannah*. "These women will attend to all your desires and needs."

"So they are servants?" I said.

"No, they are *ḥūrīyah*, virgin women. They will not be angels, but not human, either. They will be there to meet your heart's desire."

I knew what he meant. My friends had told me a million versions of how sex was done. Also, I had seen sheep and goats mating in the little barn behind our building.

But now I wondered: *What about my mother?*

I looked down the table and caught her eye. Then I turned to my father again. "You are married to my mother," I said. "If you die as a martyr and you get this many virgins, how about if my mother died as a martyr? What does she get?"

My uncles and my brothers laughed, although a bit nervously this time. Father looked at Mother, who returned his glance, then looked down.

Finally, he said, "Your mother will become one of the *ḥūrīyah*."

I frowned and looked down at the wood patterns in the table. This answer did not settle well with me. My brother Ibrahim had once told me angrily that in the Koran, Muhammad referred to women as the "ground that we walk on." We could not think of our mother that way.

I could feel everyone staring at me, waiting. Finally, I looked up at Father. "If Mother works hard in this life and dies as *al-shaheed*, why doesn't she get seventy-two virgin men?"

My uncles' mouths popped open. Then they looked at each other, threw their heads back, and roared with laughter. My father's face flushed red, and a vein on his neck began to pulse. Then, quick as a cobra, his hand closed the distance to my face. *Whack!*

"Insolent boy! Never talk about your mother that way!"

My father glared at my uncles, but the joker Khalid did not care what my father thought, and he snorted out loud. Mother did not say a word.

My question ended *madrassa* that day. But a week later, I was out on the roof chasing lizards through the liquid sun when my father emerged through the door from the living room and walked to the wall overlooking our street. I went over and stood beside him. Below, a vegetable merchant slowly wheeled his cart past a knot of giggling girls. Marie, the Christian girl from next door, was down there.

My father pulled a lighter from the pocket of his white shirt and lit a Kent. Leaning his elbows on the wall, he turned his head toward me. "Do you remember what you asked me about your mother?"

"Yes, Father."

"Your mother will become the head of the ḥūrīyah, the head of the seventy-two," he said. "She will be in charge of them all."

Father never told me where he got that. Maybe he went to the mosque and asked the imam. If he did, I learned later, the imam most certainly told him, "The woman gets nothing."

But Father could not come and tell me that.

5

People traveled to Beirut from all over the world, and the richest ones rented chalets—colorful tents on the seashore. Yellow stripes, blue stripes, white, red, like candy dotting the sand. Americans called them cabanas. The rich people jetted across the cobalt water on their big boats with wooden skis, nearly naked in their western swimsuits. It was the fancy life.

"These people bring evil with them," Mother told me. "When the flesh is exposed, the devil gets loose."

I nodded solemnly, but was secretly fascinated.

During the summer, Saturday was my favorite day. The whole family would get up at the crack of the sun and walk the short distance to the shore. I remember those walks, my heart beating, excited to visit the sea again. From my dreaming window, the Mediterranean had always called to me, inviting me to explore its endless blue depths. To come and dabble at its cool, clear edge was to me like ruffling stars at the fringe of another universe.

At that hour, the infidels would not yet have defiled the water, Mother and Father told us, having stayed up too late the night before indulging in their debaucheries.

I walked along the shore with my brothers and sisters, collecting seashells and watching tiny crabs scurry across the wet sand. Rising over the mountains behind us, the sun turned the sea foam pink as it tickled our ankles. My aunt and sisters waded into the water wearing bathing suits underneath long shirts and snug pants down to their ankles. They did not remove these outer garments even when they swam. Afterward, they were careful to wrap up tightly and quickly, not wanting anyone who might be out early to see their hair or skin.

On these days, my father tried to teach me to be a man. He would grab me and throw me into the water with just one instruction: "Swim back if you want to live!"

6

In *madrassa*, when we learned about Sura 99, "The Earthquake," my father sat with us again.

"At the day of judgment, Allah will bring all your good works and your bad works together and put them on a scale," he said, looking pointedly at me and each of my brothers as we sat on the kitchen floor. "If your good works outweigh your bad works, you will go to heaven more quickly. If your bad works outweigh your good works, you will go to hell."

My own works flipped through my mind like snapshots: fighting with my brothers and sisters . . . helping myself to guavas and plums from my grandfather's garden . . . the "medical games" I secretly played with Marie next door.

I am in bad trouble. . . .

I glanced across the table at my younger brother Omer and saw no concern. Nothing fazed him; he was always happy as a little rabbit. But Ibrahim would not look at me. I could see he was as tormented as I, stuck somewhere in his thoughts like a mouse in a trap.

Father had talked to us several times about the flames of hell and the tormenting giants who would use meat hooks to rip you apart. We had already learned that, according to the Koran, every Muslim, except for *al-shaheed*, has to pass through hell. There, Allah purifies you through burning. After a long time, if you were not an altogether bad Muslim, Allah would excuse you and admit you to a dry place between heaven and hell. Finally, if you pleaded many times, Allah would let you into *jannah*. You would be among the lowliest and receive only a few virgins and a little bit of food. But Mother assured us that even this was much better than earth.

After *madrassa* was over, I scurried to the bathroom and climbed up into my secret place, the attic where we stored rice and grain and kept blankets in the summer. My heart was melting completely because I knew I had no hope. I was not even good enough to make it to the dry place.

My breath came short and quick as I thought about the demons with the meat hooks. Leaning back against a sugar sack, I thought, *My deeds will have to make a place for me.*

I remembered the teaching about *al-shaheed,* the martyrs for Allah. My mother had taught us that one Muslim man has the strength of ten infidels, just like Prince Ali Baba in *The Arabian Nights.* As the comforting smell of wheat and rice seeped through the cloth bags all around me, I looked up at the rafters and meditated on legendary Islamic warriors. One would charge at hundreds, knowing he was going to his death. The idea, I had learned, was to take as many infidels with you as you could. I imagined myself as the great Muslim general, Khalid ibn Walid, or as Omer ibn al-Khatb, the second caliph. Father had told us that wherever Omer walked, Satan ran away.

I could be a great warrior like that.

I knew I did not want to grow up to be an evil man, not like that bandit who had dishonored his mother. And I remembered what Father had told us: "The first drop of infidel's blood you shed, you can provide atonement for seventy of your loved ones."

No matter how bad and evil I am now, I thought, *one day I can save myself and my family.* One afternoon during *madrassa,* my mother taught us something amazing. She was reading from her treasured Koran. Omer was only about four at the time. Mother sat on the floor at the end of the kitchen table, and he stood at her side, tracing the words with his tiny finger. She was reading the Sura 9:5, which teaches that infidels do not deserve to live.

"Fight and slay the pagans wherever you find them," Mother read. She then looked up to expound.

"My sons, if you kill a Jew, on the day of judgment your right hand will light up before the throne of Allah, and all his heavenly host will celebrate."

When she said this, I flashed back to an incident a couple of years before. At a young age, a sign had emerged that I was destined for trouble: when I colored with my crayons or ate my food, I naturally used my left hand. To my mother and father, this was intolerable.

In Islam, the importance of the right hand, and the "right" in general, cannot be overstated. Infidels are "the people of the Left." Muslims are "the people of the Right." We sit at Allah's right hand, the side of goodness and righteousness. The good Muslim, when he greets a friend or makes a vow or opens the Koran, or even when he eats, does so with his right hand. When he dresses for work in the morning, he first puts on his right sleeve, his right pant leg, his right shoe. When he washes at the mosque, he washes his right hand first.

His left hand is reserved for unholy business, such as going to the bathroom or having sex with his wife.

Left-handed people are shunned. So, when I began using my left hand, my mother took to stinging it with one of her welt-raising switches.

I was not yet three years old on the day I was sitting on the *nuniah*, the training toilet, when my father got home. That was the hour when my mother delivered her daily damage report: which son had done this or that, which one had gotten into the most trouble. That particular day, as she finished running down the household news, my mother and father came and stood at the doorway to the water closet where I sat.

". . . and I caught Kamal using his left hand," Mama concluded her report.

"Burn it," my father said without hesitation.

"What?" mother said.

"Burn his hand."

Burn my hand! With fire?

"No, no, no!" I cried from the *nuniah*, my pants bunched around my ankles. My mother disappeared from the doorway and returned with a small box of kitchen matches. Crowding past my father into the tiny room, she came and squatted on the floor before me. She grabbed my left hand and put it under her left arm.

"No, Mama! No!" I cried.

Mama twisted around so that I faced her back, my arm clamped in the vise between her left arm and side.

A strike. A sizzle. A whiff of sulfur.

"No! Please!" I screamed, now choking with fear.

I pushed at her and kicked with my feet. I kicked the *nuniah* and it tipped over; a pool of urine spread around my feet. The heat of flame licked near my hand, and I fought wildly.

"Mama, don't hurt me!"

Suddenly, she let go. Turning to face me, she blew out the match. A curl of bitter smoke snaked up my nostrils.

From the doorway came my father's voice: "You are a Muslim child, and you will use your right hand." Then he turned and walked away.

I cried all night long and would not allow any of my brothers and sisters to talk to me. That my mother who loved me would burn me was scarier than anything else. I decided that no place was safe.

I had not thought of that day for a long time until Mama told us about our right hand lighting up before Allah. Now I was thankful she had corrected me, that I might instinctively use my right hand to kill an infidel and not displease Allah by using my left.

"Why do we do this?" I asked.

Killing infidels is one of the ways Allah would open heaven for us, she told us. The more infidels we killed, the better our chances to move quickly from punishment to paradise.

"It is your duty," she said. "It is the duty of the faithful to punish and harass the Jews and Christians, who are thieves and traitors to Islam. They are cursed as monkeys and pigs, and their spirits are unclean. It is in the Book."

Aspen, Colorado
2007

In July 2007, Walid Shoebat and I met in Aspen to address a meeting of the Jewish-Christian Relations (JCR) on the subject of anti-Semitism and Muslim terrorism. Speaking to this audience was an extraordinary experience for me, meeting eye to eye with the very people I had been brought up to think of as my blood enemies. After leaving Islam, I had embraced the teaching that people "of every nation" were the same in God's eyes. By the time I met with Walid for the JCR conference, I had believed that for more than twenty years. The opportunity to (perhaps, in some small way) redeem some of the evil I had committed against this people was of great meaning to me.

Our stay in Aspen was brief, and the glorious summer made me wish we could stay longer. Around us, the Rocky Mountains, blue-green with spruce and pine and still capped with snow even in July, jumped out in sharp relief from the crisp Colorado sky. The morning of our departure, my wife, Victoria, and I sat by our hotel swimming pool chatting over coffee with Walid.

Walid is not Walid's real name. Born in Bethlehem of Judea, Walid's grandfather was the Muslim *mukhtar*, or chieftain, of a village in Israel called Beit Sahour-Bethlehem. While living in Jericho, Walid lived through and witnessed Israel's Six-Day War. Like me, he joined the PLO at a young age and was later imprisoned in the Russian Compound, Jerusalem's central prison, for committing violent acts against Israel. After his release, he resumed his acts of terror against the Jews, eventually continuing them in the United States, though in the form of fomenting propaganda against Israel while working as a counselor for the Arab Student Organization at Loop College in Chicago.

Though schooled in violence, Walid was also an intensely scholarly man whose *jihad* was informed by hundreds of hours of Islamic study. Ultimately, it was his intellectual bent that led him to abandon holy war. Islamist men are taught that they can marry Christian or American women in order to convert them, or to gain innocent-looking entry into a certain society. In 1993, in a challenge to convert his Christian wife to Islam, Walid studied the Hebrew Scriptures. Within six months, he decided that everything he had been taught about the Jews was a lie. Convinced he had fought his whole life on the side of evil, he became an advocate for his former enemy, speaking to tens of thousands at churches, synagogues, and civic groups, and to government leaders and media about the cause of Israel.

For that, he was marked by the jihadists for death—and by many in the American media as a bigot and a charlatan. As we sat by the hotel pool, steam rising from its surface and from our coffee cups, he told me that soon I would be marked as well.

"I have a real concern with your security," he told my wife and me. "You both need to understand that as Kamal becomes better known, you will need to eat, sleep, and breathe security."

Victoria looked at me, concern straining her eyes.

Walid had been speaking out against radical Islam for five or six years by then, but I had only recently joined the fight. I could tell he thought me an innocent who was far too willing to think the best of the other guy in the room, unworried about embracing, shaking hands, and sharing personal stories.

He had learned the hard way to be more careful. "I was targeted several times," he told us gravely. "They tried to find me and my family. We had to keep moving from place to place, hiding. To find a safe place, I eventually had to move out of the country."

Walid's grim manner sent fear spearing through my heart. He reminded us of what had happened to Zakariah Anani, the third member of our trio, who had received multiple death threats. In Canada, jihadists burned up his car and burned down his house.

"Every one of us in the Shoebat family is continually conscious of our environment, our surroundings," Walid said. "We wonder, are we being followed? Are we being watched? It is always at the forefront of our minds."

I looked at my wife and could see reality beginning to sink in on her face. Walid was telling us that if we continued on this path, our lives would never be the same.

"Move often," he urged. "Get an 800 number. Make sure that your real name never appears on any documents."

He told us to hire a registered agent to handle all our business transactions and never to reveal where we live.

"Above all," he said, "trust no one."

Beirut, Lebanon
1964

1

In *madrassa*, Mother loved to talk about how her ancestor warriors, Arabs and Turks, had used their thick and heavy swords to lop off the heads of Jews. They were men of great courage, she said. Muslim warriors were clever and strong, first piercing the enemy's armor with their swords, then severing the infidels' arms from their bodies.

"Now the Jews and Christians could not raise their swords against the Muslim fighters," Mother told us. "And that's when the Muslims chopped off the infidels' heads."

That day, during our coloring time, I pictured myself on a white horse slicing through enemy armies with my mighty Muslim sword. As a child of six, when your mother loves you so much and is nourishing you, you believe her with every part of your being. Among my brothers and sisters, I was the one who believed the most. I was the one with the big faith. I used to lie on my back on our concrete roof, drinking in the passing clouds. In them, I saw Allah's creations. Some were glorious and mighty like a snowy mountain or an eagle. Some were funny, like cartoon trees and toucans and fat elephants, as if in scrawling his art in the heavens, Allah was trying on purpose to make me laugh.

Allah must be great, I thought. *He must be big. He must be awesome!*

With the world he created as my witness, there was no question about my mother's honesty. To me, she spoke the mother's milk of truth.

That night, I had a dream so powerful that I never forgot it. I saw myself sitting on a haughty white horse, wielding a *saif*, a heavy double-edged sword, in each hand. The Day of Islam had come about, the day when Muslim warriors would cleanse the earth of every infidel and establish the true religion, the day that every infidel would convert or die, the day that *Umma* would be complete.

In my dream, I rode bareback without armor, no shoes on my feet and wearing only the white *sherwal*, bloused pants tight below the knees and above the waist, like the Ottomans. In the eye of my dream, I knew this was a battle of no return. I might die, I knew, but I would take with me as many infidels as I could. Sleek, muscular, and majestic, my horse stamped and snorted amid an army of fierce Muslim fighters, all of us ready to charge under the scarlet flags of Islam. Rank after rank in military formation, we faced off against an army of our enemies arrayed against us across a vast, foggy battlefield.

One warrior cried out, then many: "Allahu Akbar! Allahu Akbar!" One nation, one voice!

The infidels charged. Unafraid, I kicked my stallion's flanks and galloped forward, racing the wind. Setting my horse's reins free, I plunged into the enemy formation, drew my swords from their scabbards and swung them left and right in deadly arcs. Every sweep of my blades sent a man's head tumbling off his shoulders and onto the ground. At this sight, the Islamic dream warriors cheered for me, chanting, "Wa Islama! Wa Islama!" Power to Islam!

Now my dreamscape shifted so that the end of the battlefield melted into the golden carpet that, it is written, leads to the throne of Allah. I knew that I must be in *jannah*, paradise, which meant I must be dead, martyred on the battlefield. Joy seized my heart! I had done it! I had become *al-shaheed*! Now, like an offering of melons, the severed heads of Jews and Christians rolled down the golden carpet to Allah's feet, and when I looked into his face, I saw that he began to smile.

"Only my crazy Kamal would do such a thing!" Allah said to me. "Welcome! Welcome to your reward!"

2

Fouad and Amira went to *Madrassa al-Riyadh*, a private Muslim school in West Beirut. (Amira would be allowed to go until she was a teenager; then she would have to quit school and devote herself to learning to be a wife.) As a small boy, I was impressed with the way they could read and write, and I could not wait for the day when I would be old enough to go with them and learn important things. But the first day they took me there, I cried and cried until there were no tears left in my head. At first, it was because I suddenly realized that going to school meant leaving my mother. Later, it was because I learned school was a brutal place.

Winter had wrapped itself around Beirut. An icy wind charged in from the sea, whipping through the alleys to assault us on the streets. Amira held my hand as we trudged along past the shops. Rain dripped from the colorful awnings, making wet, smacking sounds on the pavement. My tears made my cheeks colder. I sniffled and tried to bury my face in the collar of my coat.

"Kamal, you always wanted to go to school," Ibrahim said impatiently. "Why are you crying now?"

"Be quiet, *inta majnoon!*" Amira snapped, calling him crazy. "He's only afraid to leave Mama. He will be fine when he gets to school and meets his new friends."

Amira tried to pull me closer. At that moment, we were walking past the open garage door of a mechanic's shop. The smells of grease and welding oozed out into the street, and I saw a man in there wearing a dark mask and holding a gun that shot blue fire.

At the sight, I sank to the sidewalk, threw my head back, and howled.

"See what you've done!" Amira said to Ibrahim. Clutching her book bag, she bent down beside me. My cries echoed off the concrete face of the building, and I could feel the wet ground soaking through my pants.

Through my tears, I saw two men emerge from the mechanic's shop to stare at our little tableau.

"It is his first day of school," Amira explained.

Dressed in blue coveralls, both men smiled and nodded sympathetically. One of them had a banana for a nose, with nostrils as big around as my thumbs. "It's going to be alright, *ya habebe*," Banana-nose said. "You're going to go to school and become smart, and the whole neighborhood is going to be *very* proud of you!"

I looked up at the mechanic and saw that he had hair sticking out of the holes in his scary nose. I screamed louder.

Now, even Fouad had had enough. He grabbed my hand and lifted me firmly to my feet. "Come, brother. We're going to be late."

Fouad dragged me along and I followed like a sheep, sobbing all the way. Finally, I looked up to see a towering double gate made of green wrought iron. Each half of the gate was shorter at the hinges, then rose in height to where they met at the center. Each pole in the gate was topped with a point like a spear.

Inside the gates, a huge concrete stairway led down into the school proper, where five buildings housed classes of all ages. *Madrassa al Riyadh* was one of the largest private schools in Beirut, home to at least several hundred kids. To me, it looked like tens of thousands as Fouad, Ibrahim, and Amira led me to my classroom, which was in a building painted baby blue. Rosebushes lined the stairs and walkways. The colors and gardens soothed me, and school began to seem more friendly.

When Amira opened the door to the classroom, music spilled out: piano, French horn, clarinet. Suddenly I was mesmerized. Fouad helped me hand over my lunchbox to the smiling teacher, who assigned me a seat with a colored sticker to remind me in case I forgot. She took me by the hand and led me to my seat. Suddenly confident, I waved goodbye to my brothers and sister.

The teacher had seated me between two boys, whose names I remember to this day: Nabil and Mukhtar. Mukhtar was a kind little boy and was always trying to think of fun things to do. But Nabil was devious. He thought about everything evil he could induce me to do. It was like sitting between an angel and a devil.

Soon we reached the ten o'clock break. In the center of the school stood a little shop with a door that opened on top while the bottom stayed shut. My brothers and sister had told me that inside that wonderful little building were candy and cakes and petit fours, and even lit-tle toys like tiny soldiers and cowboys. From inside came the smell of fresh popcorn and, best of all, freshly fried potato chips. I could see a long line of children forming at the door. Nabil and I drew near them and I saw that each student who went to the little door-gate came away with a treat.

So I got in line. My mouth began to water as other students passed by with white paper cones filled with the glistening hot chips which, my brothers and sister had told me, were dropped in a fryer, drained in a big steel net, then sprinkled with sea salt.

Child by child, I edged closer to the shop, where I saw that a teenager manned the door. He had dirty blond hair and blue eyes.

"Potato chips, please," I said when I reached him.

He scowled like a prince looking upon a beggar and handed me a wide paper cone, twisted at the bottom and filled with chips.

"Two *kroosh*," he said.

I know my face was a question mark.

"*Two kroosh!*" he snapped. "People are waiting."

"But I do not have any money," I said. I had not known that the other children were *buying* their food. Only that they got in line and that when they came out, they had a treat.

The young shopkeeper snatched the cone away from me as if I were a thief, and I heard the light clatter of chips being thrown back into a bin. "Stupid boy! Get out of the way!"

Tears squirted from my eyes. Frightened, I backed away, afraid he might box my head for trying to steal. Worried that someone might tell my parents I had dishonored them, I scurried away to find Mukhtar. School was turning out to be a treacherous place.

At the end of the break, all the classes lined up near one of the build-ings, each rank facing out, with the tallest child's back to the wall and each student going forward shorter than the one behind him. I saw the other children spacing themselves by putting their right arm on the shoulder of the child ahead. Since it was our first day, our teacher was there to show us how to do it like the older students.

At that moment, a loud squealing, like a wounded animal, cut through the general chatter. I was already standing in line and now saw the headmaster, a fat man wearing a blue suit and red moustache, striding from the direction of the snack shop. A boy trotted along beside him, dancing strangely on his toes, howling as he went. Behind those two walked a tall, dark man and a woman wearing a long red dress.

I knew the man with the red moustache was the headmaster because we had lined up and passed by him earlier that day. He had inspected our uniforms: Were they laundered? Were they ironed? And our fingernails—were they clean? I had heard from Fouad that if the headmaster found dirt or wrinkles, he would whack your hand with a ruler.

Now the headmaster turned toward the ranks of students, and I saw that the boy was the blue-eyed shopkeeper who had snatched away my chips. Tears streaked his scarlet face. His ear, the handle the headmaster had used to drag him center-stage, glowed the color of pickled beets.

"This boy's name is Amal, and he is a thief," the headmaster announced. "When we came to collect the money from today's shop sales, we found part of it in Amal's socks."

Amal's chest heaved, and I could hear his breath hitching. He kept his head down, his eyes glued to the pavement. The dark man standing on the boy's right looked on grimly. In his hand, he held a raw plank of wood, about two feet long, with a rope dangling from one end. The woman stood on his left, holding a thick length of dark-stained wood, wide at the front and tapered back to form a handle.

For the second time since I stepped through the green gate made of spears, I began to cry.

"This is the only time we will warn Amal," the headmaster went on. "If he ever steals again, we will call the police and he will be dismissed from this school."

Then he turned to Amal. "Take off your shoes."

Shaking and crying, the boy obeyed.

"Sit down and raise your legs," the headmaster ordered.

My stomach knotted. I could feel more tears sliding down my cheeks. The boy behind me in line began to sniffle, too.

Amal lay down on the concrete and raised his legs in the air. Lunging forward, the dark man placed the new plank behind the boy's ankles, and wrapped the rope around the front of his ankles. After two passes with the rope, the dark man tied it to a nail that stuck out from one end of the board.

Amal's legs were secured to the plank and the bottoms of his long, skinny feet exposed. Now the boy began to cry in earnest. "Please, I promise never to do it again! Please!"

His pleading was pitiful but they did not stop the proceedings. The woman handed the red-veneered paddle to the headmaster, then stepped up to hold one end of the plank that bound Amal's feet. The dark man held the other end of the plank. The headmaster then swung the paddle back like a tennis racket and swung it forward again, landing blow after blow on the bottoms of Amal's feet.

The boy screamed and so did I.

It was terrifying, a nightmare unfolding in the flesh. I imagined they would grab me next for one reason or another. What if Amal told them I had tried to steal chips?

3

As we got older, there were times when my father and mother taught the boys and girls separately. My father took Fouad, Omer, Ibrahim, and me and taught us some things the girls did not need to know. He taught us that we were superior to our sisters and, in fact, to all women, because the woman had sinned in the Garden of Eden. She was the weaker vessel, not perfect like Adam, and Satan was able to deceive her easily through lust.

"Satan seduced her physically," Father said. "Women are not strong. They bring sin to the house. This is why they must cover themselves from the tops of their heads to the bottoms of their feet."

Meanwhile, my mother taught my sisters how to be good wives, how to honor their husbands, how to cook and clean and serve. Among the strict Muslim families we knew, no girl was allowed to go to school beyond the twelfth grade.

Reading from the Koran, Father taught us more about *jannah*. I learned that it was a wondrous place, dripping with fat grapes so juicy and sweet that the smell of them alone would fill you up.

"If you see a bird in paradise and you desire to eat it," Father told us, "it will fall down from the air cooked three different ways."

In *jannah*, plush empty beds flew through the air, available at any moment you wanted to sleep or relax. Father read to us from the Sura that *jannah* was populated with young boys, with bodies soft like velvet and smooth like marble, reclining naked on the ground.

Why would they do that? I wondered.

When I got older and understood more thoroughly what the seventy-two *hūrīyah* and young boys were for, I asked our imam, Shiekh Rajab, "How do the *al-shaheed* have the strength to service so many women?"

He looked at me, amused. "Allah gives the *al-shaheed* extra horse-power to attend to them."

Basically, he said, the martyrs became like Superman.

4

One fall day, my best friend Eli and I were playing tag in the street, when suddenly he stopped and turned to me, huffing and puffing.

"Kamal, when I grow up, I will go on journeys and see the world. I will go places and eat delicious things, and you will not be able to go with me because Islam will not let you."

Eli was a Christian. The Christian children were allowed to go to the chalets and on vacations and eat forbidden foods. I was a little envious and wished I could enjoy life in this way. On the other hand, these were Christians and not worthy, so what did it matter to me? I knew that someday I would probably have to rise up against them anyway.

But one night, I had another dream: I was a little child running away with Eli. Strings of light like streamers fell down from the night sky. We ran through them, as though through a festival where the decorations were fashioned by angels. In my dream, I felt the cool night whispering against my skin as Eli and I ran toward the sea where, strangely, a helicopter was parked in the sand. Its blades turned around and around, slow and silent.

Eli ushered me into the helicopter, and as it floated away from the beach, fireworks lit up the heavens around me, bursting blue and scarlet, white and gold. Looking down, I could see Eli waving up at me as he receded.

The sky shimmered with chrysanthemums of light, and I heard Eli's voice echo up into the sparkling night: "Run away, Kamal! Run away!"

Beirut, Lebanon
1965

1

Life was getting more expensive for my father. He had many children now, many mouths to feed but not enough hands to contribute. In the Muslim world, the prevailing view is that it is better to bear boys than girls. Boys can go out and work, as my older brothers did. They can produce, contribute, carry on the family name. But girls cannot go out and work. They stay in the house and eat and drink until they get married. Girls are raised up for somebody else.

Where there had been joy in my household, warmth and good food, something began to change. By the time I was seven, my mom and dad had seven kids. With each new child, I watched my father change, grow old before my eyes. I did not know it then, but the blacksmith trade was falling out of demand. People were buying ready-made water heaters and washtubs and cabinets. A new world was leaving his old-world trade behind.

Suddenly, Father was not coming home until much later in the evenings. I would wait and wait for him to come with his cologne and metal scent, with bags of pomegranates from the *souk*. But now, many times, my mother would send me to bed before he arrived. Even when I was still awake, my father did not want to play with me anymore.

I did not know what was happening behind the bedroom wall, where my parents talked in private. Where I had seen warmth and affection in their eyes, I now saw tension, like piano wires tightly strung. Some evenings, I heard my father yelling at my mother about the smallest things. It seemed nothing pleased him anymore.

I sensed we were poorer now. My mother had always sewn most of our clothes, only buying ready-made ones for the festivals. Now, though, even for the festivals, we wore old and handmade things. Only Fouad got new shoes. The rest of the brothers passed his old ones down the line. I also noticed that, where meat had been a rare luxury in our home, now there was none.

As one of the youngest boys, I was in a zone where my father did not know what to do with me. The girls he treated with affection; they were not expected to earn their keep. My older brothers he treated with affection because they brought home money each week. But when I came to my father seeking his attention, he turned cold.

"Not now, Kamal. I am tired," he would say.

Then one night, he broke my heart. I had scraped together a little money to buy a new Superman comic book and was standing in the living room showing it to my brother when Father walked in from work.

He glared down at the book in my hands, then scorched my eyes with his. "You are so stupid wasting your money on this trash!" he said. "I wish you were a girl. At least then I could give you away in marriage!"

One evening, at the beginning of a new school year, my father came home early. I leapt on him to give him a kiss, to feel his moustache against my face, but he took me by both shoulders and guided me into the kitchen, where he stood in front of me and looked down. I could not read the look in his eyes, but I could see that he looked very tired, very sad.

"Kamal, you are not going back to school."

This shocked me. Why would I not go back to school? "But I love school, Father. All my friends are there."

"If you live in this house, you work," he said, his eyes turning hard in a way I had not seen before. "You have to work."

Fouad was already working as an apprentice welder. Amira had already been pulled from school for her training as a wife.

"*Please*, Father. I am making you proud in school. My grades are good!"

He kept his eyes hard. "I have already arranged a job for you, answering the phone for Uncle Abdul Al-Karim."

My uncle's plumbing business was all the way across the city, many neighborhoods away. I fell on my father's feet and grabbed his legs with both arms. "Please, Father! Please! I want to go to school! I want to make you proud!"

He pulled his legs from the circle of my thin arms, first one and then the other, and walked away, leaving me lying on the cold tile. At the kitchen door, he turned back and looked at me. The hardness was gone, and I could not tell what this other look in his eyes meant. Then he turned and went out of the kitchen. We never spoke of school again.

School started in August. The worst thing was when I passed my friends, me in my ragged clothes, them neatly turned out in their uniforms. I was embarrassed to let them see me. For the first few weeks, Sana, a girl I knew from school, stopped to talk with me. But after a while, we were not the same anymore. Not of the same class. She was a student, dressed smart and clean. I was now among the street people. Before, I had been poor but educated. Now I was only poor. Sana stopped talking to me, and instead began to pass me quickly with a hurried wave. Maybe her father told her I was not good enough anymore.

My uncle was a plumber and a pipe fitter who had landed a big job putting in all the plumbing in a tall building at the other end of Beirut. All that summer and fall, I worked until sunset, answering the big, black dial phone in my uncle's office. I was working six days for about twenty Lebanese lira—about three dollars. When someone called, I took notes. But many times, he could not read my handwriting and he could not figure out who called. At that, he would fly into a rage and punch and kick me right in my guts.

"What good are you?" he yelled. "I am stuck with you as a favor to your mother, and you are good for nothing!"

We could not afford for me to take the *serviz*, a cross between a shuttle and a taxi, so I had to walk there, leaving very early each morning. If I went the long way, I had to get up before sunrise to make it on time. If

I went the short way, through certain neighborhoods, the bad kids waited.

2

These were older boys, some teenagers, who did not go to school and hung about on the street corners looking for trouble. They cussed and spit and waited for someone they could harass to come along. I had heard some of them carried big knives, sharp and deadly knives that opened with seven clicks. One stab would put you to sleep.

"What did you bring us today, *ya ibn al-sharmouta?*" they would taunt, calling me a son of a female dog. I tried to alter my times—to get up before sunrise and still take the shortcut, running to avoid the bullies. Then I would fall asleep at work, and my uncle would beat me.

I remember the day I found my saviors. Summer and fall had passed, and the winter streets were cold and wet from the rain that sweeps from the sea up the mountainsides, only to dapple back down on the city. That morning, I got up very early to make the trip to my uncle's building. Since the day was cold, I decided on the shortest route. I reasoned that I might escape the gangs by the grace of Allah, but if I was late, a beating from my uncle was certain.

Dressed in a white shirt, hand-me-down black pants, and a black vest I had bought at a secondhand store, I set out that morning with lunch in a paper sack and my father's good umbrella. He did not usually let me use it, but with the wretched weather, I suspected he judged it better to risk losing it than forfeit my pay. My journey began pleasantly in the misty streets of my own neighborhood. The streets were freshly watered, the air crisp and cold. I headed up Verdan Street past the main police barracks, nodding at shopkeepers as they raised their roll-up metal doors with long hooks and whisked the sidewalks with home-made brooms.

I walked with my head down, zigging and zagging between the rain puddles. This was my quiet time, my safe time, the only time I was able to relax. I used it to try to keep the water from soaking through the *lira*-sized holes my brothers had worn in the soles of my shoes before passing them down to me.

Soon, though, I passed out of my safe zone onto a wide street, four lanes, two leading in each direction. The buildings were a mix of old and new, mostly houses and apartments with a couple of businesses: Bata, a shoe store, and Coiffure, a fancy hair salon. Also there was a corner bakery that sold a few groceries and was famous for its *lama-joun*, an Armenian meat dish served on thin, pizza-like dough.

That was the trouble: The Armenians. They were Christians, and almost every time I walked through there, a nasty little band of teenagers stole everything I had. On Monday, they would steal my lunch; Tuesday, the *kroosh* in my pocket; Wednesday, my shoes. Which is why I was now wearing shoes that had belonged to two brothers before me. If I didn't take a lunch, so that they could plainly see I had nothing for them to steal, they would make a circle around me and push me back and forth between them, screaming, "What's the matter, little son of a whore? Doesn't your whore mother love you enough to make you a lunch? Or did you eat it already? Steal it from our mouths?"

Once, a tall, skinny teenager slashed the palm of my hand with a seven-click knife. I screamed.

That was the time a Maronite Christian lady came running out to rescue me. In her fifties, at least, the woman was standing on the terrace of her home, which looked to me like a mansion with its tall, fluted columns and banisters of stone.

She was slim and elegantly dressed, so I was surprised when she opened her mouth. "Get away from him!" she shouted, peppering the boys with curses. "I will call the police or beat you myself!"

The gang of about five boys laughed at her.

"You will beat *us*, woman?" said the teenager. "And I will come and visit your house at night!"

But the woman stood her ground until the teenager folded his knife and signaled to the others to walk away. Then the woman hurried down from her porch, through her gate to meet me. She took my bleeding hand in both of hers and examined it for a moment. Then she put one hand under my chin, lifted it, and looked into my eyes. "What's your name, child?"

"Kamal," I said through my tears.

"Come with me, Kamal," she said. And putting her arm around my shoulder, she guided me to her terrace. After a brief trip inside, she came out and sifted a little ground coffee onto the wound. "That will take the sting out," she said. Then she wrapped my hand with a clean white bandage.

After that day, I always walked on the mansion side of the street, and the Maronite lady was always waiting, watching the Armenian boys with a falcon's eye until I had passed safely out of sight.

Now, walking down the rain-slick street, I made a straight line to her house. And at almost the same moment, I noticed two things: First, the Armenian boys were standing on the bakery corner, watching my approach. Second, the Maronite lady was absent from her terrace.

3

Quickly, I averted my eyes to the sidewalk squares, walking far to the left side of the wide street, heading east, passing with the boys on my right. My stomach jangled with fear, as though I were passing a tiger's cage and I knew the zookeeper had left it unlocked. I could feel their stares from across the street. They wanted to lock eyes with me, the signal of challenge, but I did not want to exchange eyes with them. My heartbeat quickened and I walked a little faster, hoping they would not notice.

Suddenly, a shout and the sound of shoes on pavement. "Get him!"

Instantly, I threw my lunch sack into the street like bait to wolves and sprinted down the sidewalk, pumping Father's good umbrella up and down like a piston.

The thunder of twenty feet pounded the pavement behind me. "Get him! Tackle him!"

Homes and stores flashed past. I tried to look for an open shop door, a refuge. But I knew it could not be an Armenian shop. They would only side with the bullies, who were just steps behind me now. From a cobbler's shop twenty feet ahead, a young man stepped out onto the sidewalk and looked toward our commotion.

"Farouge!" the boys called to the man. "Grab him!"

An Armenian. My heart sank. I tried to dodge to the right, but this Farouge, a man in his twenties, lunged out and snatched me by the back of my collar, dragging me instantly to a stop.

"What did you do?" he asked. It was an accusation.

The boys ran up and crowded around us.

"Nothing!" I said, panting. "I did not do anything! They just want to beat me up!"

"He is lying, Farouge," said a tall boy who emerged from the back of the pack. I looked up and saw that he was the same one who had cut my hand before. "He stole my umbrella."

I swung my head back and forth, eyes pleading with Farouge. But he only shrugged and gave me a small shove toward the others. "Take it easy, boys. Don't hurt him," he said, and walked back into his shop.

The tall teen's arm darted forward, and he yanked me toward him by a handful of my hair. "Don't *ever* run from us, you little faggot. We will *always* catch you!"

Laughter broke out around me. My eyes flickered from face to face, hoping for mercy. But I saw only mean grins. I looked at the Armenian boy who held me. He had strange slanted eyes and pockmarks in his face, like the craters of the moon. The other boys pressed in on me. Two grabbed my arms and I felt hands snaking all over my body, searching my pockets, patting down my socks, looking for money.

"I . . . I don't have any money," I said.

A hand dove down into my underwear, a good hiding place for a wallet, giving me a painful tweak when it found none.

I pleaded, still hoping to appease. "I get paid on the weekend. I can . . . can bring . . . bring some then."

"*Can—can. Bring—bring,*" the tall teen mocked, mewling in a little-girl voice. The others laughed. The teen drew back his arm and his fist smashed into my face. My back crashed down on the sidewalk. Speckles of silver light swirled before me and a warm jet of blood spurted from my nose, seeping into my mouth.

"That's for running away," the teenager said. I tried to get up, but he took one step forward and, with his square-toed black boot, kicked me in the face. Pain exploded through my mouth and nose, and I screamed. Fresh blood sprayed the sidewalk like a fountain.

Feet surrounded me and taunts showered down. "Your sister is a stinking whore! Your mother sells herself at the chalets!"

Then I heard seven clicks.

A knife blade glinted and the hand holding it belonged to the big teenager. He meant to cut me again, mark me as a trophy. Maybe this time on my face. Pushing through the ring of smaller boys, he stepped toward me.

"What are you doing, you hoodlums!" Through a red haze and a forest of legs, I saw an old man appear on the sidewalk in front of the cobbler shop. "Why do you cause trouble by my shop?"

The teenager dropped his hand down by his leg, hiding the knife from the shopkeeper's view. I heard a hard whisper from somewhere above my head. "Not this time! He will see you! Next time, if he doesn't bring money, you can cut him!"

Seven clicks again. My tormentor put the knife away.

Painfully, I stood up, cupping one hand under my nose. Blood oozed through my fingers in huge sticky drops.

"Look at this mess!" the old man fumed. "Who is going to clean it?"

I stumbled down the sidewalk, toward the shopkeeper. He stole a glance past me at the boys and seemed about to reach out to me. But instead, he turned away toward his shop, yelling, "Farouge! Come and see what those hoodlums have done this time!"

4

Tears rolled down my face as I staggered down the sidewalk, blood dripping onto my white shirt. My right eye had puffed to a slit. The metallic taste of blood slicked my tongue and I could feel that my mouth was cut inside. Glancing behind me, I saw the gang of boys skulking back toward the bakery like one animal with many legs. The cobbler was waving his arms at them, berating them, threatening to call the police. I knew he would not. He would not risk having his shop vandalized on account of a Lebanese boy.

Miraculously, I had not lost Father's umbrella. I put my hand through the wrist strap and took off my black vest. Still walking, still stealing backward glances, I used it to mop the blood and mucus from my face. Soon I had put five blocks between myself and the Armenians, and I began to think the worst might be over. It was full morning now, with a good number of people out walking. I kept my head down, not wanting anyone to see how badly I'd been beaten.

Two more neighborhoods, I thought. *Two more, and then I will be at my uncle's.*

At that moment, a pair of boots appeared dead in my path.

"What did they take from you?"

I knew the voice, and it was like a terrible dream. It belonged to a Kurdish boy named Iskendar, the neighborhood's worst bully, one who loved to shake me down for money. I looked up at his stringy brown hair and slim face. Like the Armenian, he was a teenager, sixteen or seventeen. His skinny lips disappeared into a smirk so that all I saw was teeth.

"I *said,* what did they take from you?" His tone was that of an old friend stopping for a chat.

"Nothing," I said.

Iskendar looked me up and down, then craned his neck a bit to see behind me. "What did you do with your lunch?"

I backed up a step. "I threw it away."

"You're lying," Iskendar said. But his tone was warm, as if this was only a joke.

Footsteps fell behind me. Without looking, I could feel a gathering at my back.

"I would like you to give me your umbrella and your vest," Iskendar said congenially.

With my peripheral vision, I could see that his friends now surrounded me. Still, I tried to bargain.

"You can have my vest. But this is my father's umbrella and he will hurt me."

Iskendar let his face melt into a mask of false pity. Then he laughed. "I don't care!" He snatched the umbrella out of my hand and stuffed it in his back pocket.

Suddenly, a dozen hands descended on me as the Kurds hustled me off the sidewalk into the yellow tile of a stairwell entrance out of sight of the street.

"Please! Don't!" I yelled, looking wildly around for someone who might see me, might rescue me. No one came.

Iskendar followed us into the stairwell. While the other boys held me, he stood in front of me and slapped me hard across the face. My nose and eyes burst into new pain. I held up my arms to shield my face. The other boys punched me, in the ears, the neck, anywhere they could land a blow. I tried to remain standing; I looked for a way to run, but I was caged in. Some of Iskendar's gang climbed partway up a flight of stairs behind me, and kicked me through the railing. One boy bent and pulled off my shoes to see if I had hidden money in them.

They beat me until I was lying in a heap. Finally, Iskendar reached down and grabbed the pocket of my bloody shirt, and ripped it downward. "Remember," he said. "I did that to you."

I heard laughter, and my body felt the pounding of feet on the concrete. Every spot on my body hurt. Skull, neck, back, chest. Throbbing and stabbing pain everywhere. I looked down the length of my legs and saw that my feet were bare. The bullies had taken my shoes. And my father's umbrella. For a few minutes, I simply sat and cried.

Anguished confusion tore at me. I could not go back the way I came and risk facing the Kurdish and Armenian boys again. But if I went forward, I might run into the Shia gangs. It had happened before. In the end, I based my choice on simple arithmetic: It would be better to pass through one battlefield than two. Maybe I would get lucky.

Struggling to my feet in the yellow breezeway, I peeked out. The street was empty of people. Hobbling quickly, I stole to the edge of Kurdish turf, cowering close to buildings, my bare feet slapping the wet winter pavement. At each corner, I hunched like a hunted rabbit, my one good eye ticking left and right, looking for the Shia.

Ann Arbor, Michigan
2007

The first time I met Zakariah Anani, I saw a thousand stories in his eyes. I walked into an airport hotel room in Ann Arbor, Michigan, and saw him, his back bent like the branch of a cedar tree. Zak had already joined Walid Shoebat and started speaking out against radical Islam. I had done some speaking on my own, taking leave from my job as IT manager for a large nonprofit. But this would be my first time speaking with both Zak and Walid, and the next day we were booked at the University of Michigan. When I walked into the hotel room, Zak stood to greet me, using the back of a chair to support himself. His eyelids drooped as though heavy with secrets. His skin was rough as though etched with many tears.

I stopped just inside the doorway. "You are Kamal Saleem?" he said.

"Yes."

"Where are you from?"

"I am originally from Lebanon."

"Really? Me, too."

I thought about his family name. "Anani . . . Anani. Are you not Shia?"

"No!" Zak said, sounding almost offended. He stopped to cough, hacking violently into a cloth. "We are Sunni."

"But the Ananis live in the Shia area." In Lebanon, you can know a family's tribe by where they live.

He lifted his chin, resolute. "Yes, but we were Sunni."

"Who did you fight with?"

"The Muslim fragments."

He meant militia. In Lebanon, there were the PLO and Fatah—major groups with hundreds or even thousands of soldiers. But small bands of warriors often sprang up to join the fight. When they got enough people to make a noise, they became recognized as a party or a faction.

For the first time in more than twenty years, I felt the bond of kinship. Here was someone like me, who had come out of the darkness. I crossed the room and embraced Zak like a long-lost brother. We began speaking in Lebanese, my tongue skipping happily over my native language like feet revisiting a beloved country. For so many years, I had altered my manner of speaking, concealing it behind an Arab dialect or speaking mediocre French or snippets of Spanish. Now, I babbled along with Zak, letting my heritage shine.

Zak did not tell me which militia he fought with. I assumed immediately that the militia was Shia and that he was ashamed to say it. For a Sunni to fight on the same side as the Shia is the ultimate shame, and the same is true in reverse. If you are Shia and you fight alongside the Sunni, you are never trusted, never included in the inner circle. If there is a security leak, you are the first to be suspected. If someone is to be sent on a foolishly dangerous mission, you are the first to go.

Zak told me about his first kill.

"The *fedayeen* knocked on my door," he said. " 'If you are going to join us,' they told me, 'you have to prove yourself.' They said they had cornered a man on a rooftop nearby, and they wanted me to go and take care of him."

So, Zak said, he climbed up to the top of a high-rise and threw the man off. Zak was only fourteen years old.

This story rang true with me. The factions were often like American gangs. In order to belong, you had to "make your bones," as they did in the Mafia movies.

This trading of our histories was the way we verified each other. If I was going to be in league with him, to stand on the same stage and claim a former life in *jihad*, then I wanted to know who he fought with, what he did. He wanted to know the same thing about me. Each of us would know instantly whether the other was lying.

Zak told me about his daughters, how proud he was that they were excelling in school. He was raising them on his own because his wife left him when he converted to Christianity. He also talked about his medical problems, which included severe diabetes.

As Zak told his story, he stopped often and pressed a handkerchief to his face to muffle the deep, booming coughs that wracked his small frame. Once, after such a spell, he pulled an old photograph from his shirt pocket and handed it to me, saying, "I have not always been this way."

The young warrior looking back at me from the picture was tough and muscular, his eyes awake, bright, and proud. The man before me now could not weigh much more than a hundred pounds. Suddenly, I wanted to protect Zak, to watch over and cover him.

When I met Walid Shoebat, I had challenged his experience in *jihad*, just as Walid and Zak had challenged each other. But I did not challenge Zak. Like me, like all of us, there were parts of his life of which he was not proud. He had reached his harbor of peace, but his earthly vessel was crumbling. Standing in that hotel room that day, I knew that I only wanted to see laughter return to his face before he went to his final home.

Beirut, Lebanon
1965

1

Just inside the boundary of the Shia neighborhood, I stopped and tucked myself into the vestibule of an apartment house. The boys here had robbed me many times. Should I go on? Maybe I should go back home and tell my family what happened to me. But I knew my father would be angry that I had not earned money from my uncle.

"You should have found a way!" he would say. "Take different roads!" And where was his good umbrella? he would want to know.

Huddled in the vestibule, I shivered as the chilly air bored into my bones. A mist had begun to knit itself in the air, and I looked through it across the street at mossy, old French-era buildings, their wrought iron balconies sagging like jowls on a once beautiful woman. Some of these tired old ladies squatted behind high stone walls whose tops were jeweled with broken glass in many colors, cemented down to keep out intruders.

I wish I was enclosed in a circle of jagged glass.

In the gutter before me, a sudden wind dug into a leafy drift, kicking up a swirl of leaves and sending up the scent of mildew. My head ached. I could feel tight patches of skin on my face where my blood had begun to scab. My feet seemed rooted to the dank concrete. Without seeing them, I knew the Shia boys were waiting for me—as surely as I knew my uncle was waiting—looking impatiently at the old clock on his wall.

My stomach quivered, and a new tear traced a salty trail to the corner of my mouth.

Allah, help me!

Shaking from cold and fear, I edged out onto the sidewalk. The cold wind looped through the curving streets that wound through the neighborhood, streets that did not let me see too far ahead.

I had not gone far when I heard laughter.

If I can run . . .

I could hear their laughter coming closer.

If I can run as fast as the wind . . .

I stopped and leaned against the wall of a high-rise, gathering my nerve like steam in a kettle. The pain in my head and body vanished, swallowed in a rush of adrenaline. Then, like a startled bird, a small cry flew out of my throat and I took off.

"There he is! Get him! Get him!"

How many? Ten? Twelve?

The concrete blocks drummed beneath me, the pounding of many feet as a gang of Shia boys surged across the street toward me. Shops flashed by in a blur, and my senses fed random, useless thoughts to my brain: *Military surplus. American uniforms in the window. A restaurant. The smell of hummus.*

The beast gathered speed behind me. Jingling zippers. Thudding feet.

"Faster! Don't let him get away!"

The fastest boys were only an arm's length away.

"Grab him, stupid!"

An intersection. I did not slow down. Brakes squealed. An American car, big and black, stopped inches from my hip. A man cursed in English.

I sensed the beast slip back. And ahead, I saw salvation.

Like a lighthouse, a large mosque rose in the distance. It was Sunni. Only two blocks away. Pounding and screaming about my whore of a mother, the howling animal was nearly at my heels again. Adrenaline carried me like a rushing current. I bounded up the mosque steps just as I felt the brush of fingers reaching out to grab me, then realized suddenly that Allah had smiled on me: *I am not wearing shoes!*

I was able to burst through the mosque doors without slowing down. The Shia boys had to slow down to kick their shoes off.

"Help me! Help me!" My cries echoed off the tiled ceiling in the outer court.

I saw a small knot of men, long-bearded and dressed like imams. They leapt up as a group and ran toward me. An instant later, the mosque door flew open and the Shia boys tumbled in. I reached the imams, and one of them, a tall man with fiery eyes, brushed me behind his robe with a protective arm and faced the boys, who stopped as though dropping anchor.

"What's going on here?" the imam demanded. "What do you want?"

A tall, slim boy stepped forward, jabbing a finger at me. "He stole from my father's store, then hit us and ran away! We are supposed to bring him back!"

"They are liars!" I screamed. "I did not steal! I have not been in any store! They are chasing me to hurt me!"

Another imam stepped forward. Looking up, I saw that he had hooded eyes, wise like an owl.

He regarded the boys and said, very evenly, "If this boy stole from your father, tell me—what did he steal?"

"Something from the shelf!" the slim boy answered quickly. "It belongs to my father!"

The wise man turned to me. "Turn out your pockets."

I stepped from behind the imam's robe and pulled the white fabric of my trouser pockets out. Only lint fell to the floor.

Now the first imam took a step toward the Shia boys.

"Go! Let's go!" the tall boy shouted, and the little gang spun as one and ran out the mosque doors. One of them called back to me: "We will find you later!"

The imam with the hooded eyes shouted after them. "If you come here again, we'll break your legs!"

Now the men gathered around me like a protective flock. "I am Abdul Rahman," said the man who had first challenged my attackers. "Tell us what happened."

2

I told them, neighborhood by neighborhood, my high voice echoing like a flute in the cool vastness of the outer court. The Armenians and the missing Maronite lady. The Kurds and my father's umbrella. Now these Shia boys. By the end of the story, tears of exhaustion and frustration rolled down my face. They could see from my wounds I was telling the truth.

"What is your name?" Abdul Rahman said.

"Kamal Saleem."

"Saleem? Is your father Mohammed Saleem?"

I nodded.

Above his red-tinged beard, Abdul Rahman broke into a smile, and around me the other men nodded in recognition. "We know your uncles! Do not worry. We will take care of you."

Now Abdul Rahman led me to an area called *al-wodoug*, a place of many bathrooms where worshippers cleanse themselves before *salat*, prayers. I had done this ritual countless times, washing first my hands— right then left. Then my face three times, my mouth, my nose, a dash of water to my hair, then wrist to elbows, and last my feet.

Leather-strapped wooden clogs waited outside the *al-wodoug*. I slipped my feet into them, and Abdul Rahman led me inside. Along one wall a rank of cold-water faucets stretched, poised over a long marble trough. Opposite the faucets on the other side of the trough, marble blocks marched away in a long line, forming benches on which to sit and wash.

As I rinsed away the morning's violence, weak sunlight crept in through windows set high in the wall. Icy water trickled down over my feet, and blood skated toward the drains in crimson threads. As I washed, I wondered why these men were being so nice to me. No one had been nice to me in a very long time, it seemed. For months, I had felt like a burden to my family. Like fat or a tumor. Sometimes I thought it would be better for them if I were dead.

"Does that feel better?" Abdul Rahman asked.

I nodded. "Yes. Thank you."

Another imam came with a towel, and I dried myself. Then he took off his *abbayah* and draped it around my shoulders. The robe was much too long for me and doubled down on itself, the white fabric pooling at my feet. It dragged along the ground as the three of us walked back into the inner court, an enormous space with soaring ceilings and colorful carpets. A row of curved wooden stools, or *kursi*, sat along one wall; these were used to hold the Koran while reading it. Another wall was lined with high wooden shelves filled with Muslim books.

Nearby, a small kerosene heater was burning. The other men—with Abdul Rahman and the towel imam, I counted six altogether—stood around it. The heater cast a small circle of warmth, and the imams ushered me like a duckling to sit directly in front of it.

"Sit, sit," Abdul Rahman said, and the men all sat around me on rugs someone had placed there in the shape of a crescent.

One by one, the imams introduced themselves. I do not remember all their names, but I remember two of them.

"I am Abu Azziz," said one.

"I am Abu Tawfiq," said another.

I wondered, *Are they every one Abu?*

Abdul Rahman sat to my right. "Kamal Saleem," he said thoughtfully, touching my knee. "Do you know that I play soccer with your Uncle Emad?"

My father had once touched me much as this man was touching me. But in the last year, only beatings.

"Why did you have to cross all these neighborhoods today, Kamal? Where were you going?"

"To work. It is the shortcut I take when it is cold outside. I have to work to bring home money to my family."

Abdul Rahman's brow darkened briefly, then brightened. "From this day on, no one will touch you on your way to work. Anyone who deals with you will have to deal with us."

These words both pleased and surprised me. No more long hikes to avoid the bullies? No more fear? I desperately, desperately wanted to believe him. But what would these six do, I wondered? They were not like thugs or bodyguards. They were holy men.

"After *salat*, will you take us and show us the places where the boys hurt you?" Abdul Rahman asked.

"Yes!" I said. "I will show you!"

Instantly I forgot my pain, my scrapes, my bruises. So many times I had asked my father to help me, and he had said no. He was too busy. He thought the beatings were my fault. A teaching from the *hadith* popped into my head: If one part of the body is hurt, the whole body is hurt, and good Muslims must respond to any threat to our body. My family had not honored that teaching on my behalf; but now these men, perfect strangers, had committed to do so. I always thought my family was filled with the most observant Muslims. Were these men more righteous?

Abdul Rahman spoke again into the vast space. "Would you like to spend the day with us? Here, at the mosque?"

I dipped my head in gratitude. "Thank you very much, but I cannot. If I do not go to work, my Uncle Abdul Al-Karim will beat me. If I do not bring home money, my father will beat me."

Abdul Rahman frowned. "This uncle I do not know. He is on your mother's side?"

I nodded.

"How much does your uncle pay you?"

"Three *lira* a day."

Laughter floated up from the men in the little semicircle. I looked around in wonder. Abdul Rahman opened his robe, searching for his pants pocket. When his hand appeared again, it held three Lebanese *lira*, which he held out to me.

"This should be enough to pay off your beatings for today."

I did not hesitate, but took the money as if it were water in a desert. *I'm saved!*

Now the conversation turned away from me, and the imams began discussing politics.

"I spoke with Omar Yazid in Syria," said the man who called himself Abu Tawfiq. "He said Arafat is paying *fedayeen* more money to fight now. His forces are growing."

Of course, I knew the name Yasser Arafat. Everyone did. As the founder of Fatah, a Palestinian resistance group, he was already a legend. I had heard my father and brothers talking about him, but this was different: I was included in a conversation with men who knew men who *knew* Arafat!

"The Palestinian issue is proving a good one for the Brotherhood," Abdul Rahman said. I knew from my father that the Palestinians were Muslims who had been kicked out of their homeland. "Their story is a vehicle by which we can advance the faith. We have the teachings. Arafat has the guns."

The imams laughed. Then Abdul Rahman turned to me, his eyes glowing like matched gems of dark topaz. "What do you think of all this, Kamal?"

I had no idea. But the imams knew my family and they were Muslim like me and Sunni like me, so I simply agreed. "The way of Islam is righteousness."

Abdul laughed heartily. "I can see that your heart is strong for Allah, Kamal! That is very good."

We prayed in the inner court, bowing to the east as gauzy sunlight showered down around us, turning the dust motes gold. I loved the ritual of the prayers, the holiness of the sound as it drifted up like the scent of flowers, pleasing to Allah. I sensed the strength of these men.

"Now we will go and make the neighborhoods safe for you, Kamal," Abdul Rahman said.

I smiled at him and nodded briefly. When he had first mentioned this, my injuries cried out "yes!" in chorus with my wounded heart. But now I found my mind searching for a word I had heard my brother Fouad use. It was a word for men who were very committed to advancing Islam. Something about Abdul Rahman and the Abus, as I came to think of Abu Azziz and the other imams, stirred this memory—the political talk, Abdul Rahman's luminous eyes.

I looked around at the imams and saw that their faces were somehow harder. A ghost of apprehension whispered into my ear. My injuries only stung now. I could live with them. And I had the money Abdul Rahman had given me. I could take the long, long way home, explain what happened, plead with my father.

Perhaps he will have mercy on me. Perhaps he will let me find a job in another part of the city.

Robes rustling, the imams herded me toward the front doors of the mosque. It seemed days since I had burst through them, propelled on a rocket of terror. Abu Tawfiq now spoke to me directly for the first time since introducing himself. "After we talk to these boys, they will never bother you again."

The look in his eyes. Dark. Serious. Suddenly, I knew these men did not mean to appeal to the boys in the neighborhoods on the basis of peace. What had been a whisper of apprehension now turned into a gale-force wind, and I felt as if I were a leaf blown suddenly into the swift current of a river.

Now I remembered the word Fouad had used: *zealots*.

I turned to Abdul Rahman and bowed slightly. "I thank you for everything you have done for me today, but I think I should be getting home now."

I watched as Abdul Rahman's eyes tallied my fear and discarded it. Then he smiled and put his hands on my shoulders. "Kamal, if you do not face your enemies, your enemies will chase you forever."

3

The sidewalks dried into puddles as we moved into the neighborhood where the pack of Shia boys had chased me. A chill wind coursed through the curving streets, ruffling the robes of the imams who surrounded me like a mothering flock. Abdul Rahman insisted that I tell him where I had first seen them, so I led the imams back through the Shia neighborhood.

As we approached a corner bakery, I saw the boys who had chased me to the mosque lurking by the door. When they looked up and saw us coming, they scattered like a school of spooked fish. Outside the bakery the smell of rosewater and Turkish coffee poured into the street, and I could see through the glass several customers seated at small tables, munching pastries. Abdul Rahman entered first, and I followed with the Abus behind me. On our right, a long counter ran the length of the shop; the diners sat to the left, knives clinking on plates. Behind the counter, glass cases displayed *baklava,* sesame cakes, and *kanafa* with cheeses. Suddenly, I remembered I had not eaten since leaving my mother's kitchen. I longed to be there now, safely inside the rustling of the berry tree.

A man with a small moustache squared off behind the counter and wiped his hands on the towel that hung from the bellied waistband of his white pants. His eyes roved over what must have seemed a curious group, one small boy with six large men.

"What do you want?" he demanded.

Abdul Rahman put his right arm around my shoulder and ushered me before the baker. Quivering inside, I did not resist. I kept my face even, not wanting to embarrass my protectors by showing any fear.

"Who is that large boy who was outside just now, the one who ran away with the others?"

"He is my son," the baker snapped. "What is it to you?" Beneath his bluster, I thought I sensed fear.

"Do you see this boy? Look at his face. Do you see how your son and his friends beat him up?"

The baker's face took on a look of disdained amusement. "So what? That's what boys do."

"Perhaps," Abdul Rahman said. "But this boy is our boy. He belongs to us."

The imam placed his hands on the counter and leaned closer to the baker, piercing him with a hard gaze from his superior height. The darkness I had seen flicker across his face in the mosque now burned across his features.

"We are the imams of *Masjid al-Bakar*," he said, naming the mosque. "We are the Muslim Brotherhood. If you touch this boy, you touch us."

I had heard this name, this "Muslim Brotherhood," spoken in hushed tones between my father and my brother Fouad. I did not know what it meant, but I saw the baker freeze and the insolence melt away from his face. Behind me, the diners fell silent. Around us, the whole shop suddenly seemed still. Charged. My heart thumped inside my chest.

At last, the baker drew a great breath and let it out. "I will talk to my son."

Abdul Rahman did not move, yet his presence seemed somehow to loom across the counter, pressing in on the baker. "Yes. You will talk to your son. And he will talk to his friends. And all of them will come and apologize to this boy. If they don't come, we will come and find *you*. We know where you work and we know where you live."

I did not allow any look to pass across my face, but my insides had turned to jelly. I did not know what I had expected. The imams exercising their spiritual authority, perhaps, the Sunni over the Shia. Talking. Reasoning. But as the baker seemed to shrink inside his clothes, I saw fear in his eyes. I could smell it on him, a metallic tang. He said something else to Abdul Rahman. I couldn't hear what exactly, but it was something very humble. They continued talking, but I do not remember what else they said at that moment—only my own trembling amazement at the power of the imams.

"I will take care of this today," the baker finally said to Abdul Rahman. Now he turned to me, his face a salad of anxious kindness. "Come back here tomorrow," he said. "I will make sure my son apologizes to you . . . Would you like something to eat?"

I shook my head and looked down at the flecked tile floor. All I wanted to do was go home. This was more than I had bargained for.

I did not know it was only the beginning.

4

Iskendar, the Kurdish bully, had beaten me up many times, and I knew where he lived. Abdul Rahman insisted that I tell him. After a short walk, we arrived at a shanty house—bits of plywood and tin pieced together to extend a small house sitting on a corner. Thin strips of nailed tin held the wooden door together. Abdul Rahman stood before me and rapped twice on it. The rest of the imams formed a crescent behind me.

The door cracked slightly and a woman's face appeared, her *hijab* exposing the front of her hair in the style of the Kurds that my mother thought brazen. In the woman's face, I could see echoes of the bully's bone structure—the wide cheekbones, the forehead that jutted too far forward in its skin.

"Yes?" the woman said, revealing gold among her upper teeth.

"We are the imams of the mosque. We want to speak with your son," Abdul Rahman said.

"He is not here," the woman said, opening the door a little wider. She wore a long skirt made of a patchwork of fabrics, some in screaming prints like the Gypsies wear. Most of the Kurds were poor immigrants who had come to Lebanon illegally from Turkey, Syria, and Iraq seeking any kind of work they could get. Their homes and clothes were often makeshift, cobbled together from whatever could be had cheaply.

"What do you want with my son?" the woman said.

As he had at the bakery, Abdul Rahman put his arm around my shoulder and ushered me forward. "This boy belongs to us. And your son beat him up today."

The woman looked down at me, seeming to catalogue the injuries on my face. Then she looked back at Abdul Rahman. "If my son beat him, the boy must have done something to deserve it."

"*Deserve* it?" Abdul Rahman said, biting off the words. "He *deserves* to be beaten every time he passes this way?"

His voice grew louder, and I could see from the corners of my vision that passersby had stopped to listen. Abdul Rahman spoke as if the woman was dust. "This is not even your country, and your son pretends to guard a territory here?"

A shadow play of emotions flickered across the woman's face: disdain, the dawn of understanding, then panic. Slowly, she pulled her arm from behind the door. In her hand, she held a stick.

"Get away from my house! Get out of here!" she shouted, waving the stick and salting her words with curses.

From behind her, I heard a guttural yell and saw movement. A worn print drape that served as an interior door was swept aside. Out came Iskendar, waving a banana knife. Instantly he spotted me standing on the sidewalk.

"So you have come to cause me trouble? You have broken into my house! Now I will cut you!"

"That is him!" I shouted, pointing and backing away. "He is the one!"

Abdul Rahman did not hesitate. He flung the door wide with his right hand, pushed the woman aside with his left, took three steps forward, and kicked the boy straight in the gut. A noise of wind escaping, and Iskendar collapsed on the concrete floor.

The woman screamed. "Don't hurt my son!"

The Abus now crowded into the tiny space. A single raw lightbulb swung over their heads, throwing wild shadows onto the fruit box slats that patched holes in the woman's walls.

"Please! Please don't hurt my son!"

But Abdul Rahman swooped down and snatched the banana knife, and the imams were on Iskendar like a pack of wolves, kicking and kicking, each blow lifting his body off the ground. Their fury terrified me. To the imams, this was not only an issue of territory; this boy was a Kurd, which meant he was no better than a dog.

The beating I got was nothing like he got.

Wham! Blood burst from his nose in a stream as one man's foot crashed into his face. Instantly, the skin around his eyes turned red, then purple.

Wham! Burgundy patches bloomed in Iskendar's dark hair, matting it together in stringy ropes.

Wham! His face went slack, then pale underneath the bright scarlet of his wounds.

His mother screaming, screaming, drawing a little knot of Kurdish neighbors who did not dare interfere.

My own heart screamed inside me. One part of me was glad for vengeance, but the savage assault horrified me. Part of me was proud to have champions. Part of me wished I had never run into the mosque.

In a low voice like thunder, Abdul Rahman bent and spoke into the boy's bloody ear: "If you ever threaten this boy again, we know where you live. We know who your mother is. And we know the police. I will call them myself, and they will deport your filthy little clan back to whatever Iraqi cave you crawled out of."

"My son will not touch your son!" the woman cried. "We only want to make a living. I promise this will never happen again!"

Now Abdul Rahman tangled his fingers in Iskendar's hair and jerked his head off the pale yellow concrete. He laid the blade of the banana knife against the boy's cheek and pressed the tip into his nose. Terror shot through my belly—I was afraid Abdul Rahman was going to cut the boy's face, a permanent symbol of Sunni victory and Kurdish shame.

"Apologize to this boy," Abdul Rahman said. "Right now."

A sob of fresh hope burst from the woman. "Yes! Tell him you're sorry! Ask him to forgive you!"

Revulsion seized me as a slimy swirl of spit, blood, and mucus streamed from the boy's mouth and nose, and he blubbered through it. "I'm . . . sorry. . . ."

Then I saw that his eyes were dry. No tears, no remorse, no defeat. From beneath battered, swollen lids, his eyes pierced mine with a gunmetal glint. Only his mother and I were in a position to see it. A new wave of fear rolled through me.

Abdul Rahman dropped Iskendar's head, and it thumped on the floor. Then, in a flourish of robes, the imams sailed out, like a storm cloud that has fired its lightning bolts and spilled its rain.

5

The sun had come out, playing among fat white clouds, sucking the water off the pavement. Still carrying the Kurdish boy's banana knife, Abdul Rahman walked at my shoulder, hurrying me along. I could feel a charge in the air, a spark snapping among the imams, as though they had drawn energy from the violence.

Because of that, I did not tell Abdul Rahman about the look I had seen in the boy's eyes. I was afraid he might go back and kill him.

When we reached the Armenian neighborhood, I saw a group of boys standing in front of a *cadout*, a gift shop that sold decorative items like statues and bowls and figurines. I recognized the ringleader, and as we approached, he recognized me. Like leaves in a wind gust, the boys scattered.

"Was that them?" Abdul Rahman asked me.

After seeing what the imams had done to Iskendar, I was afraid to answer. But how could I now turn against these men when they had become my defenders?

"Yes," I said.

Abdul Rahman ushered me along faster. When we reached the door of the gift shop, he did not slow down but entered in long strides, extending his arm and raking an entire shelf of merchandise off onto the floor. The crash filled my ears as crystal and ceramic pieces shattered against the tile.

A dark, curly-haired man ran from the rear of the store. "My shop! What are you doing!"

"Infidels!" Abdul Rahman roared. "You are picking on a young Muslim boy, a son of Allah! Why don't you come and deal with us?"

"What are you talking about!" the shop owner roared back. "I don't know what you're talking about!" He surveyed the sparkling mess on the floor, and rage simmered on his face.

Abdul Rahman advanced a step toward him. "Those kids outside. Every time this boy walks through your neighborhood, they beat him. This is a Christian crusade against us! You lose your country, and now you are coming to possess ours!"

"Those kids are not mine! They were just standing in front of my shop!"

Outside, I heard raised voices, and when I turned to look, my stomach flipped. Five or six Armenian men had come running, armed with sticks and pipes. Behind them, I saw two of the boys who had beaten me.

A woman's voice came from somewhere above, a window or a balcony. "The police! Someone call the police!"

Abdul Rahman barreled out the front door, robes flying, and surveyed the area like an emperor. "Yes, call the police!" he bellowed toward the upper floors of the surrounding apartment houses. "Let me show you what I will do while the police watch me do it!"

The imams waded in among the Armenians like sharks among minnows. Suddenly, in my mind, a puzzle piece snapped into place: Abdul Rahman and the other imams were trained fighters. Abdul Rahman swept the banana knife in wide arcs, forming around himself a protective space. One of the Abus—Azziz, I think—now revealed himself a martial artist, delivering a straight-armed blow to the throat of a blond Armenian man. I stood beside the shopkeeper gaping. The dozen men tangled before me, a savage knot of flailing arms and legs. Each time Abdul Rahman whirled in my direction, I saw *madness* in his eyes.

Then one of the Armenian boys picked up a rock and hurled it, striking Abdul Rahman in the chest.

Time froze. A warble of sirens broke the air. In seconds, two Jeeps carrying paramilitary police arrived amid a whir of engines and squealing brakes. Four officers with automatic rifles spilled from the vehicles and waded in to separate the fighters.

"Who would like to explain this?" a man with many decorations on his shoulders demanded.

Abdul Rahman spoke up immediately. "This boy belongs to us," he said, nodding his chin toward me.

I now hoped the earth would crack open and swallow me whole. *The police will have my name forever*, I thought. *They will think I'm a criminal.*

"Every time he comes through this neighborhood, the Armenian boys beat him!" Abdul Rahman spat out. "We try to live in peace with you, and this is what you do to us!"

"Which boy beats him?" the police commander said.

"Many of the boys! All of the boys!" Abdul Rahman said. "Especially *that* one." He pointed at the boy who had thrown the rock at him.

The police commander closed the distance to the boy in three long steps, drew back his arm, and delivered a rough slap across his face. A spot of blood appeared on the boy's lip. The commander drew back his arm and delivered another blow. Now blood trickled from the boy's nose in a scarlet stream.

This violence shocked my sense of fairness. Did not the policeman want to hear the Armenians' side of the story?

"*You* did this, and your neighborhood doesn't deserve this trouble!" the commander bellowed at the boy. "You don't know who these people are. You're going to get yourself killed! You're going to get your family killed!"

Suddenly, I realized the policeman was protecting the boy. All of the Armenians. He was showing the Muslim Brotherhood that he would take care of the problem, that there was no need for retaliation. With a bloody nose as a deposit, the policeman was buying this boy a future.

Houston, Texas
2007

I was sitting in the Houston airport browsing Internet news when I spotted an Associated Press item out of Cairo: "Two lawmakers from the banned Muslim Brotherhood were arrested Wednesday, officials said, in an intensifying crackdown on the nation's most powerful opposition movement."[1]

State security forces, the news story said, had stripped the two men of their parliamentary immunity, accusing them of participating in the Brotherhood's illegal activities: "Authorities have increasingly clamped down on the Islamist group since December including sending 40 of its top financiers and businessmen to a military tribunal on charges of money laundering and supporting terrorism."[2]

The Brotherhood does more than support *terrorism, I thought. They are its lifeblood.*

Among the groups and factions in which I had moved as a jihadist, it was well known that most Islamic terror groups have at least some roots in the Muslim Brotherhood, or *al-ikhwān*. The Brotherhood, the Muslim imitation of European fascism, had been around since 1928, founded in Egypt by Hassan al-Banna, a schoolteacher. The Brotherhood has always been strongest in Egypt, but it spread rapidly through other Muslim countries, setting up its Lebanon chapter in 1936.[3]

The Brotherhood is a Sunni movement with a stark and violent credo: "Allah is our objective. The Prophet is our leader. The Qur'an is our law. *Jihad* is our way. Dying in the way of Allah is our highest hope." As a young boy rescued from ethnic street violence, I drank in this teaching in all its simple, childlike clarity. The teachings of the Brotherhood gave me power, authority, and ultimately, a gun.

As a young man, I imported this credo to America. I was not alone. During the late 1970s, I was among a wave of Middle Eastern students who washed on to American shores, carried along on oil money and easy visas. We were the first wave, the vanguard, planting the seeds of *jihad* with groups like the Muslim American Youth Association (MAYA). It was easy for me to connect with MAYA because some members believed—and still believe—the same thing I did: that the Western world is evil and must be destroyed. MAYA held U.S. conferences that attracted Islamist groups who openly proclaim their hatred for the Jews, for Christians, and for America.

At a MAYA conference in 1994, a man named Bassam al-Amoush was delivering a fiery message when someone interrupted him to hand another speaker a note. "We have good news," the speaker proclaimed. "A Palestinian policeman has carried out a suicide bombing in Jerusalem. Three were killed and fifteen wounded. Hamas claims responsibility for the incident."[4]

The crowd erupted in rapturous chants: "Allahu Akbar! Allahu Akbar."

Sheikh Ahmed Yassin, an Islamic cleric from Gaza, founded Hamas in 1987. It is the same Hamas written about in today's newspapers, with terrorists blowing up civilians in the Middle East and Europe. And it is the same Hamas that now has organized cells in Tucson, Houston, and New York City, as well as Columbia, Missouri; Springfield, Virginia; and Santa Clara, California.

Sheikh Yassin designed Hamas on the model of the Muslim Brotherhood.

I closed my laptop and scanned the airport waiting area. When I came to this country, there were only a handful of mosques in Houston. Today, there are more than eighty. There in the airport, several groups of Middle Eastern men and women sat or stood in groups, the women revealed by their *hijabs,* the men by their general look.

How many Kamals are there in this group? I wondered.

A better question: how many Kamals were in the group of young men I had seen in the Atlanta airport in 2006 chanting, "Khaybar, Khaybar, ya Yahud! Jay'sh Muhammad saufa ya'ud!" Khaybar was an ancient battle in which Muhammad's armies annihilated some Jewish tribes. The chant taunts the Jews and warns them that "the army of Muhammad will return!" Among the Atlanta travelers, I had been perhaps the only one who understood that these young men were chanting a *jihadi* death song to Jews in an American airport.

No matter how many terrorist acts are carried out by young Middle Eastern men, it is a cultural taboo for an American to sit in an airport and wonder whether the young Middle Eastern men they see are terrorists. This is why radical Islamists love America: she has replaced her generosity toward all cultures and religions with an unquestioning embrace of "multiculturalism."

We like to think the best of our neighbors. A lot of people thought of Mohammed Atta as a fine young neighbor. That was just before he and eighteen friends killed nearly three thousand people using passenger jets as missiles. It is good to think well of our neighbors, but that does not mean we should be willfully blind to the historical demographics of *jihad.*

Which is why I was sitting in the Houston airport on my way to a string of speaking engagements in the Carolinas. My topic would be the same as it was in California, Michigan, Colorado, and elsewhere: America has an enemy within her walls. People who are like I was. Islamists working as taxi drivers and grocery clerks and university professors. People who are planning attacks such as those exposed by the American government since 2001:[5]

• **May 2002:** Jose Padilla, an American citizen accused of seeking a "dirty bomb," was convicted of conspiracy. Padilla, a former member of a Chicago street gang, attended a mosque in Fort Lauderdale with Adham Amin Hassoun, an illegal in the United States who was later charged with providing material support to terrorists. In other words, a man like I used to be.

• **September 2002:** Six American citizens of Yemeni origin were convicted of supporting Al Qaeda. Five of the six were from Lackawanna, New York.

• **June 2003:** Eleven men from Alexandria, Virginia, trained for *jihad* against American soldiers. They were convicted of conspiracy and violating the Neutrality Act. One of the men, Randall Todd Royer, was a former spokesman for the Muslim American Society, which claims to be a "charitable, religious, social, cultural, and educational" organization.

• **August 2004:** James Elshafay and Shahawar Matin Siraj planned to bomb New York's Penn Station during the Republican National Convention. Elshafay was a nineteen-year-old American high school dropout recruited into *jihad* by a person like I had been. Siraj was a twenty-two-year-old Pakistani national who had been in the United States illegally for six years.

• **August 2005:** Four homegrown Los Angeles terrorists—Kevin James, Levar Haley Washington, Gregory Vernon Patterson, and Hammad Riaz Samana—planned attacks on the National Guard, Los Angeles International Airport, two synagogues, and the Israeli consulate. James recruited Washington while in federal prison. Locked up and stripped of dignity, convicts make ripe recruits for a religion that promises them new power.

• **April 2006:** Syed Haris Ahmed and Ehsanul Islam Sadequee, both Georgia Tech students who grew up in the Atlanta area, cased and videotaped the Capitol and the World Bank for a terrorist organization.

• **June 2006:** Narseal Batiste, Patrick Abraham, Stanley Grant Phanor, Naudimar Herrera, Burson Augustine, Lyglenson Lemorin, and Rotschild Augustine were accused of plotting to blow up the Sears Tower. In February 2006, Batiste told a government agent who was posing as an al-Qaeda representative, that he and the others wanted to attend an al-Qaeda training camp and plan a "full ground war" in order to "kill all the devils we can" in the United States.

• **July 2006:** Assem Hammoud, a native Beiruti like me, plotted a mission to blow up train tunnels beneath the Hudson River.

• **May 2007:** Six men were accused of plotting to attack Fort Dix Army base in New Jersey. Prior to their mission, they recorded video of themselves at a state-owned shooting range in Pennsylvania, firing semi-automatic weapons and shouting, "Allahu Akbar!" Among the men, all of whom had Middle Eastern names, were a roofer, a pizza cook, a taxi driver, and a convenience store clerk.

• **September 2007:** Hamid Hayat of Lodi, California, was sentenced to twenty-four years in federal prison for attending an al-Qaeda terrorist training camp in Pakistan and plotting to attack targets in the United States. Federal Judge Garland Burrell Jr. said Hamid Hayat had "returned to the United States ready and willing to wage violent *jihad* when directed to do so."

Hayat, an American citizen, was somebody's neighbor. The termites are in the walls. I know because I used to be one of them. Now I am standing on the walls and shouting, "Wake up, America!" Some media and Muslim "educational" groups like to paint me as stoking "fear" of Islam. They are wrong: I am stoking fear of *radical* Islam. Given the menu of the planned violence above, perhaps it is not unreasonable to be afraid.

Had you met me before, as Allah's warrior, you would have been.

Beirut, Lebanon
1965

1

The police invited the imams and me to ride with them back to the mosque in their Jeeps. I felt very important zipping through the streets, the cool wind lifting my hair.

On the way, the police commander introduced himself to me as Sergeant Eli. "You will not have trouble with those boys again," he told me.

Then he wrote down a telephone number on a slip of paper and gave it to Abdul Rahman. "Here is the number to my station. If anything happens again, call me."

That afternoon, Abdul Rahman drove me home in his black Fiat. On the way, I prayed fervently that he would simply drop me at a corner and drive away. I planned to present the *lira* he had given me as my day's pay. My family did not need to know what had happened. My father would never believe me anyway.

But Abdul Rahman parked the Fiat at the curb and said, "Come and introduce me to your family."

My heart sank. I dreaded the moment when my father would learn I had spent the day at the mosque instead of going to work, that I had been in *fights,* that the police were called. I could not even imagine his anger.

When we reached the top of the steps, I opened the door and tried to smooth the way with false cheer. "Mama! Papa! We have a visitor . . . an imam!"

My father rushed to the door, my mother at his shoulder, her *hijab* shielding her face.

My father scowled at me. "What have you done?"

"He has done nothing, Sayyid Mohammed Saleem," Abdul Rahman said, addressing my father formally. He introduced himself and gave a brief explanation of what had happened and how the imams handled it for me.

My father glowered. "I'm sorry our son has made such trouble for you," he said. I looked down at the ground. I knew he would not believe it was not my fault.

"Kamal did not do this," Abdul Rahman insisted. "It was these boys. You must believe me. I am his witness. And if the same boys don't beat him again, it will be a different group next time. Maybe he should look for a job closer to home."

"Yes, you are right, Sayyid Rahman," my father said, and relief poured over my soul like a cleansing rain.

2

Summer seared in with fierce desert winds that sometimes blew from the south of Syria and baked the city to a shimmer. After Abdul Rahman visited my mother and father, I did not have to work across town anymore. But that did not mean I did not have to work at all. Another uncle of mine got me a job with a plumber, a competitor of my uncle's who also worked high-rise buildings. By the time the new man, Omar al-Basha, hired me, a construction crew had already erected a building ten floors high. I was hired as a seven-year-old errand boy. I had only worked there for three months when Omar announced a key part of the job: supplying each floor of the new building with the materials the men would need to install pipe for drinking water, sinks, and bath-rooms.

Omar stood outside with a small group of men and some older boys, teenagers. "We need pipe and sacks of cement for each floor," Omar said. "Kamal, you will help. There is the truck. Let's get it done."

He pointed to a rusting pickup truck that had once been painted the color of the sky. In the bed, sacks of cement sat in high stacks. We did not have elevators or conveyors of any kind. We were to carry them up, two, six, ten flights.

One of the other workers, Qassim, looked at me skeptically and then at the boss. "These sacks are as big as this boy is!"

"Do not worry," Omar said. "Kamal will do what he can."

At that moment, I vowed in my heart to do as much as the men. I was excited to do this manly work, to prove myself to the others. I could not lift the sacks high, but Omar lifted one for me and set it on my shoulder. Up the stairs I climbed, one foot in front of the other. I carried the first few sacks up with a pasted-on smile, making up with testosterone what I lacked in strength. But soon the sacks got heavier, and I watched tall, muscled workers crowd past me up the stairs again and again.

Qassim passed me up three times. The final time, he glanced back and said, "You should move faster, little one. You are being paid money just like us."

All morning long I trudged up and down, until my shoulders sagged under the weight of the sacks. I tried to think of the raise I had gotten. Omar was paying me more than my uncle—twenty-five Lebanese *lira* a week, about four American dollars, which I hoped would make my father happy. But mostly, I thought about school. I thought about my mother. I thought about Marie and Eli and playing seven stones.

By lunchtime, I felt as if my shoulders would slide off my body. White dust coated my face and arms. I sat down by the blue pickup and ate a sesame cake my brother had given me the night before. Chewing it in the hot shade, it tasted like cement.

After lunch, Omar said, we would begin moving pipe. Again, we had no machines. Instead, we were to pass the pipes up from the ground vertically, from man to man, hand over hand on the unfinished balconies.

"Kamal, go up to the ninth floor to the center balcony facing the main street," Omar said. "The pipes up there will be small and light, only for drinking water."

The breeze had shifted; it now came off the sea instead of the desert, and the air was cooler. Still, my shirt was soaked. A thin mud of sweat and cement coated the back of my neck. Up the stairs I went again. Crossing the bare concrete floor, I slowed when I reached the balcony because I saw that it had only a low rail, exactly as high as the top of my thighs.

Beyond the balcony's edge, I could see down on many rooftops of the older part of Lebanon that extended toward the sea. Leery of the low railing, I took one step, then another, until, at the middle of the balcony, I lay down on my chest and peeked over the edge. Up here, the air was cooler, the sea breeze set free from the labyrinth of alleys like doves from a cage. Far below, I could see Omar directing some of the workers to begin carrying pipe to the foot of the building. Hundreds of cinder blocks were stacked in rows down there, awaiting transport to the upper floors. Two cement-mixing machines churned near a pile of gravel.

"Ready!" came the shout from below. I stood and waited. I did not look down again. Omar had told me to reach out and grab the pipe and raise it hand over hand up to the next balcony.

"Kamal!" Now the voice came from above. I looked up to see Qassim grinning down at me. "You will be fine! The pipe for these floors is light."

I nodded, but did not smile. I did not like Qassim. And the balcony was so high.

The voice from below again: "Here it comes!"

More quickly than I would have thought, a single thread of long, silver pipe rose before me like a snake before an Indian charmer. I reached out and grasped the metal tube and, hand over hand, kept it moving straight up. Qassim was right: it was not so heavy. And, almost at once, he had grabbed the load from above, relieving my arms.

"See?" he called down. "I told you. No problem."

Pipe after pipe appeared before me, and I passed each one up, only briefly bearing the weight from the man below me, before Qassim took it from me in turn. But after many pipes, my shoulders remembered the cement sacks and began to ache, then scream. Soon, I felt lightheaded and my breath came in short bursts.

"Hold on!" The voice from below. The pipes stopped.

A thick summer heat replaced the cool breeze, as if the sea had stopped breathing. Minutes passed. The rooftops shimmered before me. My mind drifted to Marie and Eli again. What were they doing right now?

"Ready!"

The next pipe that appeared before me was not silver, but dark, dully reflecting the sun. I reached out to grab it, but overbalanced. My feet slipped. My mind flashed to the concrete blocks below. *The mixers. The gravel.*

My thighs rotated over the balcony's top rail.

Mama!

I let go the pipe and pinwheeled my arms.

Allah! I will see Allah!

My head and arms tipped out over the long drop, then something jerked my collar back hard. Suddenly I was sitting in the center of the bare balcony, heart pounding.

Qassim came from behind and knelt before me. "Are you okay? I came to check on you, my young friend."

I blinked back tears. He ruffled my hair. "We are almost finished. Come . . . I will help you."

Qassim did not return to the tenth floor. Instead, he moved to the edge of the balcony, pulled the next pipe over the rail and began forming a stack. Petrified and still sitting exactly where I had landed, I watched the sheen on his skin, his shoulders flexing in the heat. Glancing down at my own skinny arms, a thought came to me: *I should not be here. Maybe it would be better for my father if I were dead.*

When the pipe stopped coming, Qassim turned to me with a wink: "We will move it upstairs tomorrow," he said. "Just don't tell Omar."

3

Omar let us go home early that day. I trudged along the hot, narrow streets, exhausted and ashamed, wanting desperately to fall into my mother's arms and tell her what had happened. White cement dust still covered me. I could feel and taste the grit in my teeth.

Pushing open the front door, I smelled the blessed scent of *yaknah* and rice, and heard my mother call to Amira: "Bring the oil . . . no, the big jar. . . ."

"Mama?" I said, coming around the corner into the kitchen.

Her eyes widened in surprise. "Kamal! Why are you home early? Did you run away from work?"

"No, Mama. They let us go home early."

"Will they pay you for a full day?"

Tears welled in my eyes, and my mother frowned.

"Kamal, I don't have time for your complaining today. Your uncles are coming for dinner and there is much to do." She turned away. "Amira! I said, bring the oil!"

Behind me, my brothers crowded through the front door.

Fouad: "Mama! Azzizz paid me extra today."

In the kitchen, pots banged.

Mother: "Good, *yah ibny*. Give the money to your father tonight."

A cabinet door slammed.

Amira: "I can't find the big jar, Mama."

Ibrahim: "*Move*, Kamal! Why are you always standing in the way?"

After my uncles left that night and my family had gone to sleep, I slipped through the door from the living room and out onto the roof, my sanctuary, a refuge for my heavy heart. All through dinner, I had kept quiet, my eyes downcast. I wanted someone to notice me and someone did.

"Kamal, what's the matter with you tonight?" my father snapped.

I lifted my head and looked around the table. "At work, I nearly fell ten floors. A man saved me."

A beat passed. Then laughter burst out from all sides of the table. "Another tall tale?" Father said. "I think you are allergic to work!"

My uncles laughed even louder. Only Amira had looked at me quietly, concern in her eyes.

Now, a clear night stretched over me, a black velvet dome, each star the size of a tea saucer. A crescent moon gleamed like freshly poured silver. The sea had come alive again, its cool breath floating across the rooftop, carrying the faint taste of salt.

Then I did something no good Muslim would do. I stripped off all my clothes and knelt before Allah. I came in my nakedness, desperate. My father had turned his back on me. I had become my mother's milking cow, dispensing money instead of milk. I felt dirty and unworthy, left with only one hope. I raised my hands before my face toward the eastern sky, palms upturned to receive a scrap from heaven. Tears streamed from my eyes, blurring the stars. My heart cracked inside my chest and I cried out: "Allah! Allah! If you are not for me, who will be?"

4

The day Abdul Rahman came to my house, he invited my father to attend *salat* at the mosque that evening, and my father accepted. I went with them. I also attended the following evening and the one after that, and kept going, nearly every night. My father did not. But both my parents seemed happy to let me go alone; whether it was for spiritual instruction or to keep me from underfoot, I do not know.

Now that I did not have to worry about the bullies anymore, I walked through the neighborhoods after work. At first I was afraid to do this, but Abdul Rahman encouraged me to take a stand.

"If you show fear to your enemies, they will always try to intimidate you," he said. After a few trips I noticed that the boys who had attacked me before now hurried to the other side of the street when they saw me coming. Even Iskendar, the Kurd who had speared me with the devil's eyes when he was supposed to be apologizing.

The teaching at the mosque was like the teaching at my mother's kitchen table, only brought to full flower. True Muslims, the imams said, were to complete the conquest Muhammad had begun, to establish a global *calipha*, or world dominance. The imams taught us that the life call of the devout Muslim is to become a missionary zealot. To do the world a favor and rip it from its sin and lust and idolatry, whether by conversion or by death. If we did not, we learned, Allah would someday judge us.

We also learned about the value of forming cells of committed "brothers" and the importance of joining a small enemy against a greater enemy. We learned the doctrine of *al toqiah*, or lying to our enemies for the sake of Islam. And we learned that all our enemy's property—his women, his children, his money, his house—belonged to us. We were to sleep with the enemy's women and populate the world with faithful Muslim children.

"No army should be more powerful than the army of Allah!" one imam or another would shout from the pulpit, sometimes brandishing a stick or a sword. "No nation should be richer than a Muslim nation. And in whatever nation you live, you must call for *Shariah* law!" Religious law, the law of Islam. I did not know the word *theocracy* then, but that is what the imams meant.

In response, we shouted the slogan of the Muslim Brotherhood: "Allah is our objective! The Prophet is our leader! The Koran is our law! *Jihad* is our way! Dying in the way of Allah is our highest hope!"

Often, Abdul Rahman took me aside for individual instruction. I felt singled out, special. And it was Abdul Rahman who taught me that hatred itself is important.

"Allah examines the heart of the true believer," he told me once, his eyes blazing over the pages of an open Koran balanced on a *kursi*. "In order to be pleasing to Allah, we must hate our enemies with our whole heart."

We hated the Jews, of course, and that was the reason for our hatred of America. Besides despising her loud, gaudy women and loose ways of living, we knew that if it were not for America, Israel would not exist. In relation to this topic, the imams spoke often about the Palestinians and about what the Jews, in league with the Americans, were doing to them. Over time, I would learn that the Palestinian "issue" was a carrot.

The truth was that most Muslims saw the Palestinians as a scrubby little minority group, a burden on the rest of us. But their cause gave the Muslim fascists a reason to bark at America.

I did not know that then. Instead, I drank in all this teaching like a sun-scorched desert wanderer who, finding water, does not pause for a sip, but flings his whole body in, letting the healing moisture soak into every inch of his skin. For me the teaching of the Muslim Brotherhood and, even more so, their protection and acceptance quenched the thirst caused by my family's rejection.

I had become part of something important. I belonged. These men had vision, passion, power. Perhaps most importantly of all, they seemed to care about me in a way that my father did not.

One day about three months after I first found refuge at the mosque, a Palestinian man named Abu Jihad came to visit. It was on a Sunday morning, and I had gathered in a circle by the kerosene heater with Abdul Rahman, some boys a bit older than me, and a man from my neighborhood who owned a flower shop. Gray-haired with a thick, matching moustache, Abu Jihad sat on a *tesat* next to Abdul Rahman and across from me, his back to the heater. He was one of the smallest men I had ever seen, as small as a woman. But when he spoke, it was with learnedness and authority.

Through the high windows, shafts of bright morning sun speared the dim light of the inner court. I do not remember all of what we talked about that day, but I recall that Abu Jihad was fuming about the continuing dominance of Christians in the Lebanese government.

"We are in the majority now," he said, jabbing his small index finger around the circle at us. "We, the Sunni. And yet the Maronite Christians still run the country. It has been so since the 1920s. Even though there are more of us, they still make the laws and veto the laws we want to make. Now they imprison my people inside squalid camps like Sabra-Shatila while they enjoy the profits from the fat, rich, infidel tourists who love to spend their money in Beirut!"

When I was growing up, Beirut was known as the "Paris of the Middle East." Not only did tourists flock there, but, my father told us, powerful politicians from all over the world flew in for secret meetings in an area called the Hamra District. The streets of the Hamra were filled with fine restaurants and cabarets, and like New York City today, with people from every nation: Swedes, Egyptians, Danes, Americans, Nigerians, Greeks. Everyone rubbed shoulders on the boulevards, and all were fashionably dressed.

But Sabra-Shatila, though also in Beirut, seemed a world away. About ten years before I was born, Lebanon became one of the destinations for the 750,000 Palestinians displaced after the 1947–1948 Arab-Israeli War extended the boundaries of the new Israeli state. Sabra was a poor neighborhood near Shatila, one of several Palestinian refugee camps established by the United Nations. Over the years, though, the boundaries of the neighborhood and the camp melted into one another so that the two became a single sprawling ghetto, a bedraggled collection of shacks and unfinished apartment buildings lining dirty, potholed streets. Piles of scrap metal and wood framing lay heaped on the sidewalks with no public services available to haul them away. Power lines tangled crazily along the roadways as though someone had flung spools of wire at the wooden utility poles, let them unroll in wild loops, and left them where they landed.

Sabra-Shatila and other Palestinian camps had been part of Lebanon all my life. Like most Palestinians, Abu Jihad resented the Lebanese government's leaving the camps to deteriorate while the rest of the city flourished. But I later realized he was also a propagandist who used the Palestinian issue to stir up rank-and-file Muslims.

"The Maronites are becoming more corrupt," he now told us. "They will never give up control, and they will never let the Sunni observe the true law, *Sharia*. Sooner or later they will come and arrest us in our homes."

Abu Jihad paused and peered around the circle, pausing to make eye contact with each of us. The kerosene heater ticked, as if timing his silence. Then he said: "You must learn how to fight, how to use weapons, how to defend yourselves."

"And where are we supposed to do that?" the flower shop man said skeptically. "I have children to feed, a business to keep. I cannot run off to some desert camp to play *fedayeen*."

Abu Jihad smiled patiently. "You do not have to go anywhere, my friend. Because you are Sunni, Fatah will train you here, inside Sabra."

Sabra? I knew that part of Fatah, Arafat's armed force, operated from deep inside Sabra, where even the Lebanese police feared to tread. But I did not know they were training new soldiers. The very thought thrilled me. But I was sure Abu Jihad did not mean they would train someone as young as me.

At that moment, Abdul Rahman looked across the circle at me. "Kamal," he said, eyes twinkling. "Would you like to go, too?"

Atlanta, Georgia
2007

At speaking engagements in Michigan, California, and elsewhere, protesters from groups like the Muslim Student Association began showing up to accuse Zak, Walid, and me of preaching a message of "intolerance" and "hate." I liked Walid's response to these attacks. When the 3 Ex-Terrorists, as we became known, appeared at the University of California Irvine in May 2007, Walid told the audience, "Do I promote hate speech? Sure. I hate terrorism."

In another confrontation that August, this time on a sunny public sidewalk outside a Seattle mosque, a Muslim man squared off against me, nearly nose to nose: "How dare you speak against Allah and the Prophet?" he sputtered, eyes flashing. "We are converting twenty to twenty-five thousand Americans every year to Islam. We will seed your women, educate and convert your children, and have this nation! By the grace of Allah, we have nothing but time!"

A statement worth studying for those who wonder about the recent explosion in this country of the "religion of peace."

The Seattle man's remark about converting children came during the same week that news agencies reported the arrest of a fifteen-year-old boy in the northern Gaza Strip. I was crisscrossing the country again and read the story on the Internet while waiting for a flight in Atlanta. The boy had approached Israeli Defense Forces (IDF) troops carrying two improvised explosive devices. The soldiers overpowered the boy, arrested him, and carted him off to be interrogated.[6]

"The thwarting of this attack illustrates how teenagers in the Gaza Strip are involved in terror activities and are sent by terror groups to carry out operations, including ones from which they may not return alive," an IDF officer told an Israeli reporter. "The recruitment to terror groups does not start at age eighteen."[7]

Indeed it does not. And it never has.

Yasser Arafat's use and training of child soldiers is well-documented. During the First Intifada—a 1987 Palestinian uprising against Israeli rule in the Gaza Strip, West Bank, and East Jerusalem—Palestinian troops included elementary schoolchildren.[8] During the Lebanese civil war, I saw the PLO send out boys as young as ten and twelve armed with rocket-propelled grenades. The Israelis came to call them "the RPG kids." In the 1970s, Arafat established all-child camps where elementary schoolchildren learned to shoot rifles and navigate obstacle courses. My own unit sometimes used young boys during urban assault operations; they were small and agile, perfect for climbing into buildings through small, high windows to plant bombs.

Arafat trained child soldiers for thirty years. In 2000, when American boys headed to summer camp to learn kayaking and archery, America got a glimpse at what Palestinian boys did: They attended one or more of ninety different two- and three-week camps to learn the arts of kidnapping, ambushing, and murder. *New York Times* reporter John Burns attended such a camp in the town of Nablus, run by Arafat's psychological warfare team:

> *They allow no . . . fun in the sun by a cool clear lake, no rousing sing-alongs beside a roaring campfire. Instead there is a chance to stage a mock kidnapping of an Israeli leader by masked Palestinian commandos, ending with the Israeli's bodyguards sprawled dead on the ground. Next there is the mock attack on an Israeli military post, ending with a sentry being grabbed by the neck and fatally stabbed.*[9]

I remember the same training. But with real blood.

Beirut, Lebanon
1965

1

The assault camp lay deep inside Sabra, secreted in the southwest corner near a wooded area where the sewers drained. Huge metal gates guarded the entrance, reminding me of the high gates at school. But where I had feared school, now I felt in my chest only a thrill of anticipation.

Abu Jihad had collected quite a large group for training, people I had never met before. I thought they must have come from his mosque, which was near the home of my grandmother, Fatima, in the fancier part of Beirut. The group was mainly a mix of young men and teenagers; there were also a couple of thirtyish men, like the one who owned the flower shop, and a couple of boys around my age, seven. I wondered if they too had lied to their mothers and said they were only going to mosque.

Outside the camp gates, two *fedayeen* stood guard with AK–47s. But when they saw Abu Jihad, they swung the gates open wide, revealing the biggest playground I had ever seen: walls with climbing ropes, hand-over-hand jungle gyms, mud holes with ropes overhead for swinging, climbing ropes suspended between two poles. I saw an obstacle course and also a barbed wire net staked about a half-meter off the ground. I imagined the *fedayeen* would crawl under it, commando style, and hoped I would get the chance.

The whole picture sent a charge through me. I could not have spoken this at the time, but I sensed a moment, an opportunity to leave behind my powerlessness, worthlessness, and fear and become someone who would make a difference in the world.

A group of about a dozen men walked up to us.

Warriors, I thought, instantly awestruck. I had heard about these people. They were fearless, not like me, a coward in the streets. A tall man with a curly bush of hair spoke first to Abu Jihad. "*Ma sha'a Allah, jinood Allah*," he said.

Allah willing, His army.

As Abu Jihad talked with this man, I gazed around at the others with open admiration. Although they wore pieces of military uniforms—olive T-shirts or dirty white ones, fatigue pants, army boots—these men did not look clean and orderly like American GIs. Instead, they wore massive beards they had not shaved in many weeks. Their odor was stout and pungent. Some carried AK–47s strapped across their backs. All wore knives on their hips. These men drank poison and ate fire, I was sure. They looked as fierce as if they had cut their way up from hell.

The warriors stood facing us, unsmiling. The man who had spoken to Abu Jihad was roped in muscle, fit as a jaguar. He now addressed us all. "This is not a place to come and play!" he said. "If that is what you think, you can turn around and go back home. By the end of this day, we will know how many of you are warriors and how many are only men."

Suddenly he pointed down at me. My breath caught and his finger seemed to cut through my soul. His eyes blazed down into mine. "Child, do you want to be a warrior?"

I stared back up into his eyes and instantly yearned to impress him. I raised my hand and smacked my own chest. "I *am* a warrior!"

He threw back his head and laughed with pleasure. "That is good!" he said, glancing at the other warriors who allowed small smiles to escape. "We have a true zealot here!"

In a smooth motion, he slung his assault rifle off his back and knelt down, presenting the gun as if holding an offering. "But you know, you cannot be a warrior unless you know how to use your weapon."

He laid the rifle in my arms. I did not know it at that moment, but it was an AK–47. My heart pounded with the weight of it, my eyes roving over the parts that any boy knows—the muzzle, stock, and trigger. I could smell the steel, its bold scent blue and oily, invading my senses. I knew this smell from my father's shop, a masculine scent as familiar as family.

"Kneel down," the warrior said. With the others looking on, he placed the butt of the rifle against my shoulder and guided my hand to the magazine. Like a magnet, my finger moved to the trigger. Gently, the warrior blocked my finger with his own. "No, no. First you must learn to make it safe for yourself."

Kneeling behind me, he spoke softly into my ear, showing me how to safe the weapon as gently as a father might show a son how to mend a bicycle tire or hammer a nail. Around us, the other boys pressed in. I could sense each of them wishing it was him the warrior had chosen.

"This is single-shot and this is automatic," the warrior said quietly, flicking a small lever. "Are you listening carefully?"

Guiding my arms, he gently turned the muzzle toward an array of man-shaped targets lined up in front of the woods. Then, as though we were dancers, he put his hand over mine, slid my finger back to the trigger, and pulled.

The sound was sheer power searing through my body, each shot a tiny flame in my heart. The percussion of the piston; shell casings rattling out onto the ground as the rifle chewed through an entire magazine of bullets. In my ears, the weapon's roar was like fresh air in a smoky room, a lighthouse to a lost ship, a healing drug to a patient who had not known he was dying. An alarm sounded in my heart, and at that moment, my childhood slipped through my hands into the rifle's hot steel.

Everything I knew had changed.

2

The large crowd of men and boys who had arrived with Abu Jihad that first day thinned quickly. After the novelty wore off, many lost their enthusiasm and desire. Others found themselves in the press of ordinary life, school, or work. But I had found my calling.

I no longer had to walk to Sabra after work. A *fida'i,* a single soldier in the *fedayeen,* named Sarri Habbal sometimes picked me up in his dirty red Mercedes. Other times, Abdul Rahman slipped me enough money to take the *serviz* and sometimes even a taxi. In a few weeks' time, I completed several phases of training. Some days, I sat in lecture-style classes learning weapons fundamentals. Other days, I reported with the remaining trainees to the target range, where we live-fired 7mm and 9mm pistols and various Soviet-made Kalashnikov rifles.

In our camp was a leader named Abu Yousef who seemed to take a special interest in me. Though I was only seven, I had inherited my father's lean blacksmith's frame. I was much taller than other boys my age, and as tall as some much older. My size combined with my fiery, unquestioning faith may have been what drew Abu Yousef to me.

He appeared to be in his thirties. A thick cap of jet hair curled over his head and he had skin of a color we called *esmar*—not white, not black, but the color of Turkish coffee touched with cream. He wore a full moustache, and his thick dark eyelashes framed the most intense eyes I had ever seen. Abu Yousef wore stars and a crown on the shoulders of his fatigues. When he gave orders to the *fedayeen* fighters at Sabra, I noticed that he spoke in a low, calm voice that seemed threaded with steel. He had only to speak once and the thing was done.

Abu Yousef hated the Jews so intensely that it physically pained him. Whenever he mentioned them, he also mentioned the Christians. "They are deceivers, Kamal," he said to me one day after evening prayers at the mosque. "These people, the Jews and the Christians, will kill us someday if we don't kill them first."

I thought about Eli and Marie, my Christian friends. I did not want to kill them. But had not Abu Yousef and the Brotherhood loved me unconditionally? Did they not talk to me about important things, grownup things, while all my family did was take my money and send me back out to work and be beaten again? In the *fedayeen,* I had found vision and clarity and purity of love, a growing certainty of what was right and what was wrong and to whom I belonged. And so I believed Abu Yousef. I believed him absolutely.

After a couple of months, he began treating me as a leader of the "young brothers," the boy recruits, and seemed to trust me. When he stopped to take a smoke, he often asked me to follow him into the large, flat-roofed hangar at Sabra. Sometimes, he quizzed me on what I had seen and heard around the camps. Other times, he thought aloud about Arafat, the Palestinian struggle, and what was going on in the larger world.

Abu Yousef told me he had met Arafat in Egypt some years before, even before he founded Fatah. The son of a Cairo textile merchant, Arafat was a university graduate, a civil engineering major with an idealistic streak. In the mid-1950s, he connected with two Palestinians, both members of the Muslim Brotherhood. Arafat the Egyptian quickly adopted the Palestinian cause as his own and by the late 1950s had founded Fatah, a group dedicated to liberating Palestine from the Zionists through armed struggle. I was young and could not follow the thread of Arafat's relationship with Abu Yousef. But I gathered that Arafat trusted him enough to place him in a high-ranking position with *al-Asifah,* the armed Fatah element to which I now belonged.

Still, Abu Yousef had a trusted circle of his own. More than once, I heard him call Arafat a fool with dumb luck. Only three years before, Arafat had moved Fatah from Egypt to Syria after Egyptian President Anwar Sadat refused to allow Arafat to launch attacks against Israel from within his borders. The Syrians, it turned out, had no such qualms.

"He made the move to feed his ego," Abu Yousef said one day to a small knot of men in the hangar. "To show the Arab leaders he did not need their help. But he is a fool. The Syrians are vipers. I would not trust one of them to clean my boots."

It was dangerous talk, I would learn. People who spoke against Arafat had a way of turning up dead. But Abu Yousef knew I would keep my mouth shut.

"He likes you very much," a *fedayeen* fighter told me one day. "You remind him of his brother."

This *fida'i* told me Abu Yousef's brother had been killed. I do not know how or even whether this was true, but Abu Yousef continued to befriend and mentor me. One day, he told me about an article that appeared in a Christian newspaper in Beirut. The article repeated a mocking claim that had been circulating in Tel Aviv: our *fedayeen* and the Lebanese army were so weak that if the Israelis sent a hundred women on bicycles to fight us, they would defeat both Lebanon *and* Syria.

Abu Yousef took a long pull on his cigarette and gazed at me, eyes twinkling. "What do you think of that, Kamal?"

I drew myself up tall and puffed out my chest. "That is not true!" I said. "They are women. We are *men*. There are more of us and we have Allah!"

Abu Yousef chuckled. "You will make the difference someday, Kamal. You are loyal. Whomever you serve, you will make him successful."

3

At first, I did not know any of the younger boys in training. But I soon made friends with a boy named Yahya (John, in English) who was in my training group. He was not from my neighborhood, but I knew who his family was and where he went to school. Another kid had recruited him and brought him to the camp. Yahya and I had become fast friends through many weeks of training together. Our hearts were alike, each searching for something we were too young to name. In Fatah, we had found a cause to rally to and an enemy to rise against. We had also found a common code. And even though the code's beating heart was violent death, we considered it a code of honor.

One night at twilight, the *fedayeen* staged invasion training. The course, made of barbed wire stretched like a net about a half-meter off the bare ground, simulated a booby-trapped enemy perimeter. At intervals, our trainers had buried a series of flat, round stones that were about the size of Israeli land mines. Our test was to belly crawl beneath the wire, probing the dirt with the points of our knives to check for these false mines along the way. To simulate the danger of the explosives, our trainers would fire live ammo over our heads. I was a little nervous about that part; it would be the first time anyone had shot at me. But so far, the training had seemed more like camp or a game. I had not yet grasped the high price of a real bullet.

By the time the exercise began, most of the light had already leaked down over the horizon. I stood with Yahya and a couple dozen other boys and men at the mouth of the wire. We wore khaki pants, white T-shirts, and green canvas boots.

Fedayeen warriors stood alongside the course, aiming AK–47s over our heads. One man wielded a Russian DShK (pronounced "Dushka"), an anti-aircraft gun. I glanced at the big weapon, then lined up behind Yahya to enter the course.

"Ready!" cried the *feda'i* holding the DShK. I looked straight ahead and took a deep breath.

"Go!"

Yahya dove under the wire and I fell in behind him, pulling myself forward with my elbows, the bottoms of Yahya's boots in my face as I dragged my belly across the rocky ground. Bullets snapped overhead and above the rifles' rattle, our trainers' voices boomed. "*Ya-ela! Ya-ela, enshi!*"

Hurry! Go faster!

The DShK roared, drowning out the rifles. Red and green tracers zinged just above the wire. I kept my head down and crawled forward madly. The gravelly hard pack chewed into my elbows and knees, and I was right on Yahya's tail, willing him to move, move, *move*! I sensed the train of others behind me. Without warning, a sharp pain lanced into my back. I thought I had been shot, just below the right shoulder blade. But it was only a bite from the barbed wire that caged us in.

The din of the weapons increased as the *fedayeen* shot more rounds. This was both nightmare and dream. I wanted to quit, and I wanted to win. I wanted to cry, and I wanted to bellow in triumph.

A stray round bit into the ground beside me, kicking dust into my face. For the first time, I slowed down, real fear spiking my heart like needles. Yahya now scrabbled along ahead of me by about the length of two men, stopping at intervals to poke the earth with the point of his knife.

Suddenly I saw Yahya stop.

I do not know why Yahya did what he did next. I saw the back of his head rise up over the bottoms of his boots. I froze in disbelief as Yahya seemed to be crawling *up*. Up a small incline, a rise in the dirt. Then Yahya's head exploded in a gritty mist of blood and bone.

A DShK round had blown off the back of his head.

Horror knotted my gut and I vomited, making a small brown pool in the dirt. Terror buzzed through my veins, and I burst into tears. But I had to crawl forward again because of the live fire. The *fedayeen* must not have seen Yahya die because they kept shouting and firing. I squeezed shut my eyes and dragged myself past his body, holding my breath to block out the coppery stench of his blood.

When I was a man's length beyond Yahya, underneath the rattle of automatic fire, I heard someone behind me wretch. Still we had to keep moving. The finish line seemed a continent away, and I belly crawled at double speed, straining to reach the end as a sleeper strains to wake from a nightmare. Finally, I saw the end of the course, an escape hatch from the hellfire and the horror that was Yahya's corpse.

As I crawled the last few meters, I scrubbed my face against my sleeves, not wanting anyone to see that I had cried. One by one, the trainees behind me reached the end, and when the last boy emerged from beneath the wire net, we ran together and told the leader about Yahya. When they pulled him out, his head was almost completely gone.

It was nearly full dark. Some *fedayeen* whisked Yahya's body away, and the rest of us gathered around a campfire that someone had built near the edge of the woods. Even in its circle of warmth, I shivered as my friend's death replayed itself in my mind over and over again.

Within a few minutes, a middle-aged man I had not seen before materialized to address us. He was wearing a suit and seemed to be some sort of doctor, yet without warmth. "You all are alive because you did the right thing," he said matter-of-factly. "You did not take shortcuts. You found the mines and dug them up. On the other hand, Yahya did not do it correctly. He crawled over a mine. If you make the same mistake in the field, you will end up the same way." Then the man in the suit turned and walked away.

4

Yahya's death shocked me, but never once did I think of leaving Fatah. Perhaps this was because Abu Yousef and others mothered me for the next couple of weeks, praising my performance in the invasion training and telling me I was a warrior prodigy.

"You proved your worth that night, Kamal," Abu Yousef said. "You have proven you deserve to be here, fighting for Palestine and for the glory of Allah."

A false spring crept in, melting the edges of winter. My training at Sabra continued, but now when I drilled with rifles or climbed the ropes course, I heard rumblings among the *fedayeen*. Something about striking Israel. Always in these times, I overheard the word "Syria."

One day in the hangar, I asked Abu Yousef about it. Leaning against the tripod for a crew-served machine gun, he touched the end of a cigarette with his lighter flame. "We are planning a mission into Palestine," he said. Abu Yousef never called Israel "Israel." To him it was Palestine, occupied by thieving dogs. "We must provide aid to our Palestinian brothers there so they can throw off the yoke of the Zionists."

A mission! It was the first time Abu Yousef had told me about a mission.

He pulled his cigarette from his lips and gazed down at it, rolling the filter tip between his forefinger and thumb. "Arafat is sending weapons into Palestine, and he wants us to help." Then Abu Yousef looked up at me for a long moment as though weighing whether he should go on. At last he spoke. "I was thinking of asking you if you would like to go on this mission."

My heart leapt. *I now know how to shoot! I know how to fight!* This was what I'd been waiting for. "Yes, Abu Yousef!" I said instantly. "I will do anything you ask me to do for Allah!"

Looking back on it, I wonder at the horror of a grown man asking a seven-year-old to run guns into a foreign country. But at that moment, I was completely on fire, overjoyed at my good fortune and my high place of honor. It turned out I was not the only boy selected for such a high honor. Early one morning a few days later, I reported to the hangar at Sabra to find about ten boys just like me, but I still felt happy to be included.

I was disappointed to learn that Abu Yousef would not be going with us. Instead, the mission would be led by a loudmouth named Abu Ali, a convert from Shia to Sunni whose fatigues drooped on his slight frame and whose hair wrapped itself around the sides of his prematurely bald head like a bird's nest.

In the hangar, Abu Ali commanded us to fall into ranks, then paced back and forth in front of us with his chest puffed out. "I am in charge of this mission," he proclaimed. "You will listen to me carefully and do exactly what I say at all times."

He went on to explain the plan: We would ride in trucks into Syria where we would be given knapsacks and *dish-dashes,* the robes worn by Bedouins, in order to disguise ourselves as shepherd boys. The knapsacks would be loaded with weapons, some disassembled, magazines, TNT blocks, and hand grenades. Guided by Syrian collaborators, we would infiltrate Israel through tunnels dug under the Golan Heights, rendezvous with Palestinians also dressed as shepherds, and hand over the knapsacks.

When Abu Ali finished his explanation, he drew himself up importantly. "We are going to deliver destruction to the Jews, to fight for the liberation of Palestine and the glory of Allah!"

"*Allahu akbar!*" we shouted as one. "*Allahu akbar!*"

Abu Ali marched us out of the hangar into the cool sun toward a pair of vegetable trucks, each with high sides of welded metal bars, lined with plywood to form a bed. When I saw Abu Ali climb into the cab of the truck on the right, I climbed into the back of the truck on the left. He reminded me of a drum, full of noise and air. I did not enjoy being around him.

A light furry mold lined the truck bed, the residue of a thousand loads of cucumbers, and it immediately coated my pants with ick. Slowly, we rumbled out of Sabra, southeast toward Syria. At the border, the highway ended abruptly, with only desert beyond. Guard-houses, flanked by military encampments, stood on both sides of the blunted road. The trucks slowed briefly, and I could see through cracks in the wooden sides when the Syrian border guards waved us through.

I could smell mountain air as we trundled slowly up into the Golan Heights. We rolled through barren desert, a vast, ascending hard-pack strewn with boulders, gravel, and sand, as if time existed only to grind the land down into its smallest parts. We chattered among ourselves, snacked on food we had brought with us, and listened to transistor radios that a couple of the boys had. The mood was light and cheerful, as though we were only on our way to camp.

I thought of the trip as my first chance to make my mark for Allah. To make Abdul Rahman and Abu Yousef proud of me. And maybe even my father.

Morning passed into afternoon, and finally, the trucks gurgled to a stop at the top of a shallow valley. Abu Ali appeared at the rear of our truck, his head covered in a black *keffiyeh,* and began pitching bundles at us. The *dish-dashes.*

"*Ya-ela! Ya-ela!*" he said, urging us to hurry and change. Abu Ali was always urging someone to hurry.

One by one, we jumped down from the vegetable trucks dressed as Bedouin boys. The air was crisp, the sky a hard blue. I stopped and looked out across the valley to the Israeli side. Excitement rippled through my fingertips. I couldn't see them now, but I knew our *fedayeen* brothers waited for us on the other side.

"*Ya-ela!*" Abu Ali snapped. Shuffling forward with the other boys, I began walking down the shallow slope. Soon a group of five men appeared, walking up toward us from the valley floor. Syrian Baathists. They all wore civilian clothes, their faces shielded with *keffiyeh*. Each man carried a pair of knapsacks made from thick, cream-colored canvas with strangely long straps that hung all the way to the ground.

Abu Ali walked briskly ahead, meeting the men a few yards ahead of us. Introducing himself, he told them officiously, "Here are the boys for the mission. I am in charge. You cannot do anything without my approval."

One man, who seemed to be the leader of the Baathists, regarded Abu Ali with black eyes that appeared somewhat amused at his posturing. "Thank you for bringing the boys," he said. "We will let you know when we need your instructions."

Abu Ali was suddenly quiet. The Baathist leader pushed past him and stood before us, eyes twinkling. "I am Mezin," he said. "You must be the brave young warriors Abu Yousef has been telling me about."

Pride welled up in my chest. "*Allahu akbar!*" I said, and Mezin laughed.

I looked longingly at the knapsacks which I knew to be our cargo. Seeming to read my mind, Mezin motioned for the other Syrians to pass the knapsacks out to us. I took a moment to peek into mine. Inside were two handguns—one 9 mm and one 7 mm—a couple of TNT blocks already fused, and several AK–47 magazines. I cinched the sack closed and turned so that another boy could help me strap it on. The strange, long straps hung down into the dirt behind me.

"Ya-ela!" Abu Ali said. "Ya—"

Mezin silenced him with a look.

Soon enough, all the boys were ready and we began our descent, a single file line of "shepherd boys" carrying enough weapons to wipe out a village. We followed the Syrians as they led us down to a cluster of bushes, taller than men, that seemed to grow more closely together than others in the terrain. Like a magician, Mezin plucked one straight out of the ground and set it aside. It was only camouflage, concealing the entrance to a tunnel.

Mezin turned to us. "You are doing a great service to occupied Palestine," he announced. "When you return to Lebanon, you will be hailed as heroes."

With that, the Syrians produced Russian military flashlights and handed one to each boy. Then, with two armed Syrians before us and two behind, we plunged into the long hole in the earth.

5

The tunnel felt wet and cold. The ground was smooth, as though the boots of many armies had passed through before. For most of the journey, we could stand upright and walk, but in some places, we had to hunch over like old men. Once, we had to get down and crawl with barely enough space for our knapsacks to squeeze through. Twice, I had to stop when my legs became tangled in the long straps.

We had only been underground for about fifteen minutes when I saw, up ahead, light streaming down and the dangling end of a knotted yellow rope. One by one, we climbed out, blinking like moles against the Israeli sun.

"This way," one of the Syrians said, pointing down a gentle slope. Ahead, I saw grazing land and could smell dung, evidence that Bedouin herds had come through. We began walking, shuffling along through the weeds in our *dish-dashes*, the knapsack straps trailing the ground behind us. A cool headwind blew, and I caught the scent of earth, animals, and once, I thought, tobacco.

After about one kilometer, I started hearing sheep, and soon after that I saw a small group of Bedouin shepherds. As we drew closer, I counted five men standing with a large flock. One of them was the ugliest man I had ever seen.

He was tall with dark skin tinged with the reddish hue of burnt brick. His eyebrows ran across his forehead like black carpets. His nose was the size of a pyramid, and in the crevice between it and his face sat a fuzzy black mole.

"Welcome, young brothers," he said around the cigarette that dangled from his mouth. As I stared at the man's mole, he greeted the Syrians and exchanged a few words. Then he motioned for us boys to turn around so that he and the other shepherds could remove our knapsacks.

Now the reason for the long straps became apparent: Working quickly, the shepherds tied the knapsacks underneath the bellies of the sheep, then worked the animals' long wool around with their fingers to conceal both the knapsacks and the canvas straps. Then, without another word, the shepherds began to shoo their flock west. They did not look back.

The return trip through the tunnel was uneventful, but when we arrived back on the Syrian side, Mezin greeted us with kisses as our Syrian guides fired their rifles in the air. "You are the children who will change the future!" he said.

That night, we slept in a Syrian military camp. News of our conquest sped ahead of us to Beirut so that when we arrived at Sabra, we were greeted as heroes. As the vegetable trucks rolled through the neighborhood toward the Fatah compound, a Palestinian woman stepped onto her front stoop, put her hands to her mouth, and sent up a victory yodel. As we drove past, I saw another woman step out and join her, and then another and another, until the street rang with a celebration of the kind I had only heard at a wedding.

My heart soared! I had done it. I had completed a mission. That day, I felt like James Bond. And that night, when my father heard what I had done, he pulled down from a closet a sword with our family crest on it, and danced in the streets.

6

Often, I knelt next to Abu Yousef during *al ashat*, the last evening prayer at the mosque. One night, after we said *amin*, he turned to me and it seemed I could see a new intensity in his eyes, a fiercer brightness. "Do you remember our victory before, on your first mission? Now we have a new mission, and it is coming very soon," he said. "We need all the young brothers to meet at Sabra. This mission will last two days. Three if we have any issues."

Across Beirut, the Muslim Brotherhood was organized into cells, with the young boys placed in cells in our own neighborhoods so that we would not have to travel far to meet. The leader of my cell was a man named Abu Ibrahim, a Palestinian *fida'i* who had set himself up in my neighborhood as a civilian. I remember that he seemed very old to me—in his forties, at least. Part of Abu Ibrahim's job was to rally the young brothers, to get them fired up, as they say in America. Many times, I would help him by gathering the children to meet at his home for a dinner of mixed nuts and *shiska*.

After Abu Yousef told me of the new mission, Abu Ibrahim arranged such a feast. I went around the neighborhood inviting the children to come. "It will be like a camping trip," Abu Ibrahim told the boys as we munched on the *shiska*—hamburger cooked with mint and red onion, served in a pita with cucumber and tomato. "We will camp at the River Litani."

I sat next to Abu Ibrahim as he told the glorious tale of the other mission, my first. Only a couple of the boys in the room had been with us then, but all had heard how we dressed like Bedouin shepherd boys and tricked the enemy, carrying destruction into their midst right under their noses!

"This trip will be even more successful," Abu Ibrahim concluded. "You have joined our brotherhood at an exciting time!"

7

In my neighborhood lived a round-faced boy named Mohammed. Although at eight he was a year older, Mohammed was just gaga over me. Now that I was with the Muslim Brotherhood, he roamed the streets looking for me as though he were a lost puppy and I his master. I did not see him that way, though. I loved Mohammed and knew that he only wanted to be in my presence. To do what I was doing.

"I begged my mother to go with you to Sabra," he told me one day. Mohammed burned to join the Brotherhood. "I am strong in Allah! I can fight like you, I know I can!"

We sat on the curb outside a gelato shop. Now that I had money whether I worked or not, I had plenty to buy my favorite pistachio cones for myself and my friends. I licked one carefully while Mohammed, between bites, told me about his stubborn mother.

"She said I cannot go with you. That it is too dangerous."

His mother's name was Salma. His father, Omar, was a thin, weak man who hung about outside the tailor shop, smoking cigarettes with a klatch of old men.

"I will go and speak with your mother," I said.

After we finished our cones, I walked with Mohammed to his home, a makeshift add-on on the ground floor of an apartment building in West Beirut. I had visited often, and Salma loved me. Now, though, I approached the front door as confidently as if I were a *sheikh*, learned in Islam, come to direct Salma on some spiritual matter.

Mohammed sprinted past me to open the door. "Mama, Kamal is here!" he called, his voice echoing off the high ceiling and cream-colored tile. "He wants to speak with you!"

Salma was a proper Muslim, very conservative like my mother. She entered the front room, her *hijab* covering the lower half of her face.

"Welcome, Kamal!" she said. "What brings you to visit, *yah ibny*?" That was what she always called me—"my son."

But I was not interested in her usual endearments. Instead, I was brash and conceited, puffed up from my association with the *fedayeen*.

"Your son is a warrior and you do not even know it!" I said. "Let him come with me. He will be a hero!"

Salma regarded me with a look that I later understood as bemused. Looking back, I do not think she really believed Mohammed's stories about what I was doing in the camps.

"Whatever you do with him, go ahead and do," she said, smiling. "But bring him back alive to me."

"I will, *em Mohammed*. He will be safe with me."

8

A week passed. On a Thursday, all of us met at Sabra dressed in our fatigues. We numbered about twenty boys and eight adult *fedayeen*, including Abu Yousef. After loading into a militant-looking caravan of pickup trucks, Jeeps, and technicals—pickups with machine guns mounted in the beds—we journeyed through Lebanon to the Syrian border, an easy trip. I rode in the rear of a Jeep next to Abu Ibrahim.

At the border, the highway ended abruptly, with only desert beyond. Two kinds of Syrian soldiers stood watch that day. One group of about a dozen men wore gray, white, and green camouflage with green berets. A smaller group wore the same clothing, but their berets were the color of blood.

To me, those men looked as tall as mountains, serious and disciplined with their fit frames and freshly trimmed moustaches. Abu Ibrahim saw me staring and leaned over to me. "Elite Syrian army," he said.

I listened as the blood-beret Syrians spoke with Abu Yousef in clipped tones. I was used to seeing others defer to him. These men did not. Instead, I thought I smelled anger in their sweat.

Two of our adult *fedayeen*, Ahmed and Qaffin, shepherded us out of the smaller vehicles and into a big Russian truck, its bed covered with a canvas canopy the color of green olives. Chattering like schoolchildren on a field trip, we crowded in next to each other on benches that ran along the sides of the bed. I saw bullet boxes and a DShK stacked against the back of the cab. Mohammed and I sat down next to each other, near the split where the canopy opened to the outside. After a short wait, Abu Yousef threw open the canopy flaps.

"We are going into the occupied land," he said to us grandly. "You will carry weapons to our brothers in Palestine. We have done this before and achieved a great victory," Abu Yousef continued. "This time, we will go farther, to the outskirts of a village beyond the Syrian border. This time, we may engage."

A shiver charged through me, anticipation mixed with a whisper of fear that skated around the edge of my heart like a spark. I had seen much live fire in the camps, but had never faced a live enemy. However, I did not let my face show any tremor to Abu Yousef, who was beaming at me like a proud uncle. At that moment, I felt I was his trophy: *See?* His eyes said to the young brothers who had not been tested. *Kamal has done this before. There is nothing to worry about, only victory in store.*

Looking around in the dusty light of the canopied truck bed, I found all eyes on me and rose to the occasion. "This is going to be powerful!" I said. "We are going to put the Jews under our feet!"

"Allahu akbar!" the little boys shouted. "Allahu akbar!"

Abu Yousef broke into a rare, full grin. He nodded at me, then flipped the canopy flaps closed. I could hear someone securing them from the outside—*snap, snap, snap.* Soon the truck's diesel engine began its throaty churning and we rumbled into Syria, bouncing along on skinny tires that were as tall as Volkswagens.

During the journey, we were not allowed to look outside. Gradually, the threads of sunlight seeping through the canopy seams turned gold, then pink, then drained away altogether. When it was full dark, I switched on my flashlight, brushing its slim beam across the faces of the boys. Some had already gone to sleep, draped on each other like kittens. Mohammed leaned against my shoulder, his breath soft and even. Soon my eyes grew heavy, too. I snapped off my light and leaned my head against Mohammed's.

It was morning when the truck driver choked the big truck's engine into silence and Abu Yousef threw back the canopy flap. As I blinked against the light, it quickly became clear that we had arrived at a place much different than the mission before.

9

The truck had rolled to a stop at the highest point of a barren valley of rock and scrub. Mohammed and I clambered down from the bed and, standing next to Abu Yousef, looked down over a series of rugged earthen tiers that stepped down into the valley and bristled with military men and equipment. Syrian soldiers roamed among camouflage nets concealing cannons. Truck beds supported full batteries of Katyusha missiles. Gray concrete bunkers hulked against the land like boulders.

Cool mountain air skated up the valley wall, ruffling my fatigues. Glancing up, I noticed thick clouds gathering above, shadowy slabs that slid slowly across the sun. On the plateaus below, the soldiers began to notice us. Some stopped and stared up, shielding their eyes with their hands in the flickering light. As the rest of the young brothers gathered at the valley rim, Abu Yousef leaned down and put his lips next to my ear. "Kamal, keep the brothers together and stay alert."

Two Syrian soldiers appeared. I heard one of them tell Abu Yousef that our Bedouin disguises waited for us lower in the camp. They led us down the terraces, down ladders and across concrete pads, crissing and crossing our way deeper and deeper. We descended past small knots of soldiers who sat smoking and cleaning their rifles. They looked up and said to us things like, "You are the soldiers of the future! The Jews will pay the price!"

But their eyes glittered, and they sounded to me as if they were reading from a script, as we had done once at school. Suddenly, I wished I were already grown. Love for Allah burned inside me, and I knew he blessed those who waged *jihad*. But here with these cold men who were not like my *fedayeen* brothers, a shameful whisper blew through my heart: *Do you not wish to be at home again?*

Afraid my doubt might radiate through the back of my head and frighten Mohammed, I glanced back at him. His eyes were wide and uncertain. I dropped back and fell into step with him, our boots now crunching the dirt in time. "You are my shadow," I told him. "Do what I do and say what I say. If someone asks you a question, I will answer it. If you do not know what to do, look to me and I will show you."

Mohammed only nodded and turned his eyes to the earth.

At length, we came to one of the concrete bunkers. Abu Yousef stepped aside and our Syrian escorts herded us inside where I nearly collided with the belt buckle of a towering man.

"Change clothes, you little sons of whores!" came a voice from above my head. "Rise up to your deaths!"

My head whipped around to find Abu Yousef, who, I was sure, would cut the throat of this Syrian who had insulted our mothers. But Abu Yousef had not come inside. I then looked up, hoping to challenge this man with my eyes, but the Syrian seemed as tall as a cedar and did not return my glare. I hated him immediately.

The young brothers hurried over to the pile of *dish-dashes* and changed quickly as the Syrian lorded over us, sweeping his ice-blue eyes around the bunker like a king. His wide shoulders seemed to fill the cramped space. He carried a thin, leather-handled stick, like a riding crop, and barked orders.

"Do your jobs well, you mules! There is no room for error!" he thundered. "Your first mistake will be your last!"

I had thought that we were in league with the Syrians, but this man stripped away my illusions. I suddenly understood the subtle mocking of the soldiers outside: to them, al-Asifah was trash. And if we were trash, were we disposable?

10

Coming down the valley wall, Abu Yousef had leaked out more details of the mission. This time, we were going to go deeper inside Israel where we would rendezvous with some *fedayeen* brothers, Palestinians who lived among the Jews in their stolen lands. At that time, many Palestinians lived inside Israel, working in the same villages, eating at the same places, running the same kinds of shops. They did not seem to mind coexisting with the Jews, Abu Yousef told me, grimacing as though tasting rotten meat. But Yasser Arafat wanted to nurse a split, and so we were taking weapons to some Palestinians who had trained underground and were prepared to stir rebellion.

Now, inside the bunker with the hateful Syrian, I slipped a *dishdash* over my head and went to help Mohammed. When all the boys had dressed, a sheikh, a man formally educated in Islam, entered the little building. He wore an army uniform, except that instead of a beret, he wore a white skullcap. I noticed right away that this man had a beard but no moustache, in the style of the Muslim Brotherhood. Instantly, I felt better. Here was an ally. I smiled at him and he smiled back.

The sheikh looked around at all of us and spread his arms in welcome. "Gather round, sons of Islam," he said, gesturing that we should kneel together. He then sat down before us, raised both arms high, and looked to the heavens.

"So we build a dam before them and behind," he chanted, reciting the Sura. "We made them so confused that they became blind."

We all raised our arms. *"Amin,"* we said in unison.

"Tell the infidels that they do not worship what we worship, and whatever they worship we do not worship," the sheikh said.

"Amin."

"Remember *al-shaheed*. Death for Allah is noble! He who gives his life for Allah will redeem seventy of his family."

Fear wormed into my belly. *We did not pray these prayers last time.*

The sheikh continued, his face and arms still lifted high. "If you are to die, say the *shahada*. The gates of paradise will open for you, and you will enter gloriously to find your *ḥūrīyah*, seventy-two who have never been touched before."

I flashed to the day I had leaned against the sugar sack in my hiding place and dreamed of dying gloriously for Allah. Now I knew I was not ready. I glanced at Mohammed and saw tear tracks on his face. Suddenly, I wished I had not spoken to his mother.

After the blessing, Abu Yousef met us outside and supervised as the two Syrian escorts passed out to us duffel bags made of thick khaki. As on my first mission, each bag contained weapons and parts of weapons: 7 mm and 9 mm handguns, AK–47 parts, magazines, and boxes of bullets. Some of the bags contained TNT blocks, fused and dressed with ball bearings. We hoisted them on our backs and lined up like a loose platoon. The Syrians took point, and Ahmed and Qaffin followed, leading us down toward the Israeli border.

Soon we came to a clump of dry bushes that looked like any other in the thirsty land. The Syrians quickly swept them aside to reveal a mouth in the earth, a dark hole surrounded by gray rocks that reminded me of teeth. A bright yellow rope, staked at the tunnel entrance, led away into blackness.

Abu Yousef now appeared before us, and a hush descended over the young brothers. "This is what separates man from child," he said. "What you do for Islam. What you do for your homeland. Today, you become men. Go with courage and for the glory of Allah!"

"Allahu akbar!"

Ahmed and Qaffin were to serve as our scouts and guides. They stepped into the tunnel first and I followed next. Holding the rope with my left hand, I reached out and touched the tunnel wall with my right. It felt cool, almost wet. The smell of dank soil filled my nose.

"Mohammed!" I whispered over my shoulder. "Do not let go of the rope!"

"I won't," he said.

"If you have to let go of the rope, find my bootlace and hang on to me," I said. "If you stay with me, you will be safe."

"Okay," he said, sounding uncertain.

I looked back at the Syrians, at Abu Yousef and the other *fedayeen*. They would not be coming with us.

The first mission was simple, I told myself. *We do not need Abu Yousef.*

Still, disquiet bit at my insides. I could not define it because my child's mind did not have words for what my belly knew. Later, though, I understood. Later, I saw that the adult *fedayeen* taught us a theory they themselves were not willing to practice. They wanted to liberate Palestine, but they did not want to die doing it, even for paradise, even for the seventy-two. They had jobs and children, lives, and much to lose. We were someone else's children. Abu Yousef and his men poured their hate into our hearts in hopes we would do the work they could not fulfill.

11

We plunged into the tunnel, the sound of our footsteps swallowed up by the mud in the walls. Meter by meter, we edged away from the entrance, moving from gloom into blackness. We were able to walk upright for a time, but in some places had to lie down against the cool earth and wriggle forward through tight passages as if through the belly of a snake.

It seemed we had been crawling forever when I felt damp air blow across the back of my neck like the breath of a phantom. Chills quivered down my arms and a sensation of space opened up on my left. I switched on my flashlight and aimed it. Utter darkness yawned out of this new hole, beating back the weak beam. Mountain lions lived in these caves, didn't they? My mind conjured a giant, fanged cat roaring out of the new passage and biting off my head. I stopped crawling and squeezed shut my eyes. My heart thudded against the tunnel floor. Now I knew the rope was my lifeline and I gripped it in my fist like treasure.

"Kamal!"

At Mohammed's frantic whisper, I forced myself to swallow my terror. "Yes?"

"Are we almost there?"

"Yes, my brother. I think I see light up ahead."

I did not see light. The tunnel seemed to me an eternal nightmare, but I did not want Mohammed to be as afraid as I was. I began to inch forward again, trying hard to focus on the best things that ever happened to me, the happiest things. The days that my father taught me special tricks for bending and squaring the metals in his shop. Playing seven stones with Eli. Breathing in my mother's perfume when she hugged me. But those things seemed far away now, as if they had happened to someone else.

At last, I saw a tiny beam of daylight, and within a few more minutes we were climbing out of the tunnel, shimmying up its vertical ending using a second yellow rope. Squinting against the light, I emerged into a land of sandy soil and scrub. Qaffin stood alone at the top of a shallow gully, a slope that led gently down before rising again to a crest about a kilometer away.

"Ahmed has gone ahead with his compass," Qaffin said. "We will wait for the others."

A moment later, Mohammed appeared beside me, and I laughed. He was as dirty from the tunnel as a real Bedouin boy. One by one, all the young brothers climbed out and soon we were underway again, walking downhill, quiet now that we had crossed into enemy territory.

When we had gone half the distance through the gully, a strange buzzing seemed to tickle the edges of my hearing, almost as if I were imagining it.

"There, up ahead," Qaffin said. "The rendezvous."

Following his gaze, I could see a small flock of sheep about 50 meters away, all of them lying down at rest. But I did not see any of the *fedayeen* "shepherds" we were to meet. As we advanced, the buzzing grew louder, like a thousand electrical voices. And now I smelled a peculiar smell, one I knew but could not name.

At about 25 meters away, a flood of images came into focus at once:

Ahmed lying on the ground, the dirt under his head dark with blood.

Beyond him, the sheep. Not resting, but slaughtered. Blood from gaping round holes in their bellies drenched their wool.

Among the sheep, dead men torn nearly in half. Bleeding from wounds made with large-caliber weapons.

And green flies. Clouds and clouds of them, gorging on a feast of blood.

Qaffin whirled to face us, his face a mask of panic. "Retreat!" he screamed. "Go back! Go back!"

But it was too late.

From behind us came a high screaming whistle. Instantly, my brain turned to ice. My air passage shut down, and I stood rooted in place. A rocket slammed into the upslope of the gully and my world erupted into a gray storm of earth, smoke, and shrapnel. The blast wave blew my mouth open. Gravel flew at shrapnel velocity, embedding in my face and hands.

My legs dissolved into jelly and my knees knocked together. My bladder let go.

Now I was seeing in slow motion, frame by frame. A squadron of spinning shrapnel, black steel coils with teeth like a saw, screamed past my head and—*Phhhht! Phhhht! Phhhht!*—sliced into three boys behind me. They fell dead.

Terror tore through my chest. "Mama! Mama! Mama!" I cried, and my bowels let loose.

Behind me, children screamed and ran in wild circles like fleeing lambs. Concussive *booms* split the air as shells thundered down on our position. More shrapnel spun through the air like bedsprings. Smoke swirled around me.

"Mama! Mama!" I screamed.

I could not run. I could not even move. All around me, the lambs fled and I realized many were also crying for their mothers. In the stampede, Mohammed and I locked eyes.

"Kamal!" he cried, running to me, his face twisted in fear.

"Here, Mohammed! Come here!" I stretched out my arms to my friend, and he ran up to me and stopped. Then his shirt exploded. Some great force lifted him up and back, nearly folding him in half. His eyes snapped back and his mouth flew open, but he did not scream. Mohammed fell backward at the speed of the shrapnel and bounced once off the dirt.

"Mohammed!" I screamed. "I promised!"

In that moment, terror released its grip. My legs worked again, and I bent over my friend, hoisting him up over my shoulder, the way we had learned in camp to carry our wounded.

Mohammed. I've got to save Mohammed.

Shells exploded around me, sending up dirt volcanoes. Struggling under Mohammed's weight, I stumbled through the firestorm back in the direction of the tunnel.

Suddenly, the shelling stopped. Now only bullets whistled past. Behind me, I heard the trammel of boots.

Israeli foot troops. Chasing us!

Ahead of me, a boy blew apart as a round pierced the TNT in his pack, turning him into a human bomb. Chunks of his body rained down around me. Mohammed's legs bounced against my chest. His torso hung down my back, soaking my Bedouin disguise with blood.

A crackle of gunfire. *Pffft! Pffft! Pffft!* Israeli bullets meant for me pierced Mohammed's body. Fresh terror peeled my eyes open wide as I searched frantically for the tunnel entrance. But I could not find it. My heart pounded in my ears. The boots were louder now. I could hear the soldiers calling out to each other in Hebrew.

I gave up on the tunnel and ran toward some mountains I knew to be on the Syrian side. Then I saw two rockets blaze over me from the west, toward Israel. The Syrians were engaging! The rifle fire behind me stopped, and I could hear the Israeli boots running in the other direction.

"Mohammed, hold on," I whispered to my friend as I stumbled through the desert scrub. "I will take you home to your mother."

Mohammed did not answer.

The instant I set foot in Syria, I spun my friend off my back and laid him on the ground. He felt as flat and limp as a doll made of rags. His face was grey, his *dish-dash* a shredded, scarlet mess.

"Mohammed, wake up!" I yelled into his face, my own tears streaming. "Wake up! I promised Salma!"

Mohammed only lay there, the whites of his eyes pointed up at the Syrian sky.

I thought that if I talked to Mohammed, he would somehow be jarred from his sleep. He would stand up and brush off his clothes and we would march home to tell the harrowing tale of how he had almost been killed by the Jews.

"Mohammed, speak to me!" I yelled into his face. "Wake up! I promised!"

The echo of rockets and machine guns subsided until the only thing I could hear was my own wails. Dimly, I became aware of Syrian soldiers gathering around me, reaching down to pull me away.

"He's dead," one of them said. "You cannot bring him back."

"No! No!" I screamed, fighting off their hands.

He could not be dead. My worst nightmare could not be true: That the friend I was supposed to save had saved me instead, shielding my body with his own as I fled like a coward. I thought that maybe that was how hell would be: a black chaos that echoed with screams and a beast feeding on children who could not run fast enough.

Our band of *fedayeen* made the bloody trip home, and it was dark when we arrived back in Beirut. The news had traveled faster than we had, and women lined the streets, their screams of grief echoing off the buildings.

Mohammed's body rode in a cart, along with other children who had been killed but not blown apart. I walked beside this cart all the way to Mohammed's house. His mother stood on the street, waiting for me.

She looked down at me, the dark night a frame around her head, the moonlight picking out tears on her cheeks. "You promised," she said.

My stomach rolled with shame, but I did not look away. "Yes, I promised."

"He is in a better place," she said. "He is before the throne of Allah."

Then she put her fingers in her mouth and began screaming. Not a scream of grief, but of celebration. That her boy Mohammed had died a hero's death, a martyr's death, the death of *al-shaheed*. Her son was in paradise. Little by little, other mothers joined her screaming until the streets echoed with a chorus of keening, celebrating grief.

None of the mothers knew that we "brave" soldiers had dissolved into little boys, crying for our mothers. They did not know that Qaffin ran for his life, leaving the children, slow and many carrying heavy packs, to be mowed down by the bloodthirsty Jews. Mohammed's mother did not know that I had stood locked in place, peeing myself while her boy took the shrapnel.

No one knew of my cowardice. They saw me as a hero, rescuing my wounded friend, risking my own life to carry him back to his own country.

But I knew.

Kamal, the warrior prodigy, the future of Islam, had not even had the courage to pull a gun from my knapsack and shoot one bullet back. I loathed myself. Shame tore at my soul. I thought of hell again, the darkness, the screams. I did not know why the beast of the desert had taken my friend and left me. Maybe his belly was full.

12

For kilometers along the Mediterranean shore, the cliffs of Beirut kiss the sapphire sea. Before Golan, I went there often, sitting atop the cliffs looking out at my blue friend, my refuge, my freedom. After Golan, I sat up on those rocks many times thinking, *Why didn't I die? Why did I live when Mohammed did not?*

I gazed out at the sea where my father had taught me to swim, the sea that embraced me when my father would not. It would take only a running leap to balance the scales again.

This cliff is high enough to kill me, I thought. *What would stop me from throwing myself off?*

But I knew that would be a sin against Allah. Also, the imams had been filling my ears with a different song.

"Allah saved you!" they said to me in the mosque and in the camps. "You are chosen! He is saving you for a specific time to do glorious things!"

Slowly, the anguish of losing Mohammed hardened into anger, and the seed of hatred planted in me now bloomed into a dark vine, its flowers the color of blood. Over the next year, I went on to higher and more glorious training, learning weapons and tactics that would help me fight against specific enemies—the Russians, Germans, Israelis, and Americans. I yearned to fight again, half my heart committed to proving myself, the other half still hoping to die, as I should have there on the Syrian border.

Over and over, my mind replayed the moment when the shrapnel cut down Mohammed. His mouth snapping open, the burst of blood from his chest, the rag-doll way his body hit the ground. I could not put the image out of my brain. I could not escape the fantasy of flinging myself off the cliffs that ran between the city and the foamy rocks. Would not Allah's plans succeed more perfectly without me?

Spring came, turning Beirut into a swirl of enchanting scents. The high sweetness of orange and lemon blossoms. The smooth cream of jasmine. Sharp notes of gardenia—my favorite because it was my mother's favorite and reminded me of her. Sarri Habbal had gotten me a new job, this one at a *cadeau*, or gift shop. Sarri was a gigolo who wore tight pants, silky shirts (unbuttoned to show his hairy chest), and enough cologne to suffocate a tribe.

When we worked on the same shift, girls would often drop by the store to visit.

"Mind the shop," he would say to me with a wink. Then he and the girl of the day would disappear into the basement, returning in about an hour. Sarri would then slip the girl a trinket from the store and send her on her way. In this way and others, Sarri was robbing Abdel, the shop owner, blind.

He had hinted at all this before getting me the job there. "If you tell Abdel anything," he told me one day at Sabra, "there will be a day when you do not return from the battlefield."

I kept my mouth shut, but I was not afraid of Sarri. I knew he was more interested in pleasure than revenge. Besides, he would not dare touch a hair on my head because of Abu Yousef.

Abu Yousef had been understanding of my grief, even tender, after the failed mission into Israel. I had grown to love him like a father—

and if I am admitting the truth, equal to or surpassing my feelings for my real father. I respected and adored Abu Yousef so much that if he had asked me to sacrifice myself in battle, I would have done it instantly.

Even so, I was shocked one day that spring when he called me at the store. He rarely conducted business on the telephone, believing—correctly—that the telephone wires strung across Beirut leaked information like water from a broken bucket.

"There is an emergency meeting," he said. "Everyone must come. No exceptions. Pass it on."

He meant Sarri, whose name he would not mention. I told Sarri then ran straight from the store to Abu Ibrahim's where I changed into my fatigues. Abu Ibrahim paid for a taxi to take me and four other boys across town to Sabra. Usually the taxis will not drive that way, but Abu Ibrahim paid the driver extra. Because of the driver, we did not discuss what Abu Yousef's "emergency meeting" could be about. But this had never happened before, and I was burning to find out.

Inside Sabra, I could see that Abu Yousef had made calls all over the city. Dozens and dozens of *fedayeen* streamed toward the far side of the camp. But Abu Yousef had told me to come instead to his office, which was tucked discreetly into a squat concrete building that did not look like it contained anything important. Passing the guards, who knew that I was Abu Yousef's special charge, I wound through a corridor to a small, plain office with pictures of martyred *fedayeen* on the wall.

"*Yah ibny!*" Abu Yousef came around from behind the desk and bent to kiss me on both cheeks. In his right hand, he held a crimson beret and a white scarf, both brand new. "We have a special visitor today. I want you to wear these."

With that, he put the beret on my head, then looped the scarf around my neck, tucking it into my collar aviator style. My uniform was desert camouflage with flecks of red and green. I was thrilled with these new additions and thought they would make me look a cut above the other boys, like a major or even a colonel.

Abu Yousef fussed with the scarf for a moment like a mother hen, and I breathed in the pleasing scent of his cologne. "We are going to hear a special speaker," he said. "You are going to be very surprised."

Who could it be for Abu Yousef to call so many men here in the middle of the week?

13

An underground tunnel lit with garish bulbs connected Abu Yousef's office building with other parts of Sabra. He and I descended a short stairwell to enter it, then tramped along the dirt floor until we emerged outside a camouflage-painted hangar. The hangar was fortified outside with sandbags and, I knew, inside with steel beams and concrete. Hundreds of *fedayeen* were already crowded inside, seated in wide rows facing one of the long walls where a collection of wooden cargo pallets formed a rude platform. Behind the platform stood six men in a loose port-arms stance, their AK–47 muzzles pointed at the floor. They wore complete fatigue uniforms with full *keffiyah* covering their faces. I had never seen them before.

The doors at both ends of the hangar had been thrown open wide, and dust motes danced in the streaming sunlight that played over the murmuring crowd. Like Moses parting the Red Sea, Abu Yousef parted the throng, soldiers leaning left and right to let us pass. As it became clear to me that my mentor was leading me right up to the front row, my heart was just about to explode with pride. I could see that even some of our fiercest fighters were not as privileged as I. We picked our way up to the row directly across from the pallets. Four or five other boys were already seated there, and Abu Yousef motioned for them to make a spot for me dead center. I noticed right away that they too wore their camouflage. But I was secretly delighted that, because of my new scarf and beret, I was more sharply turned out.

I squeezed in and took a seat on the hangar's cool dirt floor just in time to see the rank of soldiers behind the platform snap to attention and honor Abu Yousef with a unified salute. He returned the gesture and then walked around behind the platform. His back was to me, but I could see from the soldiers' relaxed smiles that Abu Yousef knew them all quite well. Still, they clearly deferred to him, and a fresh layer of respect for Abu Yousef formed in my breast. For the first time, I wondered where my mentor had come from before taking me under his wing. Was he more important than I even knew?

About ten meters to the left of the platform, a door opened. My breath caught in my chest as I expected the important visitor to reveal himself. A half dozen men filed in, scanned the crowd, then filed out again, leaving two men posted on either side of the door. I did not look away. Now a man wearing khaki fatigues entered, his head completely covered in a black *abbayah*, the Moroccan headpiece that covers the face from eyes to chin, then covers the head with a hood.

The boy next to me elbowed my side. "There he is!" he whispered fiercely. "Who *is* it?"

"Shhh!" I hissed, not wanting to behave in any way that might dishonor Abu Yousef in front of his important guest.

Flanked by four rough-looking men, the mysterious visitor walked toward the platform, prompting the soldiers standing behind it to snap to attention and raise their weapons, eyes dangerous, barrels pointed toward the crowd. I felt at that moment that if any one of us had moved toward the hooded guest, those men would have cut him down.

The guest climbed the platform and stood still as one of his bodyguards stepped forward and removed the *abbayah*. The air left the room as the assembled *fedayeen* sucked it all in in a single gasp.

The man beneath the hood was Yasser Arafat.

14

The hangar exploded into ringing cheers that echoed off the metal walls, the noise so loud I could not hear my own voice as I screamed at the top of my lungs.

Joy! Astonishment! Delight! Reverence! I can scarcely describe the elixir of emotions that charged through my body. It was not at all like a rock star had shown up at Sabra that day. It was as if a *god* had appeared.

Every one of my senses lit up as though I had been transported suddenly into the presence of the Prophet himself. The boys to my left and right were equally giddy, shouting and hooting and dancing about, unable to contain their zeal.

Arafat wore a khaki shirt, thick, black-rimmed glasses and a *keffiyeh*, though it was not of the checkered pattern that would later become his trademark. He had a stubble beard and a thick moustache that rode above his lips, which seemed nearly as thick. In the roaring din, the Leader smiled and nodded, while the men aligned behind him continued scanning the hangar for assassins.

Abu Yousef stepped up on the platform and raised his hands to hush us. "Brothers of the movement, I present to you Yasser Arafat, *qa'ad swoara al Palestinia*."

The leader of the Palestinian movement.

The hangar exploded again. This was not forced applause. No one was under threat of not cheering enough, as I later learned was the case in the Soviet Union. No, this was pure ecstasy.

A Palestinian anthem now blared from a bullhorn speaker mounted somewhere in the rafters. After what seemed like five full minutes of screaming, Arafat raised both arms, nodding graciously, and the *fedayeen* settled to a low murmur, then silence. I sat back down directly across from the platform, not fifteen feet away.

Then the great Leader began to speak. "Jerusalem is our target," Arafat said solemnly. "Allah has given us that land. It belongs to us. The Jews took it with the help of the English. We must take it back, through the power of Allah."

Many think the PLO was a secular group. It was not. Arafat then read to us from the Koran, although I do not remember from which *sura*. He also spoke of the Palestinian movement, the justice of the cause, and the deplorable conditions in which his people were forced to live. It would be through soldiers like us, he said, brave and committed fighters, that his people would be liberated and restored to the Palestinian homeland now occupied by the filthy Jews.

"We will achieve victory through fighters like *you*," Arafat pro-claimed, and I was astonished to see that he was pointing his finger di-rectly at me.

My heart leapt in my chest. I stole wild glances at the boys to my left and my right to see if I was dreaming, that they might elbow me awake. But those boys were staring goggle-eyed at Arafat, who now stepped down off the platform and, in four steps, planted his boots directly in front of me and reached down with his right hand.

I looked up into Arafat's face and saw that he was smiling. His thick glasses magnified his eyes so that they seemed huge, floating just below the lenses. I put my hand in his and he pulled me to my feet, turned me to face the crowded hangar, tucking me under his right arm. I could smell his sweat, the product of the warm spring day.

"It is young men like Kamal who will be our great liberators!" he de-clared grandly.

My head spun. *Yasser Arafat knows my name!*

Then Arafat turned, put one hand on each of my shoulders and kissed my forehead, his breath bearing tales of garlic and onion. The crowd screamed and clapped. Arafat released me and I, dazed and soar-ing with joy, sat back down, the boys around me slapping me on the back.

If Yasser Arafat said I would be a great liberator, maybe I was not a coward after all. Maybe Mohammed's death was not my fault. The mo-ment was a turning point, a rebirth. For months, I had wanted to drown myself or crawl into a hole and die. But now my zeal returned. My spirit for *jihad* was renewed.

It would be many years before I understood that, using only a red be-ret and white scarf, Abu Yousef had set me up.

Southwestern United States
2007

After I began speaking out against radical Islam, a number of local, state, and federal law enforcement agencies reached out to me. They wanted to hear about the Islamist mindset and tactics from the viewpoint of someone who had fought on that side of the terror war. The FBI, in particular, wanted to hear about communication tactics. For example, agents had noticed that participants in certain Internet chat rooms seemed to quote certain *sura* on a regular basis. Was this devotional in nature or some kind of code?

Very likely code, I told them, pointing out a mission to Afghanistan in which my *fedayeen* unit attacked a Russian bomber using SAM-7 rockets. From troop movement to the moment we fired, our every action was prompted by the recitation of certain *sura* over handheld radios.

Shortly after the imam confronted me in Seattle with the message that Islamists would "seed" American women and "have this nation," I traveled to North Carolina for a series of speaking engagements, so I happened to be away when four Pakistani men came to my hometown to hunt me down.

On the Monday morning after I returned from North Carolina, I was sitting in my office at work when Lily, my secretary, patched through a call from Mike, the head of security at the nonprofit where I worked.

"Kamal, we've had a series of incidents you need to know about," he said.

Mike told me that while I was out of town, a group of Pakistani men driving cars with Washington State plates cruised into town. They did not find my place of business, but went to similar organizations asking if anyone knew the whereabouts of a Kamal Saleem. What was Kamal Saleem's profession? Where did the Saleem family live?

"The people the Pakistanis came into contact with said they appeared nervous and somewhat hostile," Mike said.

Because they had asked about my family, the news unnerved me. But it did not surprise me. *There was a time when I would have done the same thing*, I thought.

"The Pakistanis also went to two other locations in town, including the bank you use," Mike said. "They sat out in the parking lot for an hour working on a laptop computer. Finally, security guards asked them to leave."

I thanked Mike, and as he left the office, I dialed my wife, Victoria.

"Call the FBI," I said.

The next day, we visited at an FBI field office with an agent who didn't look much like an agent in his jeans and pale yellow polo shirt.

"What do you make of this?" the agent asked. "Why are they looking for you?"

I told him about the incident in Seattle outside the mosque. I also told him about another verbal confrontation in Seattle near the Space Needle with a Pakistani activist from the Council on Arab-Islamic Relations (CAIR), a group that claims to be educational, but in 2007 was named an "unindicted co-conspirator" in a federal case linking an Islamic "charity" with the terrorist group Hamas. The activist and I had gone nearly nose to nose in a debate over the threat of radical Islam.

The agent agreed with Victoria and me that the Seattle incidents and the appearance three days later of Pakistanis hunting me on my home turf was more than coincidence.

Now the agent had some other news. "We interviewed people who came in contact with the Pakistanis. One of them fits the description of a Muslim engineer the Bureau has been tracking for months."

Beside me, I felt my wife tense.

"This individual is brilliant," the agent continued. "He's also nuts. If you haven't done it already, you need to beef up security at your home. Cameras, alarms, everything. Better yet, move. At least to a gated community."

The agent's words echoed Walid's warning about security in Aspen in July. Now we got serious about it. Not only did we install a professionally monitored electronic security and surveillance system in our house, we also warned our close friends and colleagues about the potential threat.

Three weeks after the FBI visit, my secretary, Lily, answered another phone call at my office.

"Hello, I am looking for Kamal Saleem," said a man with a thick Middle Eastern accent.

"Your name, sir?"

"My name is Bill," the caller said. "I am an old friend of Kamal Saleem's. I used to have his cell phone number, but I have lost it. You know how it goes."

The man chuckled, and Lily thought she heard a hard, false brightness in the laugh. And she had never met a man with such a thick foreign accent who went by the name of Bill.

"Is Kamal Saleem there?" the caller pressed. "If he is not there, I will just leave a message."

"I'm sorry," my secretary said. "We don't have anybody here named Kamal Saleem."

1

By the time I was eight, I had become a free agent. At home, as long as I handed over some money to my mother and father, I came and went as I pleased. After working with Sarri at the gift shop I got a different job, this time working for a catalog-order clothing distributor. I was a counter boy, serving Beirut retailers who came in, browsed the catalogs, and ordered garments made in sweatshops by Armenian laborers who worked dirt cheap. I worked there for about a year, then became an office boy for an import-export dealer, making coffee, running errands, and carrying documents back and forth between the office and the various embassies.

All that time, I kept a delicious secret: I was living a double life. During the day, I was Kamal Saleem, just a boy working in a regular job. At night, I was training to kill people. By then, everyone was talking about James Bond, how he would pretend to be someone else, then take out a bad guy with a poison ink pen or a karate chop. Because relatively few people—only those at the mosque, at the camps, and in my neighborhood cell—knew my secret identity, I felt the kinship of spies.

At Sabra, each week seemed to reveal to me a new element of *jihad*. Imagine a school-age boy, disassembling antipersonnel mines, removing the RDX plastic explosive, and using it to build a new bomb by adding primer and a wristwatch. That was me. At the time, C-4 plastic explosives were fairly new and, we found, more stable and easier to transport than TNT. The *fedayeen* taught me how to place C–4 in a building for maximum destruction (blowing up structural support columns worked well) and how to rig an automobile's fuel system with C–4 in order to turn the whole vehicle into a bomb.

I recruited other boys to our cause, going often to Abu Ibrahim's house to teach them how to take apart an AK–47 and put it back together again.

"If you want to shoot real ammo, you have to come to Sabra," I told them. They came by the dozens.

Several times, the *fedayeen* ferried me and a group of other boys into Syria to train young soldiers there. Adults could have done the job, but it was smarter and stealthier to drop us children off at a *souk* and let us blend into the background until local *fedayeen* could pick us up and drive us to a mountain training camp. Once the training was over, they would drive us back to the *souk* where we would again melt into the scenery until we rendezvoused with our own people, who then spirited us home.

For me, it was a boy's dream—like the American Boy Scouts, but with guns. We learned weapons instead of knots, pledged violence instead of service. But in the summer of 1967, the Muslim world sustained a blow that shook my faith to the very core. A water dispute, territorial tensions, and cross-border clashes had long simmered between Israel, Jordan, Egypt, and Syria. That June, they erupted into war.

After watching Egypt, Syria, and Jordan assemble massive armies along their borders, Israel's tiny military launched a preemptive strike against the mighty Egyptian air force. In response, Jordan attacked Jerusalem and Netanya, another Israeli city. Soon Syria joined in the anti-Zionist assault.

At Sabra, we cheered when we heard on the radio about the colossal firepower arrayed against the Jews. The Egyptian air force was 450 fighter planes strong, more than twice the size of the Israeli air force. The Egyptian army fielded 100,000 soldiers, 950 tanks, and 1,000 artillery pieces. Combined, the Syrians and Jordanians fielded more than

125,000 men, 300 tanks, and 12 artillery battalions. One hundred Iraqi tanks rumbled into Jordan to face off against the Jews.

Our *fedayeen* were on standby, ready to join the fight, as we knew our brothers in Jordan already had. But no one from Beirut was sent. Two, three, four days passed as Muslim and Israeli forces clashed in Jerusalem, the Sinai Peninsula, and in wicked dogfights over Egypt. In the hangar, we huddled around a radio and shouted at the news of overwhelming victories: Muslim fighters were killing thousands of Jewish soldiers! We were pushing them back! Jerusalem was about to fall!

It was all propaganda.

On the final day of what became known as the Six-Day War, I was at home when I heard from my Christian neighbors that Israel had defeated the fearsome armies of Islam. We had lost East Jerusalem and the West Bank. We had lost the Gaza Strip. We had even lost the Golan Heights.

Sabra was in mourning, as were many in Beirut. The streets in my neighborhood teemed with shell-shocked Sunnis. How could this have happened? How could the Jews, a tiny nation of infidel dogs, have defeated all the armies of Allah?

Three weeks after the war, Israeli Defense Forces General Yitzhak Rabin explained his theory of the victory in an address at Hebrew University:

> *Our airmen struck the enemies' planes so accurately that no one in the world understands how it was done, and people seek technological explanations or secret weapons; our armored troops beat the enemy even when our equipment was inferior to theirs; our soldiers in all other branches . . . who overcame our enemies everywhere, despite the latter's superior numbers and fortifications—all these revealed not only coolness and courage in the battle but . . . an understanding that only their personal stand against the greatest dangers would achieve victory for their country and for their families, and that if victory was not theirs the alternative was annihilation.*[10]

But our Christian neighbors, the parents of my friend Marie, had a different explanation: divine intervention.

"We are hearing of miracles!" I heard Marie's mother exclaim. "One Israeli tank took out ten Syrian tanks! Egyptian fighter planes fell from the sky as if struck down by angels. Certainly, the Jews were fighting on the side of God!"

I did not understand how this could be so. How could Allah abandon us this way? I remember that my mother was baking pastries in the kitchen when I went to ask her, "Why has Allah lifted up the Jews and not the Muslims?"

"Allah would never do such a thing," she replied sharply, wiping a spot of flour from her face. "America must have helped the Jews. America must have been hidden, lying in wait, and ambushed our soldiers. It is the only explanation."

It was not until many years later that I realized my mother did not know what to say, and so she simply made something up. But at the time, I accepted her explanation. It gave me one more reason to hate America.

2

Following the Six-Day War, Yasser Arafat shuttled between Lebanon, Syria, Egypt, and Jordan. Despite Israel's success against the national Muslim armies, groups like Fatah and the PLO were growing stronger. In 1968, we celebrated at Sabra when our brothers held their own against an Israeli attack on Fatah headquarters in the Jordanian village of Karameh. The stories came back that Arafat himself had dashed back and forth across the battlefield, rallying the *fedayeen* to hold their ground. Only 28 Israelis died versus 150 *fedayeen*. But we considered it a great victory because the Israeli troops who had vanquished Syria and Egypt had failed against us.

The same year, when I was about ten years old, I lucked into a job selling clothing in a European boutique. I had been prowling the Hamra on a tourist-packed summer day, looking for an arcade where I could waste some money, when the boutique owner, a Frenchwoman who was harried and desperate for help with a huge afternoon rush, hired me right off the sidewalk. After that, I spent two years flattering lady tourists and rich Maronite women, helping them pick out sexy outfits to wear for their men.

Throughout these years, the Palestinian refugee camps scattered around Beirut grew more and more like glorified dumps. Raw sewage drained into some areas. In another place, a slaughterhouse was erected nearby and the stench of blood hung over the camp in a sickening cloud. In response, we focused on recruiting Palestinians who had lived in Lebanon for a long time. We tried to radicalize them, inspire them to stand up and fight not only for their cause, but for Allah. For Islam.

"The Christians live like kings," I heard the adult *fedayeen* say. "The Palestinians live like their servants. The refugees are our Muslim brothers. We must support them against the infidels."

Our second recruiting target was Sunni Muslims. We went into the mosques and preached a message of solidarity, encouraging the Lebanese Sunnis to align with the Fatah and the PLO. We did not recruit the Shia, whom we considered perverse.

But as adolescence bloomed inside me, I started to worry that I was somewhat perverse as well. From afar, I watched the infidel's life and wanted it for myself. I was sprouting up physically, growing tall and broad in the shoulders. At age thirteen, I was nearly six feet tall. My hair had grown into dark waves, but my skin was light and my eyes were blue like the sea. I began noticing girls noticing me. The infidel boys dated girls—openly kissing them even while riding the bus. I wanted to try that. I wanted to be like Bond and have a beautiful redhead in a Jackie Kennedy dress, and the minute she sees me she just faints.

But every time I saw a pretty girl, I melted like chocolate. Inside, I was just about to explode. When I was twelve, my father had taken me for a walk to talk about these things. I was happy to have time with him, but it felt to me like a mandatory checkmark on his parenting chart: a quick trip with me around the neighborhood to get the sex talk monkey off his back.

Now I found my confusion growing. I had learned in Islam that women were sinful and had to be covered up. If that was so, why did I want them so badly?

Maybe Abu Yousef would know.

I found him in the hangar at Sabra smoking a cigarette, as usual. When I told him my dilemma, he tucked his Marlboro into one corner of his mouth and pulled a pen and paper from the breast pocket of his fatigues. Squinting around a curl of smoke, he jotted something on the paper and handed it to me. I read an address that I knew to be downtown. A notorious address: *Souk al-Shramit.* Market of the whores.

"Many of our warriors go there to take care of their needs," Abu Yousef said, exhaling a plume of smoke. "These are tested women. They are young and beautiful, and they are clean. Not like the secondhand whores from Syria and Egypt. And don't worry about the money. Fatah takes care of the bill. The women will take care of you."

And they did.

3

In 1969, Yasser Arafat became chairman of the Palestinian Liberation Organization. The following year, in May, a Palestinian cell crossed from Lebanon into the Israeli farming village of Avivim, where they ambushed a school bus, killing twelve people, nine of them children. Back at Sabra, I am now ashamed to say, we celebrated this mission as though Allah had given us some great victory.

That is the truth of *jihad*: It is a war in which no territory need be taken, no strategic objective seized. To shed the blood of the infidels— even children—is reason enough to party in the streets.

That same year, backed by the Soviet Union and Syria, Arafat decided to launch raids on Israel from inside Jordan. But Hussein ibn-Talal, the Jordanian king, ordered a full-scale assault on the PLO, and his army crushed Arafat's forces. It was a stunning blow, one that caused

Arafat to move his headquarters to Lebanon. There, even though he had been defeated, we welcomed him like a liberator.

I was at Sabra on the day a huge column of Russian trucks brought hundreds of rifle-slung *fedayeen* into Beirut all at once. It was like a parade, a festival. Crowds of Palestinians lined the roads that crisscrossed the camp. Women hooted—that yodeling sound of celebration. Men cheered and held up pictures of the Leader.

They have only pictures, I remember thinking. *I have been praised by the Leader himself!*

The trucks rumbled by bristling with weapons: DShKs, Katyurshas, rocket launchers. Little children darted up and down in front of the crowd, some of them waving toy guns.

Abu Yousef was not so excited. I stood beside him in the front row of the crowd and when I looked up, his mouth was smiling but his eyes were not.

"Our lives will never be the same again," he said.

He later explained more. The Palestinians from Jordan considered themselves the "real" Palestinians. Now they would come and take over the camps, wrestling the command structure away from the Lebanese and other Sunnis who had made common cause with them. The rules would change. Alliances would change.

"Now, Kamal, you must be careful to whom you talk and what you tell them," Abu Yousef said. "We will have new commanders, men we do not know. Be careful."

4

In March of 1978, a Palestinian woman named Dalal Mughrabi led the slaughter of Israeli children. She and a *fedayeen* unit from Fatah slipped into Israel on Zodiac boats, landing on a beach north of Tel Aviv. Carrying explosives and automatic weapons, the twelve-fighter unit hit the Coastal Road and hijacked a bus full of families on a day outing. During a clash with an Israeli Army force led by Ehud Barak, who later became Prime Minister of Israel, Mughrabi and the *fedayeen* began shooting passengers as they tried to escape. When she realized her unit could not defeat Barak's forces, Mughrabi blew up the bus, killing thirty-five civilians, thirteen of them children.

Historians have said the attack marked the first time women were recognized as full-fledged Palestinian militants, and they are right. But women had trained with Fatah and the PLO long before that.

I trained with women at Sabra. There were not many of them, and they were not there as a matter of equality or for any recognition of revolutionary fellowship with men. It was only that Arafat, Abu Yousef, and others had deduced that by using women, they could fool the Jews. Of course, the Israelis had long known that their enemies were using Muslim children as pack mules and assassins. And as the Americans had in Vietnam, the Israelis learned they had to kill or be killed.

But the Israelis, our leaders decided, had never seen us deploy a woman. To that point, the IDF had no reason to search beneath a woman's *abbayah,* and would have been committing a gross and unpardonable violation of a Muslim woman if they had. So we began to train a few women to smuggle weapons and wear the martyr's bomb. But privately, Abu Yousef let it be known that a woman was not a man's equal. Though research had shown they could withstand mental pressure more steadfastly than men, their tolerance for physical pain was much lower.

"The woman, if she is captured by the Jews and tortured, will quickly confess," Abu Yousef told me. And so, the game plan was that if we were captured and there was a woman in our unit, she was supposed to blow herself up. If she did not, our instructions were to shoot her in the head. Make her a martyr by murder.

Since the bus on the Coastal Road erased the evidence, it is impossible to say which was the case with Dalal Mughrabi. But I can say that the mission was not the first Fatah attempt to assault Israel by sea. In 1971, I was part of a two-boat assault team that targeted the Israeli port city of Haifa.

To qualify for the mission, *fedayeen* had to be good swimmers, and I was one of the best. I had also trained on every weapon in the PLO arsenal. I volunteered to go. It had been seven years since my failed mission into Israel, and still I wanted to redeem myself by returning to the belly of the beast.

I did not meet Nizhar, our mission leader, until a month before the operation. I had just turned fourteen years old, my face still a boy's face, a narrow strip of fuzz where a warrior's moustache should have been. A tall man with a full mouth and dark eyes strangely flecked with crimson, Nizhar was not a Palestinian, but Lebanese like me. I noted with satisfaction that he had seen battle: one of his ears looked like it had been carved with a meat cleaver.

The plan was to board a fishing boat at the Lebanese city of Sidon, a busy merchant seaport. There were cities much closer to the Israeli border, but we had learned of two networks of spies, Shia and Christian, who lived on the border and profited by spilling secrets to the Jews. So we would begin farther north and sail south until we reached the Israeli coast. In addition to secrecy, the plan boasted boldness: no one would suspect an invasion originating at Sidon, a city too far north of the target to be a practical launching pad. Yet, there was nothing impractical about the haven of international waters. From well off the coast of Israel, we would launch from fishing boats in a pair of Zodiac rafts and motor by night into the Bay of Haifa.

It was near the end of summer. At Sabra, a dozen of us climbed into a convoy of trucks and Mercedes sedans. I sat in the right rear seat of a Mercedes, the motor idling, heat baking into the seats. Abu Yousef was there to say goodbye. Standing beside the car, he looked at me, his eyes a strange brew of sadness and pride. An odd look, the way I now imagine I will look when I send my own children away to college. Except that Abu Yousef was sending me away to die.

The chance that I might not come back from this mission was something like 95 percent. Nizhar had maps and telephone numbers, contacts in Israel in case we were trapped and needed refuge. But the greater likelihood was that we would be cornered in a shootout with the Israeli army, the police, or their intelligence force, the Mossad. For that possibility, each of us carried explosives on our belts.

Abu Yousef leaned close to the car window, wafting the scent of tobacco smoke. "Don't trust anyone," he said. "Stick to what you have
learned. And if you are captured, use that thing on your belt."

My heart wrestled with the fact that I might never see him again.
Saying goodbye to him was much more difficult than saying goodbye to
my real father the night before. I was forbidden from breathing a word
about the mission, but I had told my family goodbye as if it would be
the last time I would ever see them.

I was the youngest fighter on the mission. During the hour-long ride
down narrow coastal roads, I talked with two of the other *fedayeen* who
would ride in my Zodiac: Haroon, a handsome half-Palestinian and
half-Lebanese with deep-set eyes that seemed always to simmer in anger, and Tahsein, a stout, bow-legged man who ran faster than anyone I
had ever seen. Of the dozen *fedayeen* headed for Haifa, these two were
the only men I knew well.

When we arrived in Sidon, the wharf teemed with people. Old men
mending nets, selling block ice, selling bait and provisions. Young men
painting boats, scraping hulls, muscling cargo up the gangplanks. Gulls
wheeled over the water and dove for scraps. Over the whole scene, the
smell of cut fish lay like a thick, unpleasant cloud. But behind the boats,
I saw salvation: the azure sky melted seamlessly into the cobalt sea,
which seemed to wink and smile at me. I looked forward to venturing
out into the ocean's embrace, beyond sight of land. The land was a place
of pain and rejection, factions and friendship lost. But as it had since
my father taught me to swim, the deep sea meant freedom.

Two hours later, we had rendezvoused with Lebanese fishermen who
were sympathetic to the Palestinian cause, had boarded our boat, the
Tabarea, and were headed out to sea. As the fishermen busied themselves on the deck, I stood at the bow and thrilled to the crisp salt scent
and feathery fingers of ocean breeze playing through my hair. We had
been underway only for about fifteen minutes when I saw a pod of porpoises begin to pace our path off to starboard. There were at least a
dozen of them, and they leapt through the water, piercing it with their
pointed snouts and popping up into the air again as if sewing stitches in
the surface of the sea. Ahead and to our right, a broad shaft of sunlight
cut down into the water like a blade, forming a window into the indigo

deep. In it, I saw a school of fish dart from our course in a flash of silver.

I laughed out loud and praised Allah. "Great are your works! See what you have made!"

Farther and farther, we cut through the open water, leaving the porpoises behind. The swells loomed larger, pitching the boat up and down like a carnival ride. By degrees, my joy faded as I felt the first hints of creeping nausea. I rushed to the port rail, sucked in a great gulp of cool air, and promptly vomited over the side. Behind me, I heard some of the fishermen yelp with laughter.

Night came. My stomach had surrendered all it had to offer, leaving me feeling woozy and green. I stayed on the deck. From below, I could hear Nizhar's booming voice and the other men's laughter at some battle story he was telling. I sat at the stern now, and as the air grew cooler, my nausea subsided enough for me to look around again. It was the time of the new moon, and the sky appeared as though a messenger of Allah had flung handfuls of jewels against black silk.

Another day passed. As the fishermen flung nets draped round with balls of cork to keep them afloat, Nizhar came to me on the deck, carrying two black duffels.

"Come, Kamal, let's check our weapons," he said. "After night falls, there will not be time.

He thrust a duffel into my arms. I unzipped it and pulled out a Russian 9 mm. Beside me, Haroon did the same. I could not help noticing the way his weapon lay in his thick hand, his hairy and thickly roped forearm disappearing into his sleeve. I was big and well-muscled for my age, but still retained the smooth, coltish limbs of a teenager. At that moment, a voice inside me whispered a hated reminder: *You are still only a boy.*

5

The *Tabarea* arced south through international waters, motoring toward the fishing beds and ultimately our target. On the second evening, as I watched the red disk of the sun slip over the edge of the sea, nerves began needling my belly. The *fedayeen* didn't talk much, but only slipped into our mission gear, hooded black wetsuits specialized for increased buoyancy.

As the horizon sucked the last light from the sky, Haroon and Tahsein found me at the bow again. "Kamal, help us with the rafts," Tahsein said.

Many kilometers before, the captain had killed every light on the fishing vessel. In the gathering night, I followed the other men and found Nizhar at the stern where the fishermen had already begun inflating a pair of Zodiacs using gray-green air cylinders. When each raft was inflated, they pressed a skeleton of flat plastic into the bottom to make it rigid. We then lowered the rafts over the side with ropes. By the time all that was complete, the sky had dimmed to a gunmetal sheet, and a scatter of early stars glinted like glass.

I leaned on the port rail, looking back at the Zodiacs trailing in our wake. Soon Nizhar appeared at my side in his wetsuit, a dark shape against the sky. He stood awhile smoking in the silence. At intervals, the tip of his cigarette lit up like a comet.

"Do you know what to do when we reach the shore?" he said finally.

I knew we were to invade the Bay of Haifa. I knew that each of us carried an AK–47, two handguns, one 7 mm and one 9 mm, plus grenades and knives. Each boat carried a *doctoryov*, and each man on the team carried a unique weapon of his own, capable of greater destruction. Mine was a special type of launcher that lobbed 10 mm mortars.

"We are going to hit what the Americans call 'targets of opportunity,'" Nizhar said. "That means that after we land, if we come upon a bus, we will attack it. If any passengers survive the initial assault, we may kill them or we may hold them hostage. You have to be ready to change and move at any time. You have to be flexible."

I nodded my understanding. At Sabra, we had begun to learn more about the value of threatening and killing civilians. I burned with envy when I heard of the victories of an elite group of *fedayeen*, Black September. Only a few months earlier, in September 1970, the group had hijacked three civilian airliners and held the passengers hostage for a week in Amman. Then the *fedayeen* set bombs on the jets, destroying them before the whole world. At Sabra, we celebrated madly, regretting only that the passengers had been removed before the explosions.

If we were to hijack a bus in Haifa, it would be for the specific purpose of killing civilians. We had seen the fear inspired by Black September and other terrorist groups in Germany. When you struck fear into the hearts of civilians, it turned out, they started screaming at the government to meet your demands. Do what they want! Make peace! Give them their land!

Hijacking a bus would not be as spectacular as taking airliners. But killing a couple of *Jewish* bus riders would be far superior in the currency of *jihad*.

I turned my face up into the briny wind and listened as the *Tabarea* sliced through the black water below. A thin curl of smoke from Nizhar's cigarette slipped under my nose, then a great cloud as he exhaled. He flicked the glowing butt over the rail, and the wind snatched it away.

"What if we attack a bus and there are children riding on it?" he said, peering out into the cottony dark. "Would you be able to take care of them?"

Instantly, my mind was a movie screen filled with images of fleeing Muslim boys, terrified and screaming, of small limbs raining from the sky, of my friend's rag doll form and lifeless eyes. Hatred like liquid fire surged up into my throat, pushing tears into my eyes so that the stars sprouted rays like tiny suns. I was glad for the darkness, glad Nizhar was not looking at me.

"Yes," I said. The word was a gavel.

"Good. If you kill any of the offspring of the Jews, remember to tell the mother, 'You have killed our children for generations and now you occupy our land. Today you are paying for what you have done.' Also, if you kill children, try to let at least one mother live so that she can run screaming home to her village with the fear of Allah in her heart."

"I will remember," I said.

Nizhar then told me that if we made it past the coast, we would head inland and attack the police station. If that was successful, we would kidnap Haifa's top official.

Now he turned to me with what seemed to be his final words: "You know this is a one-way mission?"

I paused for a moment, considering the sky. Off the port side of the fishing boat, night had taken hold and the stars had brightened, perhaps the last I would ever see.

"Yes," I said.

The *Tabarea* captain choked off the boat's engines, and we drifted to a stop. Minutes later, Zodiacs, loaded with six men each, sped east. In my raft, Nizhar sat at the bow with two other men behind him. I sat at the stern, with Tahsein to my right and Haroon to my left. The water was cool. The height of the swells surprised me, rising and falling like great oily beasts that dwarfed our tiny boat. I was also plunged into a new definition of darkness. I could not see the top of each swell; we had only flashlights fitted with blue bulbs, and we all took turns training slim beams on the water just ahead of the boat. But I knew we were scaling great walls of water because when we slid up one side, my back tipped and I was looking up at the stars. When we crested the top, the bow of the Zodiac pitched forward sharply and we slid down into what seemed to be a deep trough.

"Paddle! Paddle! Paddle!" Nizhar shouted above the crash of the water. "Keep the bow pointed straight east."

Which way is east? I thought frantically.

Cold seawater rolled up into the boat, sloshing into my lap, and suddenly—inexplicably—fear snatched my heart like talons. All at once, I was certain I was returning to the scene of a fatal accident, that this would be like the Golan Heights, and the Israelis would win again, killing everyone, including me. The imams were wrong; I was not a chosen warrior. My chance for redemption would drown in this ravenous sea, and my name would vanish like a breath.

Up and down we pitched. My nausea returned, and now with a fierce, swooning dizziness. I wished fervently that I could see the way ahead. Nizhar had told all of us to watch out for Israeli navy ships guarding the coast. But how were we to watch for anything when we could not see past the monstrous waves that tossed the Zodiac like a toy?

Allah! I cried in my heart. *Allah, where are you?*

Unbidden, a *sura* came to my lips, and I yelled it into the wind and into the wet, splashing darkness. "Whatever you throw at the enemy, you did not throw it. Allah has thrown it at the enemy through you!"

My head rocked back as the Zodiac slid up another dark mountain. We scaled the swell, reached its summit, then crashed down into the trough. The men screamed like terrified riders on a carnival attraction.

"Paddle! We are drifting north!" Nizhar cried. "To the right! East is to the right!"

"We make a dam before them and behind them," I shouted. "Allah has blinded them and they cannot see!"

I did not tell anyone, but I reached out of the boat with my left hand and trailed my fingertips on the water. *My friend, my friend. Be with us. Be calm. Help us sail into our destiny.*

Almost instantly, the size of the swells grew noticeably smaller. Looking up, I caught sight of the shoreline for the first time. I did not attribute the calmer seas to the closer shore. Instead I was certain Allah had calmed the water through my touch. I did not tell anyone because I did not want them to think I was crazy, but from the top of my head, goose bumps cascaded down my body. Fired by faith, my confidence returned. Suddenly I knew we would be victorious.

We are called, I thought. *Great will be our reward in paradise.*

Nizhar and the others began to talk among themselves, relief flooding their whispers. Now the men in my Zodiac unzipped their duffels and began pulling out weapons, checking to see if they had survived the journey dry. I opened the case containing the 10 mm mortar launcher and examined it by touch. I did not feel anything amiss.

I held it in my lap and looked toward the shore. Now, every time we crested a low wave, we could see lights in high places, piercing the night. My heart raced. Silently, I recited the *sura*:

Judgment Day will not come until the Muslims fight the Jews, and the Muslims will kill the Jews . . .

The Jews will hide behind stones or trees, and the stone or the tree will say: Oh Muslim, oh servant of Allah, there is a Jew behind me, come and kill him . . .

Surely the party of Allah are they that shall be triumphant . . .

And at that moment, the sea exploded around me.

6

Red and orange flares seared across the sky, lighting the surface of the water in the colors of fire. To my left the sea convulsed, sending a volcano of foam toward the black sky. Haroon fell out of the boat.

"Haroon!" I screamed.

"Get down! Get down!" Nizhar shouted. "It is the Israelis!"

The five of us who remained squeezed ourselves into tight balls, our heads ducked, trying to make ourselves smaller targets.

How can they even see us? I thought wildly. *We are a needle in the dark!*

Twenty meters to our right, with a terrible thunder, the sea rose up two stories high. The water crashed down, sending the Zodiac lurching to port and the mortar launcher sailing off my lap. I scrabbled in the bottom of the boat to find it, but I could not.

It is like Golan! It is like Golan! It is happening all over again.

Some kind of shell exploded directly in front of the Zodiac. I did not hear Nizhar cry out, but I felt pieces of his flesh splatter across my face. To Nizhar's left, another man also took shrapnel. In the eerie light of the flares, I saw a black rose bloom on his throat and he gurgled around it: "*Allahu akbar . . .*"

Then he fell face forward into the floor of the boat.

Inside my brain, a voice screamed at me: *Jump!*

Instantly, I leapt into the sea, plunging into the dark water and popping up again in the flare light. Spitting out a mouthful of saltwater,

I looked around wildly. Concussions in the water pounded into my chest. A receding swell had carried me directly behind the Zodiac, and I could see Tahsein and another man still hunkering down. The raft was sinking.

The next sound I heard was a helicopter, and a single thought flashed through my head: *It's over.*

The rhythm of its blades chopped up the night. Then, to my right, two kilometers away, I saw a bright white light boring down out of the sky, sniffing the surface of the sea like a predator.

The other boat! They're looking for the other boat!

They must have found it. Like fire from heaven, red tracers arrowed down through the dark. I knew we would be next. With all my might, I started to swim. Again, instinct took over: *Swim back and to the left! Toward the open sea.*

Wildly, I stroked the water, hoping that my black suit blended into the dark. The drumming of the helicopter grew closer. Had it turned in my direction? I dove beneath the surface and swam underwater as long as my breath would take me. *Swim to sea! Swim to sea!*

My instincts did not tell me what I would do after that—only that I had to escape the Israelis, survive the next moment. I cut into the surface chop, swimming up over swells that grew larger as I went. I did not think the helicopter would be able to see me unless its searchlight fell directly on top of me.

Suddenly, a massive explosion concussed the water around me. I felt my eyeballs push forward in my skull. My right side exploded. The sea spit me up into the air, throwing me back in the direction I had come from, then pushing me deep underwater. My vision went black and my head swam. A high whining buzz set up inside my head. Under the surface, I writhed in the dark, swallowing water, disoriented. Which way was up? Which way to air?

Let go, a voice whispered.

And I realized that if I stopped fighting, I would float to the surface. I let my body go limp and floated up like a balloon. Then I felt air on my face, but all I could see was blackness. Blearily, I looked for lights, something to orient me toward the shore. The metallic taste of blood seeped down into my mouth. From my nose, I thought. Rising to the top of a swell, I caught a glimpse of lights. Slowly, I began a painful sidestroke in the direction I thought was north.

7

As the sea cradled me in a northbound current, the buoyant wetsuit kept me afloat. Cool water soothed the pain seething in my right side, and I drifted between consciousness and a foggy dream world filled with helicopters with snapping jaws, bullet-riddled children playing seven stones in my neighborhood, and Mohammed's mother waiting at the gates of paradise.

In some moments I was fully awake, enveloped in a silent, sloshing blackness, an aloneness I have never known before or since.

I thought about Tahsein and Haroon, two more of my brothers murdered by the Jews. No more cries of pain for them; right now they were standing in the courts of Allah.

One part of me wanted to join them. But another corner of my heart whispered that I wanted to live. *Live.*

My mind cried out the rooftop prayer of my childhood, *Allah! Allah! If you are not for me, who will be for me?*

At times, I caught sight of a light ashore and tried to swim toward it. But each time, my strength quickly failed, and I surrendered again to the sea.

Time spun out like an endless, fraying rope. As I drifted through dreams, I did not know whether days passed or only hours. But I remember the moment when sunlight pierced my eyelids, and I thought I heard the distant laughter of children. Then, worried whispers.

"What is it?"

"I think he's dead."

"No, he moved!"

"You stay here. I will go and get my father!"

Briefly, I felt the earth underneath me again and the tide lapping at my face. Then: blackness.

I awoke again in a small clinic, and I later learned the current had carried me past the northern border of Israel and into South Lebanon. In a brief moment of consciousness, I told the nurse I was PLO. "Please call Sabra," I whispered. "Ask for Abu Yousef."

The next time I regained consciousness, several PLO brothers had come to take me home. I do not remember the trip.

Back at Sabra, a PLO doctor examined me. The final explosion in the Bay of Haifa had ruptured my eardrum, and the concussion had caused internal injuries to my lungs and guts. The doctor showed me in a mirror that the whites of my eyes had gone scarlet. He told Abu Yousef that he did not have the equipment to care for me. I was taken to the American University hospital in Beirut.

My family came to visit me, my mother wincing and sobbing over the look of my eyes, my father proud of my bravery. Abdul Rahman came to visit me, as did other imams who seemed to replay the same tape they had after the failed Israel mission. Again Allah had preserved my life! When I should have been killed, he spared me!

Abu Yousef said the same thing, but this time I think he knew that would not be enough. He put me on a six-month sabbatical.

Looking back, I see that it was a strange prescription: In America, convalescent leave might mean no work and no strenuous exercise. In the PLO, it meant six months without guns, kidnapping, and murder.

Beirut, Lebanon, and the Libyan Desert

1972–1974

1

We learned in Islam that when a man dies in the sea, he dies in the hand of Allah. While floating north from the Bay of Haifa to the south of Lebanon, the instinct to live had surged in my soul. But after Haifa, I wanted to die. It was as though Haroon and Tahsein, and even Nizhar, whom I barely knew, were like weights in a balance, an accumulation of death that now seemed alluring. Peaceful. During my sabbatical from violence, I often wandered from my home down to the shore and walked fully clothed into the water up to my hips. Swaying in the tide's push and pull, I sometimes spoke to the sea: "If I come farther, will you swallow me? Will you devour me?"

But I knew the answer: no.

While the sea had translated my brothers to paradise, it had spit me out. Abdul Rahman and the imams called it a miracle. I was not so sure.

Autumn came. As the trees shed their leaves, I shed my last layer of boyhood. The failed Golan mission when I was seven had somehow retained an unreal quality, like jumbled, blurry-edged images from a child's nightmare. But Haifa replayed in my mind again and again in the crisp colors of a reality from which there is no waking. There, my dreams of redemption died. I realized now that my version of the James Bond life would never feature ink-pen kills and swooning redheads, but only blood and death and whores.

Where was Allah? Where was victory in his *jihad*? Now a new anger burned deep in my bones, the accumulated knowledge of many storms. I became very silent. I opened my mouth only to insult someone, smiled only when necessary to manipulate. When I returned to Sabra, I threw myself into higher training, perfecting my skills in hand-to-hand combat, especially martial arts, studying under military experts Abu Yousef had invited from Communist China. At fifteen, I was now taller and more muscled than most of the *fedayeen* I faced. I learned how to snap a man's neck with my bare hands and hoped for an opportunity to do it. Outside the camp, I walked the streets freely, protected by both the aura of the PLO and the Muslim Brotherhood and by the look in my eyes that said I was willing to kill and willing to die. I could take it either way.

I began to volunteer for every mission. Whether it was a small errand of intimidation to put an upstart faction in its place or blowing up an entire building in the middle of the night, I raced to say yes.

It was during this time that I committed my first kidnapping. As was often the case, it was because the Lebanese government poked the PLO in the eye, this time by allowing the Syrian Baath party to open a fancy office on Verdan Street.

Arafat could not tolerate this, of course. The PLO considered the Baathists, who ruled in Syria, a mongrel party of socialists, Sunni, and the hated Shia. Some of its founders had even been Arab Christians. The Baathists favored a secular, socialist society in which even non-Muslims could participate in government. By the late 1960s, Syrian president Hafez al-Assad, a wily enemy of Arafat, had woven the Baath Party into the Syrian government so tightly that the two seemed of one cloth. And so, the Baathists setting up an office in Beirut was the same as Assad planting a Syrian flag in Arafat's front yard.

Four or five times a week, Abu Ibrahim sent our entire cell to Sabra. Sometimes it was for mandatory training, other times for meetings to discuss "jobs" that needed to be done. At one of these meetings, at the home of Haj Abdullah, a Palestinian elder, Abu Yousef announced that the Baath Party office was a direct affront to Islam and to the Palestinian people.

Members of a couple of other cells had come for a dinner of hummus and *keffeh*. After the meal, we gathered around Abu Yousef. "Whoever takes this job must infiltrate the building, gather any useful documents, then destroy the offices so completely that they cannot be salvaged," he said from his seat on a *tesat*.

"I will go," I said instantly.

Abu Yousef looked at me. "Are you sure, Kamal? You just finished with the *mukhtar* three days ago."

He was referring to a small job where I had blown up a Fiat in front of the home of a *mukhtar*, an elected neighborhood leader. It was a warning, like the horse's head in the producer's bed in *The Godfather*, a new movie out that year: work with us, or next time it will be *you* exploding. The PLO *fedayeen* loved *The Godfather*. We hated America, but saw the American *mafiosi* as our colleagues.

"As you say, I finished with the *mukhtar*," I told Abu Youself with a hint of freshly minted insolence. "Now I will finish the Baathists."

I peered around the room, waiting for a challenge. The young brothers had long looked to me as a leader. I had always had Abu Yousef's favor, and now each successful mission elevated me in the eyes of the older *fedayeen*. By snapping up every job, I was purposely building my résumé. For months, I had expected some equally ambitious *fida'i* to mount a protest. That night, no one did.

I chose three other *fedayeen* for this new job, including a wiry, brown-skinned Palestinian named Ahmed, who was an up-and-coming young sniper. A week of surveillance on Verdan Street revealed that the Baathists followed tight security procedures during the day. At night, a Kurdish concierge kept watch over the lobby. We knew he would not open the door for us because the Syrians would kill him for it the very next day. And we could not blow our way in without forfeiting our chance to sift the Baathists' documents for treasure.

The solution: we learned the concierge's home address, and, as she swept her front steps, snatched his wife off the street.

Thirty minutes later, Ahmed and I walked up to the Verdan Street office and rapped on the lobby glass. The night was cold and moonless. A brisk winter wind skated through the street, giving us good reason to cloak our faces in red *keffiyeh*. The concierge, a round man with curly dark hair, met us at a security window resembling those at a theater box office. His nametag said "Marwan." I watched his eyes narrow as he took in our dark pants, gloves, and black leather jackets.

"What do you want?" Marwan asked curtly through a round vent.

I held up a Kurdish *hijab* and a lock of auburn hair. "I have a message from your wife."

The concierge's face went pale. Ahmed, his face dark and serious, pointed to the sliding drawer in the security window. With a trembling hand, the concierge pushed it open. I placed his wife's hair and scarf inside, and he retrieved them. He stared first at the hair, then pressed the *hijab* to his nose and inhaled.

Tears sprang to his eyes and his whole body quivered. "What have you done to my Samra!" Marwan cried.

"Nothing yet," I said darkly. "But she is with two of my friends who will kill her if you do not open the door and let us in." Then I held up a two-way radio. "All I have to do is make the call."

Marwan did not hesitate, but snatched a jingling ring of keys off his belt and hurried to unlock the door. We stepped inside. The lobby light had been dimmed for the evening, and our faces were crossed in shadows.

Ahmed lifted the back of his jacket, withdrew a Makarov 9 mm, and pointed it at the concierge. "Lock it back again."

"Now Marwan, let me tell you what is going to happen," I said. "You are going to escort us through the Baath party offices. I will be collecting paperwork, and my friend here will be watching you. If you help us, you and your wife will live. If you do not, you both will die. Do you understand?"

Marwan's face had gone pale as death, and I could see beads of sweat rolling from under his hairline. He nodded quickly, but did not speak.

An hour later, Marwan, Ahmed, and I exited the front doors of the Verdan Street office. Ahmed and I each carried a fat folder of documents—maps, schedules, correspondence. We walked six blocks, the concierge with Ahmed's gun in his back. Finally, we stopped in front of a café, which was shuttered for the evening.

I withdrew my radio from my jacket and spoke into it. "We have what we need. Let the woman go." Then I turned to the concierge. "Go home."

Even in the light of streetlamps, I could see his face flush with anger. "How do I know you let her go! How do I know you did not hurt her!"

"You don't, but what choice do you have?" I said, then repeated the threat that I had first heard Abdul Rahman utter when I was seven years old. "And if you are thinking of calling the police, remember: we know where you live."

Again, the color drained from Marwan's face. He cast his eyes on the sidewalk, walked slowly across the street, around the corner, and out of sight.

At that moment, a series of explosions ripped the night. Minutes later, as Ahmed and I continued walking, fire engines screamed past us toward the Baathists' former offices, on their way to destroy with water whatever we had not destroyed with flame.

2

Two weeks later, in a meeting of cells at Haj Abdullah's house, Abu Yousef told us about a job connected with Musa as-Sadr, a Shia imam. A few years before, as-Sadr had become the first leader of the Supreme Islamic Shiite Council, a group formed to win more power for the Shia in Lebanese government. The Sunni considered the Shia to have twisted Islam centuries before, instituting idolatry and pagan rituals related to their illegitimate line of prophets.

When the Prophet Muhammad died in 632 A.D. without naming a successor, some Muslims said the role of *caliph* should pass through Muhammad's bloodline, beginning with his son-in-law and cousin, Ali ibn Abi Talib. But most of Muhammad's followers favored Abu Bakr, the Prophet's friend.

Abu Bakr was named the first *caliph*, succeeding Muhammad. Ali became the fourth *caliph*, but was murdered in 661 A.D. and so, like a spiritual fire, the battle over succession flared again. Those in the camp of Ali favored the *caliph*'s son Hussein, while the majority favored Syrian governor Mu'awiyah and his son, Yazid. The dispute led to a battle at Karbala, a city near Baghdad, and Hussein was killed, giving the *Shi'at Ali*, or partisans of Ali, a martyr. Mu'awiyah became the fifth *caliph*, and his followers became Sunni, which means followers of the Sunnah, or Way, of the Prophet.

Fourteen centuries later, we still despised their idol worship, their lurid and profane mourning every year on Ashura, the anniversary of Hussein's death when many Shia would publicly whip themselves. Now, at Haj Abdullah's house, we learned from Abu Yousef that Musa as-Sadr, the prominent Shia imam, had installed an offset printing press in a building in a Shia neighborhood in Beirut.

"He is using it to print Shia propaganda and the Shia's perverted books," Abu Yousef spat, referring to the rival sect's version of the Koran and *hadith*. "Who will go and destroy it?"

"I will go," I said as usual.

But this night a voice sounded from a far corner of the room: "Hold on."

A *fida'i* from another cell stood. He was older than I, a tall, dark-skinned Lebanese with charcoal eyes that seemed to dip too far back in his skull. I knew his name to be Issa.

"You are taking every job lately," Issa said. "You are not the only fighter here worthy of leading others."

As outrage filled me like a flash flood, the room grew instantly still. In one way, I was impressed that Issa had challenged me, since he knew Abu Yousef was like a father to me. Still, I could not allow him to humiliate me.

Seeming emboldened by my silence, Issa spoke again. "You do not even know the details of this mission, what's involved."

I leveled my eyes at him. "I don't care what the details are. I'll take it."

Abu Yousef stood. "You two work it out between yourselves. I need an answer by tomorrow."

For a moment, his lack of support stung, then burned as I saw Issa smile at the opening my mentor had given him. Then a thought hit me: *Abu Yousef cannot always play favorites. Perhaps he means I must win this job on my own merits.*

So after the meeting adjourned, I walked outside, and using what the Chinese martial arts experts had taught me, beat Issa into a bloody pulp.

A week later, as I was stealing an electrician's van to convert into a bomb for the Shia, the electrician ran out of his shop, waving his arms as he came.

"Stop! Stop!" he yelled. "What are you doing? That's mine!"

Dashing past the windshield to the driver's side door, he jerked it open and began trying to pull me from the seat. With my left hand, I grabbed his throat. With my right, I jammed an AK–47 muzzle against his lips.

"If you scream like that too much," I told him calmly, "you will lose your voice."

The electrician's hands shot into the air and he backed away, eyes wide. I slammed shut the van door and roared off. Three days later, Musa as-Sadr's printing press was incinerated in a bombing for which no one claimed responsibility.

Neither did anyone claim responsibility for the deaths of nine Syrian envoys shot dead in a four-star, ocean-view hotel, or the deaths of three foreign intelligence agents gunned down in front of their embassy in Beirut.

3

I was only sixteen when I found myself rumbling in a GMC Jimmy, an American vehicle, across an ocean of blazing sand. We were traveling through the Ribiana Sand Sea in the south of Libya. Fine as powder, the sand shone blindingly white, with hints of pale yellow and tangerine. My *keffiyeh* ruffled in the breeze, shielding my head from a scorching sun.

Finally, I felt I had ascended to something important. My zeal in Beirut had earned my place on a stage that, while secret, would make a difference for Allah. As the Jimmy bounced over the desert moguls, I flashed back to the conversation with Abu Yousef that sent me here.

"There is an opportunity for you in Libya," he told me in his office at Sabra one day about a month after the as-Sadr bombing. "Gaddafi has requested more PLO assistance in training liberation groups from around the world."

Gaddafi? Adrenaline tingled in my bones. In those days, if you were a Muslim and a rebel, Libyan President Muammar Gaddafi was your idol. He was obscenely rich, famously generous, and would finance any training, any attack, anywhere, anytime.

"He is paying for everything," Abu Yousef continued. "Fighters come from all the Arab countries, and students and radical leftists come from Latin America. Even the IRA goes there to train. It would be a great opportunity for you, Kamal, and it is the future of the PLO, the chance for us to establish offices worldwide. If we are able to establish strong ties in Latin America, we can easily reach into America itself."

All over the world, insurrection was in the air. Communism was encircling the globe: the Soviet Union, Southeast Asia, Korea, China, Cuba, Latin America. And terrorism had gone international: In 1970, the Popular Front for the Liberation of Palestine (PFLP), a socialist group, blew a Swissair flight out of the sky over Zurich. The same group in 1971 hijacked five airliners in rapid succession, negotiating the release of a captured female hijacker and three PFLP prisoners from the Zurich bombing. Even in America, rebel groups like the Weather Underground and the Black Liberation Army were bombing high-profile targets like the police and the Pentagon.

From Tripoli, Gaddafi cheered on the revolution. It did not matter whether you were a Marxist, a jihadist, or wanted to assassinate the Queen of England. As long as you were a terrorist, Gaddafi loved you. And now he was sponsoring a kind of university of terrorism, inviting rebels from all over the world to "campuses" flung across his vast chunk of the Sahara desert. For the PLO and the Libyan leader, the arrange-ment was a win-win. Arafat wanted Gaddafi's millions; Gaddafi wanted to change the world.

"These revolutionary groups are like ships with no harbor," Abu Yousef told me. "Today, we will teach them and guide them. Tomorrow, when they take power in their own countries, they will see us as men-tors and allies."

When Abu Yousef asked me if I wanted to be part of it all, I said yes in an instant, and now I was here, rolling through the smoking desert on my way to destiny.

I had flown TunisAir into the country from Lebanon and helicop-tered south to a remote base where two Libyan militia and a Palestinian driver named Faisel picked me up in the Jimmy. Two hours later we ar-rived in a small desert compound bordered on one side by a long fence of barbed wire. I later learned we were close to the border of Chad, near Niger. The fence was a hedge against Chaddian guerrillas who hated Muammar Gaddafi as much as he hated them.

As we walked through the camp, a session in hand-to-hand combat training was underway in a central open area. About fifteen men in fa-tigues sat in a circle watching as a *fedayeen* trainer dropped a larger man to the sand with a roundhouse kick. I was surprised to see a woman sitting in the circle, too. None of the trainees were Middle Eastern; I guessed them to be from Latin America. Faisel took me to meet the camp leader, Abu Mustafa. When we entered the tent, I recognized him from Abu Yousef's description: a burly Palestinian with eyes like a falcon.

"Welcome, Kamal," he said, looking me over sharply. "Abu Yousef has told me you will be a great asset to us here."

I bowed my head slightly. I knew that Abu Mustafa and my mentor had known each other in Egypt, fought together in Fatah, and remained close friends. "Abu Yousef sends his greetings," I said. "He told me I can learn much here."

Abu Mustafa smiled. "We are glad to have you. Now, go with Faisel. He will issue your weapons and show you where you will sleep. Faisel, get our new friend something to eat."

I turned to leave, but Abu Mustafa spoke again. "Kamal, while you are here, keep your eyes open for vipers and scorpions—and not only the ones that crawl through the sand."

4

After Abu Mustafa's warning, I never went anywhere without an AK–47 strapped to my back—nor did any of the 130 other PLO *fedayeen* and Libyan militia who lived permanently at the camp.

The camp itself was a small village of tents, huts, and a couple of rude cinderblock buildings used to store equipment during the day. The majority of storage lay hidden underground, in a tight labyrinth of lead-lined concrete bunkers camouflaged from above with sand. The bunkers also served to hide us from the prying eyes of western governments. We had two different satellites we dealt with, both American. At night we could sometimes see them passing in the high heavens like fast-moving stars. When the satellite alarm sounded, we scrambled down into the cramped bunkers and sat, packed in like galley slaves, until the eye in the sky had moved on. We knew the Americans knew Gaddafi's camps existed, but it was critical to hide our numbers. The Americans were devious, the Libyan leaders told us. If they found an especially active camp, they would launch a chopper attack by night and destroy it with rockets.

At my camp, we had no shortage of students. Marxist-Leninist groups, Islamic groups, upstart Sandinista rebels from Nicaragua and, just as Abu Yousef had said, the IRA. Every day was like a graduate school in terrorism, in which we helped anywhere from ten to eighty hard-eyed revolutionaries sharpen their killing skills. Hand-to-hand combat and martial arts training always took place in the open center of the camp, where I had first seen the Latin Americans. In a designated area on the camp's western border, we practiced marksmanship and sniper techniques. Regularly, we loaded up in vehicles and rumbled far into the desert to practice with TNT, RPGs, and Katyusha rockets, blowing up old Jeeps and target structures built for the purpose. Month by month, we consumed enough explosives and ammunition to fight a small war. Gaddafi cheerfully paid for it all.

But we also expended an equally valuable explosive that cost Gaddafi nothing and made him love the PLO all the more: propaganda. Every terrorist we trained hated America. That was a given and, in fact, the only price of admission. But before each revolutionary left the camp, we made sure they also hated Israel. The *fedayeen* told them the Jews were animals and showed them gory pictures of murdered women and children to prove it. In truth, we did not know where the pictures came from or even whose crimes they depicted. But they served their purpose.

Meanwhile, whatever grievance a rebel faction had against its government or another group, we embraced it as if it was our own.

"Yes!" we told the Communists. "You must subdue the imperialists and bring freedom to your people!"

"Yes!" we told the Sandinistas. "You must kill your corrupt president and bring justice to your people!"

What did it matter to us? Unless they were Muslim, both the foreign factions and their targets were all infidels worthy of death. So, according to *al-toqiah,* we made fellowship with them all, lying to the fighters and puffing them up in order to wedge Islam into future revolutionary governments and advance our faith across the world.

I remember two fighters in particular who lapped up our flattery like cats enjoying cream: Bobby and Patrick, they called themselves, two soldiers with the IRA. Both in their twenties, they were young, restless, muscular fighters with six-pack bellies and mouths that yap-yap-yapped like windup toy dogs. Bobby, a blue-eyed man with dark, spiky hair, loved to bark in his brogue about "killing the English bastards!" Blond-haired Patrick bragged so constantly about his fighting skills that when I finally went one-on-one with him in the combat circle, I nearly broke his wrist just to hear him scream instead of talk.

Gaddafi, of course, did not have to put up with such annoying daily details. He sponsored dozens of camps across his sprawling desert, often visiting them personally to observe training and cheer on the insurrection. At our camp, his people had built an observation tower on a hill, like a covered lifeguard stand. The Libyan president would come and watch us train through a huge pair of military binoculars, sometimes for the whole day. In the evening, he would sit with us and tell us how impressed he was. Gaddafi was handsome and charming and loved to pour on the praise.

Even in front of his own Libyan militia, he would say to the PLO *fedayeen*, "My own people are lazy. They do not have the heart you have."

Gaddafi loved Abu Mustafa because he had personally organized three successful attacks on the hated Chaddians. Once after such an incursion, Gaddafi came to visit and handed each of us an envelope stuffed with money.

"For your service to my country," he told me as he placed a fat packet in my hand. When I looked inside, I was astonished to find a thousand dollars. It was more money than I had ever held in my life.

5

The camp wasn't all terror all the time. Sometimes for fun, we let the air out of the Jeep tires and went four-wheeling, flying over knife-edge dunes, the powdery sand spraying out behind us like water. Several times, we made excursions to an ancient castle on the Chaddian border. Inside, the yawning rooms were in ruins, but outside the castle was completely intact, rising from the barren desert like a strange, medieval mirage.

Often, in the evening, I would commandeer a Jeep or a Jimmy and drive far off into the dunes to be alone. Far enough to leave behind all manmade light and sound, to a place where the pale sand sea glowed in the moon's alabaster light, where the silence was so complete that if I sat still enough, I could hear the stealthy shoosh of a viper's belly crossing the sand.

Sometimes, I would lie atop the hood and talk with Allah, the desert sky arcing over me like a giant tent, the stars breathtaking in their clarity. Often, clusters of shooting stars burst across the velvet sky, medleys of light in silver and fiery gold.

"Glory to you, Allah!" I prayed one night after I had been in the camp nearly eighteen months. "Finally, I am making a difference!"

Libyan and PLO intelligence filtered back good news from our brothers in arms. Since 1971, terror attacks had increased around the world, and we knew some of the revolutionaries involved had trained with us.

• In May 1972, four of our own PLO terrorists hijacked a passenger flight en route from Brussels to Tel Aviv and died *al-shaheed* in a glorious battle with Israeli special forces.

• In September of the same year, Black September killed eleven Israeli athletes at the Munich Olympics.

• In March 1973, Black September struck again, taking ten hostages in Sudan and killing three western diplomats.

• That May, the IRA killed five British soldiers with a roadside bomb in Tullyvallen, Northern Ireland.

• That same month, two Arab terrorists hijacked a passenger train in Austria and demanded the closure of a camp there for Jews transiting from the Soviet Union to Israel. After the Austrian government complied, the terrorists escaped to Libya.

In 1974, I was in Abu Mustafa's tent when he received a strange call from Libyan military intelligence: A pair of Irishmen had arrived at the airport in Tripoli on a flight from Italy. They fit the description of two IRA soldiers who had trained at the camp: Bobby and Patrick.

"These men are seeking refuge," I heard a Libyan agent say over the radio.

It was common for Muslim fighters to do a mission and then, like the hijackers of the Austrian train, seek sanctuary in Gaddafi's desert camps. But such a request was unusual for fighters from non-Muslim groups.

Abu Mustafa paused and looked up at the tent ceiling for a moment. Then he keyed the radio and said, "Let them come."

While Bobby and Patrick made the chopper flight to our midrange base, Abu Mustafa learned more details of their mission from Libyan intelligence: A bombing in England. Civilians killed, including women and children. Scotland Yard and British intelligence on the rampage. Already, foreign pressure had been increasing on Gaddafi to stop supporting the IRA. Now these two Irish buffoons had left a trail from England through Italy that ended in Libya, endangering us all.

Abu Mustafa radioed a report to Gaddafi and, later that morning, relayed the results to me: "These people don't belong with us," he said, referring to the Irishmen. "Gaddafi tells me we are to send them back where they came from. But we need to quiet them first."

I nodded my understanding.

That afternoon, I made the two-hour Jimmy trip to the helicopter base with Faisel and two PLO *fedayeen*, Majid and Omar. We picked up Bobby and Patrick, who bragged all the way to the camp about their miraculous escape from the British authorities. The Irishmen rode in the middle bench seat, with Omar and Majid behind them. I rode in the front, but turned around to encourage their storytelling with breathless admiration.

"Really?"

"That's amazing!"

"What did you do next?"

By the time we reported to Abu Mustafa's tent, I was able to confirm to him with a nod that Patrick and Bobby were connected with the England bombing.

Abu Mustafa chatted briefly with them, then said, "Kamal, Omar, these men must be tired from their long trip. Show them where they will sleep."

When we stepped back outside, the sun shimmered low on the horizon, painting the sand pink and crimson.

"It's the tent at the end," I told our guests.

Bobby and Patrick walked ahead of Omar and me, chattering like women as they had since the moment we had picked them up.

We reached the far edge of the camp.

Omar and I cycled our AK–47s.

The Irishmen whirled at the sound, but did not even have time to register their shock before we cut them down.

I cannot say for certain, but the rumor in the camp was that Gaddafi ordered Bobby and Patrick shipped back to England in body bags.

Southwestern United States

2007

A week after the Pakistanis came looking for me, I was sifting e-mail in my loft office at home when I noticed a message from an unfamiliar address. Since launching a website that published the truth about radical Islam, I had received a lot of mail from people I did not know. I had installed powerful antivirus software to enable me to interact with interested people without worrying about a computer meltdown. This subject line said "No subject." I clicked on it and was instantly glad my wife and children were not at home.

In the first of six color photographs, an angry-looking Middle Eastern man was dragging another man down a street by his jacket collar. In his right hand, the angry man held a 9 mm pistol. In the second photo, the man in the jacket sat cringing on the pavement as the man with the gun prepared to shoot him in the head.

The third picture showed a raging crowd of Middle Eastern men stomping another man to death. In the fourth photograph, a crowd that included a boy of about seven surrounded the body of a barefoot dead man hung upside down from some kind of steel tower, his blood-splotched white T-shirt protruding oddly where his tormentors had broken his ribs. A swatch of rope held the man aloft by his left ankle and his right leg was splayed radically backward so that his whole body arched in a strange arabesque of death.

The final two photos turned my stomach. Both showed crowds of men, dressed in ordinary street clothes, chanting victoriously and holding up wet human entrails and internal organs. In one picture, a man seemed to yell directly into the camera. His right hand, raised palm forward, was painted in blood; a scarlet rope of intestines dangled from his left. In the final photograph, a crowd of men, their mouths open to the sky, pumped fists in the air while one man gazed rapturously at the prize he held in his hand—a freshly extracted human heart.

A cascade of memories washed over me as I remembered seeing *fedayeen* commit the same horrors in the late 1970s, during the Lebanese civil war. Returning to the e-mail, I saw that besides the pictures, the message contained only three lines of text. It was the same nine words of broken English written three times in the colors of the Pakistani flag:

"THIS WHAT WE ARE GOING TO DO TO YOU."

Beirut, Lebanon
1975–1976

1

On December 6, 1975, I was at home in Beirut eating a lunch of pita and tomatoes when my brother burst in the front door, his face stretched into panic. "You are not going to believe what is happening downtown! The Gemayel party is shooting people! They set up checkpoints on the streets and they're checking IDs. If you are a Muslim, they kill you on the spot!"

I jumped up from the floor. It was the Christians. They called themselves Phalangists. We called them the Gemayel Party after Pierre Abdel Gemayel, the leader of *Kataeb*, a political body supported mainly by Maronite Christians. In 1958, the year I was born, Gemayal emerged as a new leader and later was elected to the Lebanese national assembly. It took him only a decade to build *Kataeb*, the party the Sunni and Palestinians hated most, into a major force in government.

Which was why Abu Yousef had recalled me from Libya. Tensions were mounting between the Lebanese government and the PLO. Arafat wanted as many guns in Beirut as possible.

As we saw it, Gemayel's sins against Muslims were legion. Long an agitator among the far-right Christian separatists, Gemayel opposed the *Nasseriyeen*—fighters loyal to former Egyptian president and PLO cofounder Gamal Abdel Nasser—and other Muslim-led attempts to gain more representation in the Lebanese government. Gemayel also supported a policy that was poison to the PLO and the Lebanese Sunni—allowing foreign troops to operate on our land. He did not want an Arab Lebanon—which, of course, meant a Muslim Lebanon. Instead, he wanted a European Lebanon with close ties to France and the West. This would guarantee the supremacy of both the Christian faith and Christian power in government. Gemayel also despised the Palestinian refugees. But in 1969, under international pressure, he signed the Cairo Agreement of 1969, which allowed Arafat and the PLO to set up their headquarters in Lebanon.

Now, in my parents' house, Fouad's voice notched higher. "The Nasseriyeen and al-Morabitun are doing it too! Killing civilians—making their own checkpoints and shooting Christians!"

I had never seen Fouad in such a state, both impotent and frantic with rage.

Abu Ibrahim, I thought. *I must go to Abu Ibrahim.*

I dashed past Fouad and out the door.

"Where are you going?" he yelled after me. "Do not go out there!"

I ignored him and ran out into the street. I had not been outside longer than a minute when I heard faint wailing and the distant crackle of gunshots. I turned the corner at the end of my long block and nearly collided with other men spilling out of doorways onto the sidewalks, some of them carrying guns. Our numbers grew rapidly as if we were forming some kind of human rapids, all rushing toward downtown.

The gunshots grew louder, as did the wailing, which now sorted itself into individual women's voices crying out names, keening with grief. It was only a few blocks to Abu Ibrahim's house, but by the time I had gone there, the whole neighborhood seemed to tremble and quake as if some great, dark beast was stomping through the sewers underneath our feet. Turning another corner, I saw women dotting the sidewalk, beating their chests, screaming toward the heavens. Men darted between them, sprinting toward some common destination.

I turned another corner. In the middle of the next block was a fabric store and next to it a tailor's shop. On the sidewalk outside the fabric shop, the owner, a man named Anis, knelt on the concrete, vomiting.

I pulled up short, aghast. *What is going on?*

"*Kamal!*"

I whirled away from Anis, scanning the crowd to see who had called my name.

"Kamal, where are you going!"

A familiar face burst into view—Adnan, my neighbor, his huge dark eyes lit like wildfire beneath an explosion of curly hair. Glancing down, I saw that he was holding a dagger.

I looked back at Anis. Violent spasms of nausea still wracked his body and he seemed oblivious to the scores of people who ran past him as though he were a large rock in the middle of a stream.

Abruptly, Anis threw his head back and split the sky with a scream. One word, again and again:

"Why!"

"Why!"

"Why!"

"The Christians killed his brother Mahmoud," Adnan told me. "I have already been downtown. I saw Mahmoud lying dead in a taxi with a bullet hole in his head."

My heart broke. I had known Mahmoud since childhood.

Adnan took off running, and I followed him. I wanted to see this outrage for myself before reporting to Abu Ibrahim. We darted between grieving women and older men who stood like statues, shell-shocked.

Between breaths, Adnan spilled out little bits of news.

"The Christians shot everyone in the taxi. Two women, three men. They told the driver . . . to bring the corpses back here so that we could see what they had done!" His throat seemed to close around the last sentence, squeezing it in the high pitch of outrage and disbelief. "The Nasseriyeen are establishing a checkpoint where the taxi is. I am going to help them. These *sharmouta* will pay for what they are doing to our people!"

Now my own anger burned. I fervently hoped Abu Ibrahim would give me a large weapon and permission to kill. We ran through the thickening crowd, rounded another corner, and arrived at a major intersection that looked as if it had simply exploded. The crossroads was a seething mass of people. Horns and women wailed. Men faced off nose to nose, shouting, arms wheeling and pointing. Robed imams ran from group to group; some seemed to plead for peace, some for violence. And in among the chaos, I saw knots of armed men who looked to belong to several factions. I did not yet see any PLO.

Someone had already set up a checkpoint, parking two cars in the intersection to form a narrow passage through which any vehicle that arrived would have to pass. Adnan grabbed my wrist and dragged me through the swarming crowd to a taxi parked on a curb. Looking inside the old four-door Mercedes 180, my heart nearly stopped. There were five bodies inside, two women in the front seat, eyes and mouths frozen open, large crimson patches blooming on the sides of their *hijabs*. In the back, three men, also shot in the head. I knew two of them—Mahmoud and another man. I had stood up for him one day in an argument with a neighbor. Now, in the taxi, the entire left side of his face was bathed in blood.

They were good men, I thought, *and they had killed them like dogs.*

Anger enveloped me like fire. I turned to tell Adnan that I wanted to avenge them, but he was gone.

Two kinds of people crowded the intersection that day—Muslims who wanted peace and Muslims who wanted vengeance. Those who wanted peace outnumbered those thirsty for blood many times over. But the radicals had guns in their hands. I knew many, many people on both sides of the argument. People from my neighborhood. That is what is difficult to understand about Beirut, about Lebanon in general. It is a small place. Everyone knows everyone, or at least someone from their family or tribe. Now this atrocity had pitted many of us against each other, not only Christian against Muslim, but Muslim against Muslim, pro-Palestinian against pro-Lebanese, pro-normal life against pro-radical change.

In an instant, I felt all those clashes within me and realized that I was among those lighting the fuse of unrest, shaking the world of these grieving women I saw around me, whose children were now in danger. A glimmer of guilt flickered in my heart. But the spark did not catch, and the moment passed.

Our cause is great, I reminded myself. *The children will be better off when the Lebanese military has been split and the followers of Allah rule our nation.*

Near the corner where the checkpoint vehicles stood, I saw a man I recognized locked in an argument with another man, a *fida'i* brandishing an AK–47. The man I knew was important in the community, though I cannot now remember why. In his fifties, he wore a goatee and thick moustache. From my spot by the taxi, I could hear him shouting pleas into the armed man's face.

"You are only pouring more fuel on the fire!" he said. "That is what they want from us! Let us not give them what they want!"

The *fida'i* let go the muzzle of his assault rifle, drew back his arm and slapped the other man across the face. Instantly, several other men wanting peace produced knives, but the *fida'i* and his comrades leveled rifles at their heads.

An imam elbowed his way forward. "You are *all* Muslims!" he cried, his arms raised as though trying to calm a storm. "It does not matter to what faction you belong! You must love your brother!"

All this happened in seconds. As such confrontations rippled through the crowd, panic rose in my chest and I glanced around wildly. This intersection was like dynamite with the fuse already lit.

Where is the PLO?

I caught sight of Adnan again. He was in the middle of the intersection at the checkpoint, dragging a man from a black sedan. Two *fedayeen* held the man, and Adnan blasted his face with his fists, cutting into his flesh with brass knuckles. Blood gushed from the wounds, but Adnan hit him again and again. Then one of the radicals lunged forward with a dagger and plunged it into the man's side. When he withdrew its jagged edge, part of the man's intestines came with it, glistening like a snake in the sun.

Horror gripped me. I thought of my neighbor in the taxi. I thought of Yahya at the training camp and Mohammed in Golan. In a moment of weakness, I wondered if my life would always be filled with blood and death. Again, though, I closed off my heart, like an emotional tourniquet.

I looked a final time at the death scene inside the taxi, then sprinted for Abu Ibrahim's, just two blocks away. When he admitted me, he was holding a green military radio, and I heard Abu Yousef's voice scratching into the air.

"This situation will work to our advantage," my mentor was saying.

At that moment, I did not know the scope of what was happening. I did not know that a thousand people would die that day, all of them slaughtered for their faith. I did not know that the two sides—radical Christians and radical Muslims—had just pushed the button that would detonate a fifteen-year civil war.

2

The day of the dueling massacres became known in Lebanon as Black Saturday. The incident triggered a full alert at Sabra. We anticipated everything: retaliation by the Phalangists, an invasion of the Palestinian camps by the Lebanese army, even an air attack from Israel. We emptied the camp and set up a perimeter around Sabra with anti-aircraft gun emplacements and rockets. No attack came, but after Black Saturday, *fedayeen* in Beirut clustered into angry hives of warring factions with constantly shifting alliances and outright treachery.

When relief shipments came in to bless the country, the factions seized control of them. The only way to get a share was to be wired into a faction. If you did not belong to a group—the PLO, the Nasseriyeen, Fatah, al-Morabitun—your family did not eat. It was a form of manipulation, a way to use fear and the survival instinct to build alliances. Many, many people chose sides not for ideological reasons, but because they wanted to keep their families fed.

While I was with the PLO, two of my brothers had joined other factions. Fouad fought with al-Morabitun, and Ibrahim joined a group led by Saeb Salam, a former prime minister of Lebanon, who was well connected with the Saudis. This was the strategy of many Muslim families, to hook into several groups in order to survive.

As part of Abu Ibrahim's cell, my mission was to split the Lebanese military, which included both Muslim and Christian soldiers. We hoped to turn the Muslim soldiers against the government and induce them to join the PLO. It was Arafat's divide-and-conquer strategy: if we could fracture the military, the Christian government could not stand against the increasingly powerful PLO.

The PLO fanned out in Beirut, beginning a strategic march to hold and protect Muslim neighborhoods. Five weeks after the Phalangist massacre, my unit had gone to investigate a Christian plot to invade a Muslim girls' school when I heard of the next outrage: Christian militias overran Karantina, the settlement near the slaughterhouse, and turned it into a slaughterhouse of its own.

Reports crackled over our radios: The infidels had invaded Karantina and were shooting Muslim civilians in the head. A Christian fighter used a knife to slice open the belly of a pregnant woman, aborting her child on the spot. Another fighter placed a boy in his grandfather's arms, then shot the child in the head. A Christian raped a Palestinian woman with a glass Pepsi bottle, then killed her by kicking the bottle up into her womb. Before the day was over, a thousand Muslims, many of them Palestinians, were butchered like animals in Karantina and two other areas in the city.

Hearing the reports, my blood turned to foam in my veins and fantasies of murder consumed every thought in my head. The urge to kill vaulted past vengeance and became justice.

The Karantina incident plunged Beirut into chaos. The PLO retaliated immediately, pounding Christian neighborhoods with mortars and artillery. But some among us lost our couth and became vampires and savages. Some PLO units and Muslim militia acted on their own and invaded Christian areas. They captured Christian women, raped them, then literally cut their hearts out of their chests to kill them.

It was as if a zookeeper had opened all his cages and the animals were tearing at each other's throats. Beirut, the beautiful city of my childhood, was being crushed into ruins as Muslims and Christians carved it into an ethno-religious jigsaw puzzle, with each side trying to annihilate the pieces they hated.

A few months after Karantina, I helped launch an attack to take a Christian neighborhood near the Beirut *manara*, or lighthouse. Early that day, Christian militia had tossed grenades into an open-air market in a Muslim area, killing seventy people. Now they would pay. On a hilltop about five kilometers away from the *manara*, we set up our batteries and started shelling. We did not care whether a location was a military target: Because Christians dominated the government, their neighborhoods had better roads, better sewers, better everything. With hundreds of artillery rounds and mortars, we set out to change that. Grocery stores exploded. Restaurants collapsed in torrents of rubble. Soon, the entire neighborhood bristled with columns of smoke and fire, and the acrid odors of gunpowder and cordite choked the sky.

Abu Yousef had issued orders that we were to take no prisoners. I passed this to my unit as we rolled off the hilltop in a Jeep to launch a building-by-building urban assault.

Imagine your own neighborhood overrun by a huge citizen militia, trained in camps on the outskirts of your town, now armed with a full array of military weapons including artillery, mortars, grenades, C–4, and automatic weapons. Imagine that militia storming every apartment house and business—*your* business, *your* apartment house—and putting a bullet in the head of anyone not like them.

That is what we did.

The Lebanese Civil War did not have a traditional battlefield of the kind Americans study in school. No: as on the day of the lighthouse battle, I often sent men and young boys into apartment houses to place timer-rigged explosives in an attempt to kill every infidel inside. After each blast, fifty to sixty men from my PLO unit and others flooded the interior and shot every survivor dead. It was not war. It was a religious cleansing. It was *jihad.*

The PLO did not act alone that day. Al-Morabitun, the Nasseriyeen, and other factions sent their own fighters. Their orders concerning prisoners were different than ours. Six hours after we entered the *manara* neighborhood, the combined forces of the Muslim *fedayeen* had mostly annihilated the Christian fighters. Now, instead of the thunder of regular explosions, only scattered small-arms fire echoed through the streets. I rolled up in a Jeep to a central roundabout, a large concrete driveway visible from many directions, and saw that the Nasseriyeen had rounded up about twenty Christian fighters. The Phalangists looked ragged and beaten, some of their uniforms already stained crimson.

My driver pulled to a stop about twenty meters from the Nasseriyeen and their prisoners. As I stepped out, one of the Muslim fighters lofted his AK–47 and sprayed an arc of bullets over the prisoners' heads.

"Line up!" he shouted. "Hands behind your head! Do it now!"

Limping and stumbling, the Christians formed a jagged line, standing side by side in the driveway, facing the street. "On your knees!" another Nasseriyeen shouted, this one also armed with an AK. "On your knees, now!"

Awkwardly and off balance, hands behind their heads, the Christians knelt on the pavement. Then, without pause or ceremony, two Muslim fighters wielding 9 mm pistols marched down the line behind them and put a bullet in the back of each Phalangist's head. With each pistol report, the Muslims cheered and another Christian fell onto his face and surrendered his soul. The sound of each round was somehow louder in my ears than the C–4 I had been using all day to fight through the streets. More personal. As I watched, each of the first seven men collapsed in a bloodless heap. But on the eighth, one of the Nasseriyeen aimed poorly. The left side of the soldier's head sprayed forward, landing on the pavement before he did.

Justice, I thought with satisfaction, and a line from the *hadith* threaded through my mind: *An eye for an eye.*

3

In prewar Beirut, the Christian population was concentrated in the east, toward the mountains, while most Muslim neighborhoods perched in the west, nearer the sea. But by 1976, the Christian militia, aided by the Lebanese army, had advanced into our neighborhoods in West Beirut, carving the city into bits. The PLO and other Muslim factions feared that without a massive counteroffensive, the Christians would completely overrun the Muslim areas and wipe our people out. We decided not only to push them back, but to push into their eastern neighborhoods and take them for ourselves.

Already, the Phalangists had taken over a portion of the district sur-rounding the St. George Hotel. An elite resort before the war, the entire area now looked like Armageddon. Where rows of swanky boutiques had once bustled with wealthy tourists, now lay heaps of rubble and twisted wreckage, burned-out cars, and low walls of snaking sandbags. The facades of historic buildings bore the scars of artillery and small-arms fire, and in the windows jagged remains of shattered glass hung like broken teeth.

The Christian militias had entrenched in the area, fortifying many buildings with sandbags and, for even more protection, with water-soaked bags of concrete, creating a maze of bunkers and gun emplace-ments. Their most strategic position was a new hotel under construction near the St. George. When complete, the soaring tower with a swim-ming pool on the roof would have dwarfed every other hotel in the city and boasted commanding views of the sapphire sea. The Phalangists had turned it into a sniper's nest, and used it to pick off any Muslim fighters trying to push east across the open road. For weeks, the strat-egy was effective. From their high ground in the tower, using 120 mm rockets, RPGs, Quad .50s, and sniper rifles, the Christians kept twenty-four-hour watch on the street and simply mowed down any Muslim fighters who showed their heads. Sometimes, their strategy was even more evil. If the Phalangists detected our fighters lurking in the area, their snipers would fire on civilians, intentionally wounding them. Then, when a Muslim fighter rushed to aid the victim, the Phalangists would take off his head.

Soon, Abu Yousef had had enough. He sent a force of about three hundred fighters to the hotel district to take it back. My unit of seven men was embedded with a larger force of about thirty more. We had one objective: take out the tower.

To get across the open boulevard that was the Christians' killing field, we devised a plan: our large force of warriors would build a thick, mov-ing wall of sandbags, dousing them with water from portable tanks as we went to make them denser.

In my unit, I assigned a man named Ali to deal with what we came to think of as the "fish bait strategy"—the Phalangists' intentional wound-ing of civilians.

"If you see a civilian injured and it appears they are going to die anyway, shoot them in the head," I said. "You will put them out of their misery, and then no one will be tempted to try to be a hero and get themselves killed."

Ali, a Shia who fought with the Sunnis, was an intimidator, a gambler. I knew he would have no problem raising his head from cover to take care of this job.

It was a cool day with clear skies. We started in the underground garage of a warehouse and began building our sandbag wall toward the wide four-lane road. Once we crossed the road, we would have to fight our way through the neighborhood to the tower, about half a kilometer away. Working in teams of two and three, we built the wall column by column, stacking the bags five feet high and three feet thick. Behind us, a team of about thirty men advanced with caches of armaments drawn from a large pool in the garage: 120 mm rockets, grenades, assault rifles, and hundreds of kilos of TNT. Snipers advanced with their Seminovs. The most deadly was Ahmed, the man who had helped me with the Verdan Street job. By now he could put a bullet in an enemy's eye from a kilometer away.

The Phalangists quickly caught on to our strategy, and before our wall had extended five meters, the sky began raining lead. I did not hesitate, but directed traffic: "Keep moving! Keep moving! You can die advancing or die standing still!"

Bullets sizzled and snapped over my head. Our wall-building teams scurried like ants on a hill, carrying bags from the rear position to the forward tip of our barrier. Spinning on their fins, RPGs seared in, slicing through the air with a high-pitched whine. Miraculously, the Phalangists kept missing. Grenades exploded around us, but did not hit our wall. At least twice, grenades landed on the street in front of us and clinked harmlessly to a stop, their fuses defective.

Within ninety minutes we had reached the middle of the boulevard. Suddenly, I heard a booming thunder and the sound of the heavens cracking: the Phalangists had called in an artillery strike.

"Incoming!" Ali shouted.

I could hear the high scream of a 155 mm shell bearing down on our position. The PLO-trained fighters hit the pavement, then lifted ourselves on our elbows and toes to prevent being blown skyward by the force of the shell's impact with the ground. We covered our ears with our hands and yelled as loudly as we could to stop our eardrums from breaking. When the shell hit about one hundred meters away, the sound was like the sky crashing to earth. As a hail of shrapnel and concrete peppered down, I looked up to see two of our fighters from another faction lying dead in the open street. They had not known how to brace for artillery fire, and the bucking pavement had coughed them over the sandbag wall.

Seconds later, the Phalangists began firing on the exposed corpses with a .50 caliber antiaircraft gun. The huge rounds quickly shredded their bodies into gore. The assault on our dead infuriated Ali. Crouching low, he scuttled back toward the group carrying our weapons forward behind the sandbags and armed himself with two RPGs.

Then, abruptly, he popped above the wall holding a launch tube on each shoulder.

"Ali, no!" I yelled.

As he fired the RPG on his right shoulder, a long plume of flame scorched the ground behind him. I did not see where the grenade hit, but saw Ali's upper body disintegrate as three .50 caliber rounds hit him in the head, chest, and shoulder. He collapsed behind the wall in a bloody heap.

"He is in *jannah!*" I cried instantly, not wanting the others to shrink back. "Move! Keep moving!"

Quickly, our warriors started building again, extending our protective barrier across the boulevard, moving closer to the Phalangists meter by meter. Now we had perfected our movements, and it took only an hour to extend the sandbag wall across the boulevard. Once it was complete, hundreds of *fedayeen* poured across in a furious stream. Now we would take down the neighborhood—one alleyway, one building, at a time.

As always, my job was demolition, blowing holes in buildings that were Phalangist strongholds, clearing them, marking them cleansed with a painted code, and pushing forward. The deeper we penetrated toward the tower, the more the retreating Christians strafed us with panic fire. Heavy fire came in from snipers embedded in the hotels, bullets chipping away the concrete on building corners.

I had ducked into an alleyway, preparing to move my team up the next block with Ahmed providing cover fire, when a rocket whistled in, smashed into the corner of the building, and sent a shard of shrapnel winging into the back of my head. I did not fall, but my hand flew to the wound, and my eyes watered as the hot metal burned in my scalp.

Ahmed stepped forward, brushed my hand aside, and plucked the metal from my head.

"It is not deep!" he yelled as the sound of more incoming echoed in the alley. "Just a cut!"

For two blocks, we pushed the Christians back, fighting our way up the street through a metal storm, returning fire with RPGs, rockets, and sniper fire. By the time we reached the tower we had lost at least twenty men. The Phalangists guarding the base of the tower had already retreated inside, but they pounded us from above with .50 caliber guns. I dashed for cover behind a building column. Above, about fifteen floors up, I could see two fighters, their heads popping into view and quickly gone again.

"Fareed! RPG," I yelled to one of the *fedayeen* bearing weapons. Crouching low, he scuttled forward with grenades and a preloaded launcher. I took aim on the fifteenth floor and fired. I drew back in surprise when the entire floor erupted in a flash of fire that splashed out of both sides of the building. There must have been stored ammunition barrels there.

In all, seven groups—some PLO, some Muslim factions—entered the building. The Christians who had not already retreated had no place to go but up. We pushed them higher and higher with small-arms fire and RPGs, blowing men off the floors still under construction and into the street below. We also cleared floors using "sticky sacks," bags filled with a pasty explosive compound and shrapnel, and fitted with a short fuse: light the fuse, fling the bag up to the next floor. When the bag exploded, it cut everyone in range to ribbons.

The fight raged for two hours before we had pushed the Christians to the tower's roof. Now they had no place left to run. But the roof provided them with a great advantage: it was split into two levels, with the still-dry swimming pool on the lower portion and the hotel's utility sheds and giant air-conditioning units on the higher. From that metal maze of cover, the Phalangists were able to pick off three of our fighters as soon as they emerged on the roof. We knew they would be able to hold out there as long as their ammo lasted, which could be days since we had no cover on the lower level.

The only solution: blow the roof.

Working quickly with a team of two other demolitions experts, I wired massive amounts of TNT to the support columns of the floor just underneath the roof, fusing it all to Russian-made military batteries that would serve as detonators. It was the most TNT I had ever used for an operation; between the three of us, we used hundreds of kilos. We only had one chance, and we wanted to ensure complete destruction.

We ran the wire down four floors, hoping that would put enough distance between us and the explosives so that we would live and the Christians would die. Helpfully, the Phalangists had already built a kind of sandbag bunker on that floor, perfect for us to take cover behind. Even so, most of the *fedayeen* descended several floors lower in case the operation went wrong and the whole building collapsed. Only I and the two other triggermen stayed high.

On a three count, we pushed the buttons. For a long second, an eerie silence enveloped us as the current sped up the long lead wires to its destination.

Then hell came to earth.

The explosion that ripped down from above sounded like the collision of planets. It was the eruption of Mount Vesuvius, Everest in an avalanche, a roaring tidal wave crashing through an earthquake. A thick cocktail of black smoke, white dust, and rubble blew down through the stairwell, turning us all instantly white. The gargantuan blast distorted the air into violent, undulating waves that sucked my breath away, deflated my chest, and seemed to scramble my internal organs. Spontaneously, I vomited and dimly noticed the other fighters doing the same. A storm of devastation raged over our heads, the squeal of twisting steel, the roar of massive concrete slabs breaking loose, tumbling, thundering closer and closer as accumulating tons of wreckage broke through floor by floor.

A moment of panic gripped me: *Did we take cover far enough down?*

I tried to stand up and run but had to grab a support column because I had lost all equilibrium. In that moment, I heard the ceiling of the next story up smash down onto the floor over my head. Instinct sent me diving to the floor again.

Allah, save us! I prayed, then tensed my body and prepared to die.

4

The chain reaction of destruction lasted for a full minute. Gradually, the noise died away leaving above us the silence of what had to be a literal tomb. I raised my head off the floor and coughed up puffs of dust. In the smoking air, I felt I could not get a full breath. The two other *fedayeen* stirred, rising slowly amid the dust and gravel like ghosts.

My guts ached. But I knew I had to shake the pain off quickly—all of us did—in order to advance to whatever remained of the roof.

I heard the rest of our force rumbling up from below, ready to finish the attack. The upper stairwell was a tumble of wreckage. Armed and moving in relays to cover potential attacks from above, we climbed it like a concrete mountain. It was a short trip to daylight. I emerged into the sun to find a tangled mass of masonry, utility sheds, air-conditioning parts, and bodies.

Picking my way quickly through the rubble, I moved to the edge of the tower that faced the main road and looked down. Cars parked below looked the size of credit cards. I was about to call in a report to Abu Yousef when a slight movement caught my eye. Turning swiftly, I spotted a Phalangist lying on his back about five meters away, his fatigues burnt black and stained crimson. Had the blast carried him another meter, he would have been blown over the edge of the tower. Now he lay on his back, slowly turning his head back and forth.

I keyed my radio and gave Abu Yousef a victory report, then a footnote: "We have survivors."

Abu Yousef did not hesitate: "Make an example of them," he said. "Dead or alive, make an example of everyone you find."

I knew immediately what he meant. Walking across the wreckage, I closed the distance to the Christian fighter and stood at his right side looking down. His eyes were closed and he moaned softly. His guts peeked out from a wide gash that ran down his left side from chest to hip. I bent down and grabbed his wrist and his knee.

His eyes snapped open. I lifted the Christian's body perpendicular to the ground, swung him to my right, and launched him out into space.

Stepping toward the building's edge, I leaned out and watched his silent fall. For a long moment, he turned in the air like a plane in a flat spin. Then the weight of his torso pulled him down head first. When he hit the street, his right arm came off.

I turned around to see several men staring at me through the smoke. "We have orders!" I shouted. "Make an example of everyone you find!"

For the next few minutes, at least seventy bodies sailed off the top of the tower as the Muslim fighters disposed of the living and the dead. Some Christians made the trip to meet their God screaming.

5

In the beginning of the civil war, the battle lines were clear: the Lebanese army and Maronite Christians, led by the Phalangist Party and militia, allied themselves against the Palestinians, who were mostly Muslims. But those alliances swiftly shifted, crumbled, and shifted again. Syria, whose army had opened the way for Fatah assaults on Israel from the border, now played both ends against the middle. They pretended to support the Palestinians but in truth hoped to arm the Shia and establish a separate Shia government in the South of Lebanon.

Meanwhile, I saw criminal gangs becoming powerful, stealing and selling relief shipments to buy drugs and weapons. As the situation deteriorated, I could soon see there would be no winner. I grew confused about a lot of things. I did not see myself as a grunt soldier; I was a jihadist. People go to university to become teachers or to a carpenter's shop to learn woodworking. I had trained in Beirut to advance the cause of Islam with a gun. This dirty war of treacherous nations had ceased to be about Islam and had become only about survival.

I wanted to get out, to a country where my back was safe. I wanted to start fresh, to establish an Islamist movement somewhere else. Sweden seemed a prime destination. I had heard it was clean there, and ripe for a spiritual takeover. Many *fedayeen* talked of moving to northern Europe, quietly invading the cities in a cultural *jihad*. To establish a movement there would be a step toward reclaiming for Allah what the Ottomans had lost.

To save my own skin and not be labeled a traitor, I confided my feelings to Abu Yousef. He agreed that I had labored long for the Palestinian cause and would benefit from another sabbatical. I did not tell him I meant to get away forever.

In late 1976, I applied for a work visa to Sweden. While I waited for the wheels of international bureaucracy to turn, I continued to fight. But where I had fought with fierce resolve in the past, now my heart betrayed me.

By this time, a "Green Line" split the city from the seaport to the mountains. It was a line of demarcation, a burned-out no man's land that divided hate from hate. The Christians dug in on one side, holding their end. We dug in on the other, holding ours. Pavement formed the dividing line: eight lanes and a concrete median plus sidewalks. If you crossed the line, you were crazy. Snipers on both sides would take you out.

At times during the long civil war, the warring sides would call for a temporary peace—a day to claim your wounded, resupply, and take a half-respite from the constant vigilance that wore us down like acid.

The Christians called these days a cease-fire; the Muslims called it *hudna*. Generally, each side honored the temporary truce. I remember the day we did not.

It was a mission of opportunism. Why should we honor this code of war when our enemy had shown time after time that they had no honor? Along the Green Line, large sections of downtown Beirut were unoccupied. Our plan was to cross into Phalangist territory in an area filled with empty theaters and cheap hotels. In previous battles, we had blown holes through the buildings; now we had ready-made tunnels we could use to penetrate deep into Phalangist territory without being seen in the streets. Then, while the Christians were off-guard, we would do what we called "combing"—killing all the Christians we could find.

Three leaders took a group of eighty to ninety fighters from three factions. We rallied near the theaters where we would begin our attack. I led the largest group, a PLO unit of about forty men. The rest of the force was split between two men, Hamza, who led about twenty *fedayeen* from al-Morabitun, and a Syrian named Abu Zayed.

The Syrian and I disliked each other instantly. Over the years, to blend in with the PLO, I had taken to speaking in a Palestinian dialect, Arabic with a different slang, a different accent that was closer to Egyptian. When my face was covered with camouflage paint, people could not tell I was Lebanese. Abu Zayed seemed to think I was Palestinian and because of this, suspicion dripped off him like sweat. As it had been on my first mission into Israel, the Syrians still thought of Arafat's fighters as trash. Now, for me, the feeling was mutual: a Syrian, I felt, would sell his mother in the streets at a discount. Abu Zayed matched the stereotype. Looking into his eyes, I could see a hunger for blood.

Now, our force climbed fire escape ladders to the top of the theater and scrambled across the theater roof, our boots crunching sun-warmed gravel. Reaching the opposite edge, we dropped into an alley on the Christian side of the Green Line. Now we were able to run through the connected buildings undetected. We often had to step across the corpses of soldiers killed in past battles, some so old their flesh had worn away.

For about an hour, we advanced through the building interiors until we came to a building I knew to have a balcony that looked over a large public courtyard.

I turned to Hamza. "Keep watch here. We will go up and have a look." I motioned to Abu Zayed to follow me, and together we climbed six flights of stairs, emerging in a large empty room. I did not want to go with him, but I also did not want to let him out of my sight.

When we reached the highest floor, Abu Zayed and I got down on our bellies below window level. Slowly, carefully, we crawled to the balcony door and pushed it open. Below, I could see thirty or forty young men wearing the uniform of the Phalangists. But their small unit was completely off-guard, snacking, talking, and laughing, their weapons laid aside, enjoying the peace.

I knew it would be the perfect invasion. I knew we could kill them all.

I carried a Seminov rifle that day. I raised it and peered through the scope. A quick count revealed that I had brought two men for every one of theirs.

Abu Zayed spoke quietly. "It's perfect. An easy kill. I will get the others."

But then, in my heart, a quiet voice rose: *Don't touch them. These are mine.*

I did not hear a voice. I *felt* a voice. Was it Allah speaking? I did not know. What else could it be? Who else?

Whatever it was, my resolve to attack dissolved. I was not afraid, but I knew instantly and without question that we should abort. I had a problem, though: Abu Zayed lay beside me transmitting tension, ready for battle. My brain sorted through excuses to give him, a reason to abort.

An ambush.

"This is an ambush," I whispered, my mouth forming the words as soon as they popped into my mind.

Zayed whipped his head toward me with a hard stare.

"They saw us coming," I said carefully. "Their commanders sent those boys out there as bait."

Zayed peered back out at the scene. He raised his rifle and scanned the area with his scope.

"Where is the ambush?" he said skeptically. He motioned for my binoculars and swept them across the buildings and streets. "I see nothing."

I raised my arm and pointed to a random apartment building. "There, in the higher floors. If we move forward, they will see us immediately." I spoke evenly, firmly, full of false facts. "If they have Katyushas, we'll be murdered right here, and those who crossed with us will be dead."

"You're dreaming!" Zayed pointed to the young Christians with his rifle. "They are right there for our taking. We can *do* this. Besides, if we die, we will be *al-shaheed.*"

"True. But I am not ready to die today."

With that, I moved off the balcony, sliding backward in a combat crawl, then stood and headed down the stairs. Abu Zayed was on my heels all the way down, spitting whispers in my ear. "You are a liar and a coward. There is no ambush!"

Emerging onto the lower floor, I called retreat. Immediately, my men and Hamza's formed a loose group and began moving out, back in the direction of our tunnel system. But Abu Zayed's men stood still.

"Don't listen to him," he said. "It's not an ambush! It's the perfect attack. He's a liar!"

I whirled on him and stared, looking him up and down. For the first time, I noticed how clean he was, how unlined his face. Suddenly, he struck me as a man who had never engaged, who had never crawled in the dirt, never spilled a drop of blood. All at once, I knew his heart: he wanted glory for this battle, glory he had never tasted.

"Palestinian traitor!" Abu Zayed hissed. "You cost us a victory!"

I turned away and moved to follow my men through the hole. I had taken only three steps when a bullet seared into my back. I knew it was Abu Zayed who pulled the trigger. I kissed the ground immediately and laid there, still as a rock, feigning death.

But the Christians had heard the report and now gunfire lit the alley outside. Abu Zayed and his men pounded past me in retreat, hurrying to get through the tunnels back to the other side of the Green Zone. Then I heard the high scream of an artillery shell. Seconds later, an explosion shook the building.

I staggered to my feet, felt blood running down my back, pooling in the waistband of my pants. Hamza ran back through the hole toward me.

"Kamal! Let's go!" He put my arm over his shoulder and helped me through the hole into the alley outside. Gunfire snapped around us, and I noticed a bizarre sight. A pair of boots sat in the alleyway with feet still inside them.

"Abu Zayed," Hamza said.

Southwestern United States
2007

As my fight against radical Islam became more public, tension grew inside our home. My wife, Victoria, found herself rising several times each night to check on our daughter. Both of them had grown to dread my speaking trips, as it seemed each new venue brought more who attacked and tried to discredit me.

After a 3 Ex-Terrorists speaking engagement at Stanford University, a student named Adnan Majid, who was vice president of the school's Islamic Society, wrote an op-ed in the *Stanford Daily*. Young Mr. Majid, by his own account, was a devout Muslim who prayed five times a day, but who, despite video beheadings, suicide bombers, and more than a dozen thwarted terror attacks in the United States by radical Islamists following 9/11, wished his readers to know that the 3 Ex-Terrorists were lying about the threat of radical Islam.

"Our community at Stanford can easily reject such fear," Majid wrote. People can "easily dismiss the first two speakers, Zak Anani and Kamal Saleem, for offering us nothing but that fear." [11]

Rejecting fear is a simple matter for a student who has likely never looked down the barrel of a gun. Not so simple for us.

In late 2007, while I was away speaking in California, our home telephone rang. It was an administrator from Tamra's school. "Tamra nearly fainted in class, and she can't catch her breath," said the woman on the phone.

Tamra's teacher had run to her aid, catching her before she collapsed on the hard tile. "Her pulse is racing, and her heart rate is around two hundred beats per minute," the administrator said. "We've already called an ambulance."

While driving to the school, Victoria called me on my cell phone to tell me the news. And when she arrived on the school grounds, images hit her: A white ambulance. Spinning red lights. And Tamra sagging in a wheelchair, her face completely drained of color.

The paramedics diagnosed Tamra's episode as a panic attack. Later that evening, Tamra told Victoria that she had been sitting in science class thinking about the Seattle confrontations and the Pakistanis hunting me near my home, when an avalanche of terror engulfed her: *What would the Islamists do to Daddy? Behead him, like they had those hostages in Iraq? Could they find Mom? Could they find me? What would they do to us?*

"Mom, I cannot stay in this house while Daddy's not here," Tamra told Victoria.

So for the rest of my trip, they stayed in a local hotel. Our family physician prescribed Xanax for my daughter. She was only thirteen years old.

Saudi Arabia
1977–1978

1

In early 1977, I took a taxi to Beirut's embassy row, a collection of concierge-style buildings in an upscale part of the city, to follow up on my visa application. The *autostrad*, a wide four-lane divided street, ran through the area, and the taxi dropped me off in front of a building that housed the Swedish consulate and a couple of others.

I had applied for my work visa with a labor official named Gunnar Viggo, a tall Swede with white-blond hair and eyes the color of a Scandinavian lake. After signing in with the building concierge, I took an elevator to Viggo's office. But when I walked in, another man was sitting in the Swede's massive leather desk chair. Behind him, through an enormous window, I could see the rooftops of West Beirut stretching all the way to the sea.

The man in Viggo's chair did not rise or even move, but only sat back and appraised me with his eyes. He held a cigarette between the first two fingers of his right hand and gazed at me through the curling smoke. His thin, long face and slicked-back hair reminded me of Humphrey Bogart in a movie I had once seen.

I stood for a moment, unsure of what to do. "I am here to see Gunnar Viggo," I finally said. "Is he in?"

"No," the man said coolly. His accent was American. "What's your business with Mr. Viggo?"

"I am following up on a work visa to Sweden."

"I'm filling in for Mr. Viggo today. I'm Edward Redding." He flicked his eyes toward the smaller leather chair opposite him across the desk. I sat down.

Redding took a pull from his cigarette, his eyes never leaving mine. "Why do you want to go to Sweden?"

"I want to get out of Lebanon," I said. "I am a good plumber. I want to make a new life."

"Are you Sunni or Shia?" Redding asked.

What difference does that make?

"Sunni," I said.

With his left hand, Redding drew a pen from his right breast pocket and made a note in an open folder lying on the desk in front of him. I hadn't noticed it before. Had he known I was coming?

"Tell me about your family," Redding said.

"My father is a blacksmith, my brothers and uncles are plumbers. My mother is a devout Muslim woman."

Redding drew on his cigarette again and exhaled slowly, not in a hurry to fill the silence. Then: "You're not giving me enough information. You need to tell me more."

Information? His questions and his steady gaze were beginning to make me squirm. He kept a poker face, but one like a gangster. I felt he was watching my hands move, my lips as I spoke. I did not know this man's game. What did these questions have to do with a work visa? Was he an American agent testing to see if I was a radical? If he concluded that, my visa was dead.

His next question seemed to answer mine: "What do you think of this war?" he said.

Now I warmed to the game. I was used to being both screened and recruited. I returned his volley. "This country has always been one with both Christians and Muslims," I said, shaking my head sadly. "It's a shame they are fighting each other."

Redding stubbed out his cigarette in a green glass ashtray and stood. "The Swedish consulate has temporarily closed," he said. "I am with the

American embassy. We're filling in. The only way you can go to Sweden is through France. But as no visas are available for you, our business is concluded here."

His abruptness shook me. Redding had known from the moment I walked in that my visa application was dead. Why the questions? Why the game? A nervous flush rose in my collar. I remembered the armed guards posted around the building. Would I be arrested on my way out?

Redding walked around the desk, and I waited for him to pull a gun or a badge. Instead, he extended his right hand and took mine. We shook, but Redding did not let go. He peered into my eyes, never smiling, just—*knowing*.

I pulled my hand free and hurried out. I had not thought myself easily intimidated, but this man rattled me. I grabbed the first available elevator and rode it down to the lobby, where I signed out and then emerged through the glass doors into the sun. My anxiety now fused into anger. Why had Redding wasted my time with all his questions when he knew he was only going to send me away?

A taxi, a charcoal gray Mercedes 180, was already parked at the curb, the right rear seat empty. I was walking over to speak with the driver when the right rear door swung open. From inside came a voice: "Kamal. Come and share the taxi with me."

Cigarette smoke curled out onto the sidewalk. From the left rear seat a face leaned into view.

It was Redding.

My mind reeled, flashing from the office down through the elevators and the lobby, trying to mentally trace out his path to the street. *How did he get here before me!*

"I'm going to the American embassy," Redding said evenly. "Come ride with me if you want to talk."

There was no way I was getting into a taxi with this man. Except for the driver, he was alone in the car. For all I knew, he and the driver were both American agents recruiting informers from the PLO. It had happened before. If I were seen and suspected by my brothers, my life would not be worth a *kroosh*.

"I am going home," I said firmly. "It is in a different direction."

He patted the seat beside him. "Come, Kamal. I'll pay your taxi fare back home."

He had a confidence that shook me. I did not know what game he was playing, and I did not want to know.

"I have another engagement," I lied. "I cannot break it."

"I understand," Redding said. He sat up and his face disappeared.

I shut the taxi door, crossed the *autostrad,* and hurried south. I walked for a full minute looking straight ahead. When I got to the first corner, I glanced back. The taxi had not moved.

2

Two weeks later, I visited the Hamra district, a melting pot of sex, liquor, and intrigue. In the Hamra, there were no rules. You might go into a place and order a pizza, but the shop was really only a front for a gambling operation. Even ordinary-looking people sitting in the sidewalk cafés might actually be there for a rendezvous, not an espresso. I was there just blowing off steam, still plotting a way out of Lebanon, out of the dead end of this war. As I wandered down the streets, women in doorways beckoned with their eyes. Some spoke in low, smoky voices wanting to know if I was looking for a date. I was not in the mood for that.

I came to a stairway that led to an underground arcade, which was attached to a bar. I wasn't interested in the bar, but mindless diversion seemed attractive. I went down the stairs. The glow of pinball and slot machines lit my way as I wove through the darkness. Coins jingled as someone won on a nickel slot. A Rocky Balboa pinball machine caught my eye, then a gambling contraption I hadn't seen before: beneath glass was a movable sheet of glossy wood with variously sized holes in it. Each hole had a money value printed underneath. Using handles at the end of the machine, the player was to tip and rock the wood sheet this way and that, guiding a large ball bearing toward the big-money holes. I had just dropped in a coin when I felt a tap on my shoulder.

"Fascinating machine, isn't it?" a man said. "The kind of machine that will take your money and give you nothing in return."

Redding. *How did he find me?*

Slowly I turned to face him, recovering enough to smile. "Yes, it is a waste of time and money. But it *is* entertaining."

Redding took a long pull from a cigarette, his eyes amused, confident. "There are a lot of games where you can be entertained and also make a lot of money."

In the Swedish embassy, Redding's off-kilter questioning had knocked me off balance. There, I had worried about the guards, about who he was, really. Now, though, he was on my turf, in my country. He knew I wanted to leave Lebanon, and he had searched me out. I decided to play along.

"I'm listening," I said.

"How would you like a job where you can make some real money?"

"I'm still listening."

"It would require some travel."

"I like travel."

"I thought you would. If you're interested, meet me tomorrow at Marroush. We'll have lunch."

Marroush is a café in Beirut, famous not only for its sumptuous food but for the many deals made there. After Redding approached me in the arcade, I spent the evening wondering what he wanted with me. Did he want me to spy for the Americans?

When I arrived the next day, Redding was seated at a patio table covered in a white linen table cloth. He had already ordered for us, roast lamb.

He began with a question. "Kamal, what's the most money you've ever made?"

"Six hundred dollars a month," I said.

It was a complete fabrication. Redding knew it instantly and burst out laughing. It was the first time I had seen any other side to him than cool. "Kamal, I've been checking," he said. "I know that you have worked odd jobs most of your life. Let me tell you what I do. I work for a large American company that builds recreational villas and hospitals all over the world. Some of our biggest contracts are in Saudi Arabia, and our customers are Saudi sheikhs and generals. I know that many Lebanese work in Saudi. I also know that you are well-connected with people who have reason to dislike the Saudis."

Redding reached for a wedge of pita, dipped into a saucer of olive oil and herbs, and took a strangely small bite, chewing as he continued. "I think you would do well in my company as someone who hosts my Saudi customers, who gets to know them. Who gains their trust."

Redding was right that my faction disliked the Saudis, whom we felt were the enemies of true Islam. They controlled the black gold and could have leveraged it to conquer land after land for Allah. Instead they had sold out to the American infidels, even allowing the infidel army to occupy and operate from Muslim territory. Redding had piqued my interest. I nodded, indicating that he should go on.

"If you're interested, we'd like to train you to be a translator and interpreter for us. You would be in charge of one of our recreational villages in Riyadh. You would have your own apartment, lavish benefits, and your own car. The salary is between $16,000 and $18,000 a year, tax-free."

The number shocked me. In 1977, a $20,000 salary was like $100,000 today. Only engineers or professors could aspire to such an amount. I actually felt dizzy. This could be my way out! The way to escape this war and recommit my life to serving Allah and not the factions.

"Your job would be taking care of the customers at the villa, who are mainly from the Saudi upper class," Redding went on. "They have certain—preferences. They do not trust Americans to see to those things."

Redding swirled his pita in the oil again, took another nibble, and leveled his eyes across the table. "But they would trust you."

3

Redding set me up in a deluxe apartment in Riyadh. Every day, his company sent me private tutors, two American and one Egyptian. I learned conversational English. I learned etiquette, how to behave around the royal family, around generals, around international executives. I was tall and muscular, so I learned how to minimize my presence with my body language. Then there were the details: the American teachers taught me the finer points of Arabic as it was spoken in Saudi so that I could better pick up on the nuances of a meeting. Also, I learned how to listen carefully to conversations to record time, dates, numbers, dollars, fuel.

When my training was complete, my work began. At first, it was low-level industrial espionage. I was to combine my inborn expertise in Middle Eastern culture with my new training—all under the guise of being an errand boy to the high-powered executives. Redding met almost weekly with Saudi officials to negotiate new contracts and nurse contracts already underway. I slipped in and out of ornate conference rooms with polished tables the length of boats, discreetly refilling the sheikhs' water pitchers, replenishing wide bowls of figs and dates, spiriting in fresh paper and pens, making copies of documents. All the while, I pretended that my English was poor, and my Arabic of the Lebanese variety only.

Soon the sheikhs and generals regarded me as furniture and spoke freely in front of me when Redding visited the restroom—which he sometimes did on purpose. I listened to every word and passed it all to the Americans.

At the recreation villas, my job was much different. Originally the villas were built for international travelers coming to do business or work on projects with Redding's company. As general manager, my official job was to oversee the service staff. My unofficial job was to arrange unimagined pleasures for the Saudi sheikhs and generals. Many nurses, technicians, teachers, clerks, engineers, and other professionals applied to work in Saudi. But many of them, once they arrived, practiced their true professions: pool girl, escort, dancer, dominatrix. The company set them up at the villas with good Muslim family men who had never dreamed of women who looked like this, women of many talents from all over the world—Belgium, Denmark, Britain, Sweden, Egypt, America. For good Muslim men who were supposed to remain sexually pure, America provided every sexual favor and flavor, including young men.

The purpose? To buy influence. For commercial contracts. For military contracts. For royal contracts. And even to influence Saudi-American relations. That was Redding's purpose, anyway. But I quickly found another purpose: extortion.

Every room in the villa was fitted with hidden cameras. And each day, I visited a nearby mosque bearing photographs. My contacts from the PLO took them back to Arafat, who used them to finance the Palestinian cause with oil money extorted from guilty Arab sheikhs. I had left Lebanon, but was back in the business of *jihad*.

4

By 1978, I had quit Redding's company and was living and moving through the United Arab Emirates, Europe, Oman, Saudi Arabia, and Lebanon raising money for *jihad* from Arab sheikhs. Some of my connections were willing donors I had met at the villas. Others knew I had pictures. Whatever the source, I funneled huge sums back to the PLO. Though I bounced around the Middle East, Saudi Arabia was, from a financial standpoint, unquestionably a terrorist's paradise. Oil was the new gold, and prices had shot into distant galaxies. During the 1970s, the Saudi royal family and anyone with ties to the nation's petroleum industry saw their wealth double, triple, then explode by nearly 2,000 percent.

For jihadists with the right connections, it was like dipping into a bottomless pool of money. I intended to make sure my brothers got their share. I began spending long days at local mosques in Riyadh, teaching from the Koran and the *hadith* as the Muslim Brotherhood had taught me. Only now, I placed an emphasis on money.

"The Koran teaches that the righteous Muslim will 'make ready your strength to the utmost of your power, including steeds of war, to strike terror into [the hearts of] the enemies of Allah, and your enemies,' " I said, quoting from Sura Al Anfal, also called The Spoils of War, Booty. "In former days, horses represented wealth. Today, we count wealth differently. And the Koran teaches that the true Muslim will contribute his wealth to advance true Islam. Remember that it says, 'Whatever ye shall spend in the cause of Allah, shall be repaid unto you, and ye shall not be treated unjustly.' "

At a mosque in Riyadh, I met a young man named Aamer whose father was connected to the Saudi royals. He came to the mosque and sat with me during the day as I spoke from the Koran to small groups of men. I spoke with force and conviction—with the same uncompromising fire as a cultist. Aamer was a year or two younger than I. He became infatuated with my zealotry. I became infatuated with him when I learned he went to school with Sa'ad Fahim, the son of a sheikh who was a cousin of the royal Saudi family.

Immediately I began plotting how I could use Aamer to get to Sheikh Fahim, who was supposed to be a stout Sunni Muslim. Aamer often visited his villa, which was really a palace, he said, perched on the edge of Riyadh.

In Saudi, there were and are two kinds of royalty: the pro-American, westernized kind who want to travel and enjoy life, and the Wahhabi Muslims who are radical to the bone. The second breed was angry and resentful over the decline of Islam, over the crumbling of the male-dominated culture. Then, as now, they believed fervently that America was destroying Islam, and they were happy to pour their wealth into bringing our great faith back to its full glory, donating their millions for *jihad*.

Aamer and I became close friends, as close as two men can become when one of them has an ulterior motive. One day, we were shopping in a gold *souk,* really a gleaming mall where in shop after shop, thousands of chains and bracelets lay in endless rows, shimmering like the treasures of ancient Egypt.

"Aamer," I said. "You know I am going back to London soon to meet with the Muslim Brotherhood. I was wondering if you could talk to Sheikh Fahim for me."

I was quite familiar with the etiquette. The sheikhs were extremely generous, but the secret was that you did not ask them outright for money. You told them about your cause, about the pressing needs, and let them suggest how they might help. If a sheikh was to become your benefactor, you must both pretend it was his idea. It was like a waltz, a minuet, and each side knew it. But always, we danced the steps.

Three days after our trip to the *souk*, Aamer and I rolled in his Coup de Ville, which had been a birthday gift from Sheikh Fahim, down a black strip of freshly paved highway to the sheikh's villa. It was April. A late afternoon sun lit the desert, and the rolling dunes beyond the rim of civilized Saudi glowed rose and copper.

Aamer blasted the air conditioner and gossiped about the Fahims.

"Noorah, the sheikh's youngest daughter, is seeing someone outside the palace," he said, smiling behind giant blue aviator shades. "He is Lebanese, like you. The family knows about it, but pretends they don't."

I frowned, wondering about the power of a Saudi royal who would allow his daughter to indulge in a relationship outside the kingdom circle. "Why does he allow this?" I asked.

Aamer laughed. "Because he treasures his reputation as a good Muslim father and does not want to ruin it with a scandal. Also, he has a weakness for his daughters. They play him like a harp."

Noorah wasn't the only problem child, Aamer went on. Jaled, the sheikh's oldest son, was seeing an English woman. "Sa'ad told me she dumped him and ripped his heart out, but he keeps going back to England trying to see her. Apparently, he cannot get sex like that anywhere else."

Now we both laughed.

Before long, I saw the villa rising in the distance. It covered an entire city block and was surrounded by a high white wall. Greenery peeked over the walls, hinting at the lush oasis concealed inside. Soon we arrived at the gates, which swung open automatically. He waved easily at the guards, and we barely slowed down.

"I've been coming here since I was a little boy," Aamer explained.

Inside the gates was another world. The road itself was concrete, carefully inlaid with some kind of colored stones, pressed flush so that the Caddie didn't encounter a single bump. To the left and right, manicured lawns spread out like bright green carpets. I saw huge stands of palm trees—date, queen, and silver—as well as exotic trees I had never seen before, bearing clusters of crimson fruit. All around us flowers bloomed as though we were in the tropics. Here and there workers tended the gardens, and I wondered how they kept all this alive beneath the broiling Saudi sun.

The mosaic road opened up to reveal the largest private residence I had ever seen, a breathtaking blend of European and Middle Eastern architecture as wide as a soccer field and built story upon story. Aamer pulled through a roundabout with a huge stone fountain at its center and parked just past a pair of enormous double doors that were carved with a mural of flowers and palms.

A story flashed through my mind: the goose and the golden egg.

I tucked a small box under my arm, a gift for the sheikh, and as we exited the car, I took note of video cameras mounted above the doors and at the corners of two cupolas on the second story. (I had also noticed a series of them secreted tastefully in the landscaping on the way in.) Beside the main doors was a smaller door. Two men stepped through it onto the covered portico and began chatting with Aamer—more guards. As they did this, I noticed a black stretch limousine with gold ornaments creeping toward us on the circular drive. It seemed to have come from somewhere behind the house, and it pulled to a silent stop directly in front of the double doors which, at that moment, opened.

5

My breath caught in my chest. The young woman in the black *abayyah* did not *walk* out of the doors. She *flowed*, like whispering surf caressing a beach. Although the clothes of Muslim women are designed to conceal their bodies, the cloth and cut of this woman's clothes revealed every curve. The *abbayah* covered only her head; her face was concealed by an expensive half *niqab*, a mask of shimmering copper fabric that revealed only her eyes.

The woman was not looking in our direction when she first came out of the villa. But when she did, her eyes blazed. Large, deep-set, and shaped like almonds, they were the color of dark chocolate and rimmed with thick black lashes that reminded me of the wings of birds.

The eyes lit up. "Aamer!" she said, her voice low and golden like a sunset. As she turned and moved toward us, I thought she walked like a royal—but a royal who carried tantalizing secrets.

I started to sweat.

Aamer turned from the guards and smiled a brotherly smile. "Fatima, how are you?"

"I am better than fine! Still living in London and spending Father's money." Then her eyes danced over me playfully. "And who have you brought with you today?"

"This is an old friend of mine. Kamal Saleem," Aamer said. "Kamal, this is Fatima Bint Sheikh Fahim."

A horn sounded from the limousine. Without removing her eyes from me, Fatima waved an impatient, perfectly manicured hand in the direction of the car. "My chauffeur," she said in a bemused tone that said good help was hard to find. "He has been driving me since I was a little girl, and he thinks he can tell me what to do."

Looking into Fatima's chocolate eyes, I knew instantly that no one could tell her what to do. My blood raced. Her fragrance seemed to displace the air. Not a sweet scent like jasmine or gardenia, but something earthy and hypnotic. I glanced up at the surveillance cameras, then back at this exquisite woman. A battle raged inside me: I desperately wanted to telegraph my attraction. But a guest of a Sunni sheikh does *not* make eyes at his daughter. With cameras watching and guards likely monitoring the feeds, I knew if I did not turn my eyes away, I would be shown the way out. Worse, I would lose the sheikh's money.

I'd rather have her, I thought, and allowed a meaningful smile to briefly curve my lips. Her eyes sparkled back over the *niqab*.

"*Ya-ela, ya-ela,* Kamal!" Aamer said, nodding toward the small door. "I do not want to keep the sheikh waiting."

In a willful act of self-preservation, I forced my gaze to the ground. "It was an honor to meet you, Fatima," I said, and hurried inside.

6

The entrance hall was large enough to hold an entire American house. Across the cavernous ceiling marched an intricate tile mosaic, a smaller-scale mirror of the pattern on the floor. On one wall, hand-painted wallpaper in thin stripes of gold, cream, blue, and crimson. On the other, a backlit glass case at least ten meters wide displaying swords and sabers from around the world. A round red couch, embroidered in gold and large enough to seat twenty people, dominated the center of the hall. Around the room stands of black bamboo rose from pots the size of small cars.

My pulse quickened. I had met many sheikhs, but their homes were not ornate. They were the pillars of old tribes, and they decorated in the Bedouin tradition. They were wealthy, but not Howard Hughes wealthy. Not like this.

As we wound through equally ornate passageways toward the sheikh's private business suite, a single word rang in my mind like a cash register bell: *billionaire.*

The sheikh's suite was a blend of Middle Eastern and European decor. On one wall of the huge main room, bookshelves climbed to the twenty-foot ceiling and featured sliding ladders of polished mahogany for reaching the highest shelves. A massive desk, also mahogany, commanded another end of the space, and intricate Bedouin carpets softened the tile floors. In one area was a large seating group with English leather sofas. And outside the suite, through a wall of glass-paned doors, I could see a sprawling, lushly landscaped courtyard dotted with bubbling fountains, conversation areas, and, in the shade of feathery palms, cages filled with birds. It reminded me of *jannah*.

"Have a seat," Aamer said, indicating the leather sofas. Leaving my gift for the sheikh on a small table by the entrance, I walked over and sat down. Aamer remained standing near the double doors.

Moments later, Sheikh Fahim entered and I stood again. "*Yah ibny*," he said warmly, embracing Aamer, who bent and kissed the sheikh's hand.

The sheikh wore the most expensive *dish-dash* I had ever seen. I marveled at the sheen of the fabric and the gossamer-thin *abbayah* he wore as a second layer, black and laced with thin golden thread. His facial features reminded me of the pictures I had seen of the royal family: light skin, bushy eyebrows, a sharply trimmed goatee, and a thin moustache. Even from across the room, I caught the scent of his cologne. It was a unique, spicy smell, probably custom-made for him in Paris.

The sheikh rested his hand on Aamer's shoulder, and the two began strolling slowly in my direction. "How are your father and mother?" the sheikh asked.

"They are fine. My father is adding to his business a new masonry contract with the Americans. He sends his thanks again for your help."

The pair drew near the sofas, the sheikh behaving as though I were invisible, and spoke cryptically about something they clearly did not want me to understand. The sheikh then sat down directly across from me, and Aamer took the neighboring seat. Finally, Sheikh Fahim regarded me regally and gestured for me to sit down.

I sat lightly, humbly, and with my knees together, intentionally making myself smaller, according to protocols I had learned working for Edward Redding. I waited to be invited to speak.

"Who is this you have brought?" the sheikh said to Aamer.

"This is my friend, Kamal, the one I told you about, the one I met in the mosque. He is a good Muslim and a warrior for Allah. Kamal travels all over the world, wherever he is led to fulfill the calling of Islam."

The sheikh nodded thoughtfully, letting a tiny smile of interest steal onto his face. He then lifted his right hand and pointed at me. "Kamal, do you know who I am?"

"Yes, Sheikh Fahim, Aamer has told me who you are and that you have a heart to advance the cause of Islam," I said. "If you had not graciously opened your doors to me, I would not be here today."

Aamer broke in, proudly: "Kamal has a gift for you."

Sheikh Fahim raised an eyebrow, pleased. It always amazed me that no matter how many possessions these people accumulated, no matter how remote the possibility that I would give them something they did not already have, they were as happy as schoolchildren to receive a gift.

"May I go and get it for you?" I said.

When the sheikh tipped his chin forward, I stood up and walked backwards, away from him. One has no permission to give his back to a member of the royal family. I backed all the way to the door to retrieve the box I'd brought, then requested permission to return. The sheikh waved me forward. I crossed to the seating area and kneeled at his feet, cradling the box on my two flat palms like an offering.

He received the gift with both hands. If the royals don't care for you, they will set your gift aside and look at it later. But Sheikh Fahim opened the gift box, extracting a polished wooden case with a glass lid.

"It is *beautiful!*" the sheikh enthused, for a moment abandoning his royal bearing.

Opening the lid, he lifted out an exquisitely detailed gold-bladed dagger, for which I had paid three thousand U.S. dollars in a *souk* in Oman. Fine tan leather wrapped its grip, and a metal craftsman had etched a *sura* into both sides of the blade.

"How did you know?" the sheikh said. "How did you know I would like something like this?"

*Because you are a wealthy, cloistered man who likes to play-act at ji-*had, I thought.

"A true warrior requires such a thing," I said.

Gently, he replaced the dagger in its black velvet nest and returned his eyes to me, now with genuine interest. "So, tell me about yourself," he said.

I did not go back to the couch. I sat right there at his feet and told him about my life, my recruitment by the Muslim Brotherhood, my involvement with the PLO. It turned out that Shiekh Fahim knew my cousin, an imam who would go on to become the highest *mufti*, or Sharia scholar, in Lebanon. I had learned to drop his name whenever I could; it always opened doors for me.

I quoted the *sura,* as I always did to remind the rich that Allah commands *jihad* and that Muslims without guns could fight with their gold. "The Shia are taking over Lebanon with the help of the Syrians," I went on. "The infidel Americans are helping the Maronite Christians and Phalangists. We have a lot of warriors, but we cannot fight on an empty stomach."

Aamer looked on, seeming proud that he had impressed his uncle and benefactor with his devout friend. Sheikh Fahim seemed riveted. I went to close the sale: "We cannot move forward unless we are blessed by Allah and his chosen people. We are already thankful that you took your valuable time to allow us to sit in your presence today. If you find it in your heart, we would be most grateful to also receive your blessing."

Sheikh Fahim turned to gaze out into the garden, and I watched his face as he considered my story. When he returned his eyes to me, it was as though someone had turned a dial: warm to shrewd.

"Many people ask for our blessing," he said. "If I help you, how do I know this money is not going to the wrong place?"

"Our brothers in leadership will confirm to you that they have received it."

His eyes tightened further. "I do not want to receive any phone calls. I do not want any traceable connection."

"Then I will give you information you can use to verify that the money went to the proper account."

The sheikh paused for a long beat, and I worried that my pitch to the richest man I had ever approached had failed.

Then he spoke again: "Today, you will have seventy thousand dollars. It will be deposited as soon as I verify who you are."

My heart raced. In 1978, seventy thousand dollars was as a quarter million today. Not only was the money huge, but this was a coup of another sort. For months, I had been fishing the bank accounts of Bedouin sheikhs, but now I had hooked a whale.

Aamer and I parted ways with the sheikh and went out the way we came. At the security station near the front doors, a guard stopped me and held out an envelope. It was made of expensive-looking cream-colored stock, and I took it from him, slightly confused. Had the sheikh changed his mind about the bank deposit, the verification, and issued a check right away?

Lifting the flap, I shook out a single sheet of paper and saw that it bore only two lines of handwriting: a London telephone number and, in a flourish of black ink, a signature: *Fatima.*

7

Only to appear to be a man in control, I waited a week before I picked up the phone. But the truth was, I counted the hours like a man in prison. My pulse galloped as I dialed Fatima's London number. She answered the call herself, and her low, tawny voice reached into my chest across two continents and three seas.

Still, I played it cool. "I keep an apartment in the Emirates and I just returned. I received your note. Very lovely. I am just getting back with you."

Fatima spoke playfully but did not waste time. "I know why you wanted to meet with my father."

Did she really know I had visited her home in the cause of *jihad?* Perhaps she had tortured Aamer until he told her.

On the phone, I brushed past her intimation. "It was a great honor to meet him and also to meet you."

"You know, as a proper Saudi girl, I am not supposed to talk with strange men—especially men like you." Across the distance, I could hear the smile in her voice, see the sparkle in her dark eyes. "But I like you very much. And I like what you do."

Her directness startled me. No woman of Saudi royalty should speak with me—a commoner, a foreigner—alone on the telephone and so brazenly. Suddenly, I remembered with exact clarity her mesmerizing scent, the rose petal texture of her hand.

"Women like me don't meet men like you," Fatima said. "A lifetime could pass first. Men like you have tasted liquor and known women. I have known since I was a little girl that I will marry my fat, ugly cousin. I also know he will not know how to please me. But you have practiced. I could see it in your eyes."

Now every pulse point in my body pounded. Her voice was like golden nectar in my ear. I imagined the face behind her veil. Remembering the few strands of raven hair that had peeked from her *abbayah*, I envisioned a thick mane tumbling down her back.

"Come to London," she said with sudden urgency. "Or Paris. This weekend. I will meet you wherever you like."

London? Paris? Reality hit like cold water in my face: a trip like that would cost money I did not have. "I cannot come this weekend," I said. "My budget does not permit."

The teasing sparkle returned to her voice. "Evidently, my father is not paying you enough."

Maybe she does know the truth.

"I do not touch that money. That is for advancing the cause of Islam." My answer was true, and would also serve me well if Fatima was playing the spy.

"In any case, you don't have to worry about finances," she said lightly. "My father pays for everything I do and I don't keep an itemized record of my expenses."

A long pause filled the line. And then, like a single raindrop breaking the still surface of a pond, it was broken.

"Come to me," she said.

8

That was on a Wednesday. But it felt as if I waited two years instead of two days for Friday to come. I worked some contacts in the United Arab Emirates, a project involving fake American visas. But even that was torture. I spent most of my time mooning around my apartment and listening to love songs by Ummu Gulsum, the legendary Egyptian singer.

Finally, Friday came. At the British Airways counter in Dubai, I picked up the first-class ticket Fatima had booked for me, boarded the plane, then sipped champagne all the way to Heathrow. A driver met me there in a limousine flying a gold-tasseled Saudi flag, and he whisked me to a grand London hotel overlooking Hyde Park. A smoothly mannered concierge welcomed me personally and ushered me into a café decorated in leather, mahogany, velvet, and crystal.

The concierge seated me at a table, and a waiter appeared with a tall, dewy glass of freshly squeezed lemonade, thin slices of the yellow fruit wedged among the ice. My seat faced a terrace banked in vines and flowers and overlooking the park. I felt like royalty. I had never been treated this way. I did not know how to react. I was thinking that I could quickly get used to it when an earthy scent stole my breath. I whirled to find Fatima standing behind me.

She wore a silk blouse in pale pink and a matching skirt, long and slim, down to high-heeled boots of expensive black leather. A scarf of pink chiffon wrapped her head, but her face was not covered. And it was the face I had imagined hidden behind her veil: Delicate feminine features. High cheekbones, skin golden. Full lips touched in an innocent pink. And those wide, dark eyes, inviting pools in a secret grotto.

There is something beyond a racing heartbeat, when the center of your soul flies outside your body and enters the soul of another. I stood and faced Fatima, grabbed her hand, and kissed it. The kiss was not polite.

A full minute passed before we were able to collect ourselves. Then Fatima glanced around the café and saw that a couple of other parties had come in to dine. "Would you like to go out to the terrace?" she said.

Outside, we settled on a bench facing Hyde Park. A number of diners turned to look at her. That's how striking she was.

"Would you like to have lunch?" she said, looking into my eyes.

"I'm not hungry," I said.

"Neither am I."

I reached for her hand again and now found it cool and trembling. For a long time, we didn't talk. We just looked. But inside me, a war raged. *Am I doing the right thing?*

If the sheikh found out, even about this rendezvous that had so far been chaste, it could be deadly for both of us. Many was the outraged Muslim father who had sliced his daughter's throat for merely sitting with an unmarried man. They did it to preserve their honor, the family's good name.

"What am I doing here?" I finally said aloud.

"I don't know," Fatima said. Then, as if she had read my thoughts, she looked around the terrace. "There are a lot of people watching here. Let's go upstairs and talk."

An elevator swept us up to a luxurious suite that must have covered an entire hotel floor. The sheikh had apparently rented it for years, or perhaps bought it, because it was decorated in the style of his villa, all silk and leather, mahogany and gold. On one wall of the wide sunken living room, a fire roared in a massive marble fireplace.

Fatima disappeared, and a moment later I heard the voice of Ummu Gulsum floating through the room. Fatima returned.

"I listened to this while I waited for you."

"So did I," I said, amazed.

She stepped close to me, so close I could feel the heat from her body. I looked down at her, reached forward, and brushed away her pink *hijab*. It fell away like air, releasing a burst of myrrh, the scent of her hair. She reached up, and like a cool fire her hand touched the back of my neck. She laid her head on my shoulder.

"I was dreaming you would dance with me," Fatima said.

Circling her with my left arm, I pressed my hand against the small of her back and pulled her to me. Her breath caught. I took her left hand in my right, and as we swayed to the voice of Ummu, time stopped and every question in life seemed answered.

We danced until sunlight faded from the windows and only the glimmering fire lit the room. When I kissed her, I drank as deeply as if I had never kissed a woman. And there before the fire, we settled on silk cushions striped in burgundy, green, and gold, where we danced until morning, the flames reflecting off Fatima's golden skin.

9

Relationships like the one with Sheikh Fahim opened more doors for me, though they would likely have turned into guillotines if Sheikh Fahim had known I had fallen passionately in love—and into bed—with his daughter. Fatima and I spent nearly two years before fireplaces up and down Europe. She kept the suite in London and an apartment in Paris, but wherever I was working, she flew to meet me. Our affair was a mad, secret string of hidden café rendezvouses, extravagant gifts, and ardent nights ending in shared sunrises.

Fatima had been promised to her cousin, Fayed, who worked as some kind of bureaucrat in the Saudi royal government. But she kept delaying the marriage, playing her indulgent father like a marionette with strings of excuses.

Sheikh Fahim and his wealthy friends, meanwhile, loved me and my European connections. They loved me because I appeared "neutral," a Lebanese who could speak French, English, and Arabic and who could blend in with other cultures. I was a chameleon. Best of all, they knew I could obtain for them—pleasures. You see, many of Saudi's powerful were drenched in lust. Radical Islam is like a moral straitjacket: do not look, do not touch, do not even *wish* for the things of the flesh. So, while the oil sheikhs pretended to be strong Islamists up front, they enjoyed the world in secret.

In the sheikhs' eyes, all this was justifiable, according to the *hadith*, which teaches Muslims to "seed" the women of infidels. For the Muslim Brotherhood and the PLO, it was a profitable arrangement: the happier the sheikhs, the more money I commanded for the armaments of war. At one point, I had over a dozen regular benefactors who pooled their money to purchase fifty thousand, sixty thousand, even seventy thousand dollars in travelers checks in my name. Once, I received over two hundred thousand dollars at one time. As always, I handed it over to my contact, Samir, a Palestinian accountant who deposited the funds in the PLO's accounts.

Saudi money was the lifeblood of our movement, along with regular contributions from sheikhs in Kuwait and the Emirates. But to the sheikhs themselves, such donations were less than pocket change. I once saw a Saudi sheikh give a Rolls-Royce to a young British woman who had only helped him when he had a flat tire on the way to the airport.

Gave it to her. On the spot. The whole car.

In early 1979, I was in London and called Fatima at the hotel. She did not answer. And she did not answer the next day or the next. This was unlike her. We had been in constant contact, even when we were in different cities. But since our affair was secret, there was no one I could ask. On the fourth day, I went down to the maibox at my flat and found a letter. The return address was Saudi Arabia.

I opened it and when I saw what was at the top of the letterhead, the breath left my body: it was the Saudi royal seal.

We know who you are. Cease and desist your relationship with Fatima Bint Sheikh Fahim. If you do not, we will cut you down.

Was this a joke? I would have thought so except for the stationery. It looked genuine. I had seen some like it in Sheikh Fahim's business suite, among his papers. I slammed shut the mailbox, bounded up the stairs to my flat, and called Aamer.

"Is the letter right?" he said, shocked. "Have you been with Fatima?"

"Absolutely not!" I said, still clutching the letter. "I do not know what they could be talking about, what this means. Maybe it is a plot against me."

"Is the letter signed?"

I glanced at it. "No."

"Make a copy and send it to me," Aamer said. "I will find out what is going on."

A week passed while the mail made its way to my friend. And during that week, I received four more letters from Riyadh. Each was on royal letterhead and blasted the same unsubtle message: Break it off with the sheikh's daughter or we will kill you.

Who is "we"? I wondered. *And where is Fatima?*

I called the hotel. I called her Paris flat. I had not heard from her in nine days, when the most I had ever gone was one. Was she safe? Had the letter writers already told Sheikh Fahim of their suspicions? If so, I was already dead. And, perhaps, so was she.

On the tenth day, my phone rang.

"Did you do anything with her?" Aamer said immediately.

My stomach dropped. "What are you talking about?"

"Fatima. She's here. In Riyadh. Her cousin, Fayed, sent the letters. Her father sent bodyguards to London. They brought her back here and put her on house arrest. She has a lock on the outside of her bedroom door and walks with a guard everywhere she goes, even inside the villa. Fayed found out she had pictures in her Paris apartment of four different men. One of them was you."

"Me!"

"Kamal, did you do anything with her?"

"Absolutely not!"

"Kamal. . . ." Aamer's voice grew indulgent, conspiratorial.

"What?"

"How did Fatima get your picture?"

I sighed, pretending to break. "Okay. When you and I first went to the villa, Fatima left me her phone number. One day when I was in London I called her. We went out for coffee. At the café, she took a picture of me. I guess she kept it."

"*Never* say that," Aamer snapped. "*Never* tell anyone that she took your picture, or even that you met. Deny everything."

"What am I supposed to say, then?"

"Say you don't have any idea how she got your picture. Say she's been living on her own, unsupervised. Say she's got pictures of three other guys, and why don't they ask them? Say she's a woman and who can believe a woman?"

Chino, California
January 2008

It was at a conference on January 11 at Calvary Chapel of Chino Hills that I first told three thousand people that one of Islam's secret evils had come to America. Ten days earlier, the bodies of two sisters, Sarah and Amina Amin, seventeen and eighteen years old, had been found in Irving, Texas, shot full of holes. The girls were students at Lewisville High School. They shared a favorite color, pink. Sarah loved science and dreamed of a career in medicine. But their father, Yaser Abdel Said, an Egyptian immigrant, was angry that Sarah had gone out with a non-Muslim boy. At one point, the girls' mother, fearing her husband would harm the girls, took them and fled. But on New Year's Day, both sisters were found dead, abandoned in the cab their father had been driving.

That's when I knew. Honor killing had come to America.

After Sheikh Fahim yanked Fatima back from Europe, Aamer convinced him that his daughter was not so much wayward as a silly dreamer with a rich fantasy life. What else could explain pictures of four different men? Surely the sheikh did not think his daughter a whore? And surely he did not think so devout a Muslim fighter as Kamal would jeopardize his mission—and the sheikh's millions—for one woman, when it was well-known he had lots of women all over Europe. The sheikh believed Aamer, and I lived to see another day. So did Fatima.

Thirty years later, the Amin sisters did not. Since their deaths, I have read in American newspapers that honor killing is not a part of Islamic religious tradition. That is a lie. Honor killing is as much a part of the fabric of Islam as is the subjugation of women, their head-to-toe covering, keeping them uneducated, and denying them the right to vote. Koranic scholars teach that if a wife refuses to make herself beautiful for her husband, or if she refuses to have sex with him, to pray, or leaves the house without a good excuse, he should beat her.

Amnesty International reports that over 90 percent of married Muslim women in Pakistan report being "kicked, slapped, beaten or sexually abused when husbands were dissatisfied by their cooking or cleaning, or when the women had 'failed' to bear a child or had given birth to a girl instead of a boy." [12]

In Islam, a married man can take another wife and ostracize his first wife simply because he has tired of her. He may divorce the first wife with a simple verbal proclamation: "I divorce you." He only has to say it, and the first wife is out in the street. But if the man chooses to keep the children, he may do so. The woman can fight him in court. But under Sharia law, the court normally views children as the product of the man's seed. The woman was only the incubator.

In Muslim societies, even a woman who is raped is not a credible witness in the courts. It takes the testimony of four eyewitnesses to convict a man of rape. But only two men, the rapist and a friend, are sufficient to deny a rape, thereby condemning the woman to a public whipping for the sin of fornication. In Saudi Arabia and Iran, if the woman is found to be pregnant out of wedlock, she can be stoned to death.

This is Sharia law, the same law of which Omar Ahmad, founder of the "moderate" Council on American-Islamic Relations (CAIR) said this: "Islam isn't in America to be equal to any other faith, but to become dominant. The Koran, the Muslim book of Scripture, should be the highest authority in America, and Islam the only accepted religion on earth."

The Amin sisters are not the only victims of violent attempts in America to preserve Muslim family honor. In 2008, Afghanistani immigrant Waheed Allah Mohammad repeatedly stabbed his younger sister because she was a "bad Muslim girl." Her offenses: wearing immodest clothing, visiting nightclubs, and planning to move to New York City.[13]

Also in 2008, prosecutors charged Chaudry Rashid, a Pakistani immigrant living in an Atlanta suburb, with strangling his daughter, Sandeela Kanwal, to death with a bungee cord. Kanwal, a worker at Wal-Mart, had planned to end her arranged marriage of six years and had gotten involved with another man. Rashid was sitting in his driveway smoking a cigarette when police arrived to arrest him. He later told police he killed his daughter because adultery and divorce are offenses against Islam.

In seven months' time, three Muslim men in America attacked or killed women for religious reasons. And yet some reporters have insisted on trying to divorce honor killing from Islam. Why is this? Do we think that by softening this connection in the name of "multiculturalism," we will somehow appear enlightened and that women's lives will be spared?

In the name of Islam, I befriended messengers of political enlightenment—communists, Baathists, intellectual revolutionaries—from three countries. Then I killed them. Why do so many Americans think today's Islamists, now teeming through their cities and actively plotting against them every day, will treat them any differently?

Police believe Yaser Abdel Said did not treat his own daughters any differently than I treated those I killed. He has not been seen since the January 2008 killings and is wanted in Texas for murder. Police believe he is armed. I believe he may be hiding with Muslim sympathizers who consider the killings a righteous act.

Afghanistan
1978–1979

1

In 1980, I flew from London to Riyadh to see Sheikh Fahim. Not only was it time to replenish PLO war chests, but for many months I had been monitoring the escalation of a savage attack on Islam. The Soviets were murdering our Muslim brothers and sisters in Afghanistan. I was hoping the sheikh would commit funds to the battle.

I had always hated the Communists. Unfailingly, they behaved as treacherous vipers, and it would prove no different in Afghanistan. In 1978, they took over the country when the People's Democratic Party of Afghanistan (PDPA) staged a coup commanded by a U.S.-educated former Afghan schoolteacher named Hafizullah Amin.

Amin and the PDPA ousted the regime of Mohammed Daoud and installed as president Nur Mohammad Taraki, who immediately began to uproot the country's centuries of Islamic law and tradition and replace it with Marxist-Leninist "reforms." The changes sparked rebellion among the village *mullahs* and tribal leaders who wished to maintain the old ways. Many Afghan traditionalists, intellectuals, and religious leaders fled to Pakistan, while others waged open rebellion across most of the country. The Afghan government, which by then was receiving assistance from hundreds of Soviet "military advisers," executed villagers by the thousands—"political prisoners," they called them.

From London, I watched these developments, outraged at the murder of my Muslim brothers and sisters. By July 1978, Taraki's requests for Soviet advisers had turned to requests for regiments including rifle divisions and an airborne unit. Slowly, a Soviet presence built in Afghanistan.

But Taraki was behind, history later revealed: the Americans had already authorized CIA paramilitary forces to aid the tribal rebels. As events unfolded, I had no idea I would meet some of these American operatives.

In October 1978, the Nuristani tribes fought back violently against Taraki's reforms. In March 1979, Afghan rebels in Herat killed ten Afghan soldiers. Taraki's Air Force struck back, killing twenty-four thousand people in the city of Herat in a massive airstrike. Soon, villages around the major cities—Kabul, Kandahar, and elsewhere—began emptying themselves of young men who joined several insurgent factions, eventually forming an uneasily allied *mujahadeen*. Four months later, the Americans began arming and training the *mujahadeen*.

That December, I watched the news as Soviet ground forces invaded Afghanistan. Within a month, they had an established force of one hundred thousand, including eighteen hundred tanks, eighty thousand soldiers, and squadrons of bombers and helicopters. The Afghan government, now led by Hafizullah Amin (who, it is rumored, had Taraki suffocated in his bed with a pillow), hoped the Soviet presence would quell rebellion. Instead, the Afghan tribes rose up in defense of their traditions and in defense of Islam. But even with aid from the Americans, then ultimately the Chinese, Soviet firepower outmatched the *mujahadeen* and thousands of Afghan rebels died in the withering fire of Russian choppers and bombers.

By then, I was a familiar face at Sheikh Fahim's villa, and the guards smiled as they waved me through the front gates in early 1980. The sheikh came to meet me in the same den where we had our first encounter, having swallowed the lie that I had not been sleeping with his daughter. I bent to kiss his ring, and he embraced me like a son.

When we had settled into his fancy sofas, Sheikh Fahim leaned forward to pluck a slice of apricot from a silver platter of dried fruits that sat on the table between us. I was surprised when he brought up Afghanistan before I did.

"If we don't do something swiftly, Muslims will lose Afghanistan because the Americans will defeat the Soviets there," he said, popping the orange circle into his mouth. "Then we will spend years trying to deliver Afghanistan from the hands of the Americans."

I gazed out the window at the sheikh's garden paradise, thinking. How could we help the Afghans? The *mujahadeen* were already fierce fighters: from the Soviets they had captured caches of RPGs and AK–47s to replace the World War II bolt-action rifles they had been using. Still, the weapons were not enough to battle bombers and tanks; they needed more. The Russians had always been our biggest supplier, but now they were the enemy.

I turned to Sheikh Fahim and shared these thoughts.

"What about the Chinese?" he said.

"Perhaps, but it would be expensive."

"Kamal, as you know by now, money is not a problem."

By this time, the sheikh was making direct deposits into a numbered account maintained by the PLO. I left that day with the promise he would pour in seven hundred thousand dollars and boarded a flight for Lebanon. Although I had not seen him in nearly two years, I knew I needed to speak with Abu Yousef.

It would have been the perfect time to stop in and see my mother, whom I missed very much. But I had not seen my father since leaving for Saudi Arabia, and I did not want to see him now. As my status with the PLO grew during the war, he had basked in reflected glory, bragging about me to anyone in the neighborhood who would listen. And the more he did that, the more I grew to resent him. My father loved me not for who I was, not because I was his son, but only because I made him look good. So I stayed away.

I met Abu Yousef in his office at Sabra, the same one where he had dressed me up in a scarf and beret so many years before. He grabbed me in a bear hug. *"Yah ibny!"* he cried.

To my eyes, Abu Yousef had not changed, except perhaps for a sprinkling of gray in his moustache. Quickly, we caught up on our personal lives—he had a new grandson, he said—then got to the business at hand.

"I have separate intelligence both from the PLO and the Muslim

Brotherhood that the Syrians have a cache of SA–7 rockets stored in a weapons depot in the northern city of Aleppo, or Halab," Abu Yousef said.

"How many rockets?" I said.

"About three hundred."

Calculating that the sheikh's money would be enough to buy them all, I told Abu Yousef of Sheikh Fahim's gigantic deposit.

He chuckled, shaking his head in a slight reproach. "Kamal, these are Syrians. I would not give a Syrian a *kroosh* for his hummus when I can steal his food from his mouth and pay nothing. The Muslim Brotherhood intelligence was able to provide us the depot hours of operation, the guard shifts, and details on all security procedures. We will save Sheikh Fahim's money for something else."

I laughed along with Abu Yousef at my lapse into thinking ethically about Syrians. It was very good to see him.

2

Stealing SA–7s (we called them SAMs) from Hafez al-Assad would be like stealing rats from the mouth of a cobra. The PLO could have done it alone. But when stealing from a cobra, it is sometimes wise to enlist the help of a crocodile.

I had long known a man named Abu Tawfiq, the bodyguard of the ambassador from Iraq. Abu Tawfiq was famous for saving his boss from at least two assassination attempts, one during the Lebanese civil war. Now his country had a new president, Saddam Hussein, a man who had long supported the Palestinian cause. I arranged a meeting between Abu Tawfiq, Abu Yousef, and myself. That led to a meeting at the Iraqi embassy with the ambassador where we shared the intelligence on the Syrian rockets and posed a question: would Saddam like to help the PLO embarrass al-Assad, his hated rival?

The answer returned to us swiftly: yes.

Saddam, who had since the early 1960s consolidated his power in Iraq, had SAM missiles of his own he could have given to help the Afghans. But he agreed to involve his intelligence forces for the sheer joy of mocking al-Assad.

A week later, posing as tourists, a unit of *fedayeen* rumbled into Syria, through the port city of Tartuse to Halab, in two buses with storage compartments concealed under false floors. Two kinds of conspirators met us in Halab: Saddam's intelligence agents and Syrian soldiers who, as secret members of the Muslim Brotherhood, had agreed to betray al-Assad and admit us to the weapons depot.

When we rolled up to the depot, the Iraqi agents subdued the Syrian guards who were loyal to al-Assad, while pretending to force the Brotherhood Syrians to give the *fedayeen* access to the SA–7s. As we loaded the rockets onto the buses, the Iraqi agents shot and injured the Brotherhood Syrians so that it would appear to al-Assad that they had put up a fight. Then we headed for the Iraqi border with three hundred rockets for the Afghans.

The PLO had not used SAMs before, but the Iraqis had. Once in Iraq, we trained for two days at an air base deep in the scorching desert. On the second day I watched a convoy of military vehicles roar onto a ramp area near a warehouse about one hundred meters away from the range area where we were training. A man wearing a khaki uniform, black beret, and sunglasses alighted from the rear of a Jeep and walked to the edge of the tarmac, an entourage trailing out behind him like ladies-in-waiting. The man in the beret held out his right hand. An aide put a pair of binoculars in it, and the man aimed his eyes at us.

"It is Saddam! He is looking at you!" the Iraqi trainers told us reverently. "Wave at him! Show him you are grateful!"

I had heard stories about Saddam Hussein. That he would toss a man into a torture chamber simply for not smiling correctly. I was not afraid to die, but I did not want to die in Iraq, the prisoner of a sadist. So when Saddam Hussein aimed his binoculars my way, I grinned and waved wildly, jumping up and down like a trained monkey.

Among Muslim warriors, the saying goes, "Me and my brother against my enemy." Saddam was a staunch Sunni brother who hated the Syrians and the Shia as much as we did. Still, on this mission, we knew we were in bed with real evil. Every one of us was glad when we loaded the SAMs on a Saudi cargo ship bound for Pakistan and left the crocodile behind.

3

Five of us went into Afghanistan. One was a Palestinian named Aassun. He was older than I, in his mid-twenties, and very good with explosives. Tall and slim with curly hair bleached gold by the sun, Aassun could also make anything out of anything. He was like an ancestor to the American television character MacGyver. Zeid, a light-skinned Lebanese with blue eyes, was an intellectual who devoured books the way other men eat meals. He understood Islam inside and out and fully embraced *jihad* as the ultimate aim of the teaching of the Koran and the *hadith*. Zeid was from an upper-middle-class family who used some of their money to finance his zealot adventures. His specialty was an ironic sort of factional diplomacy. He knew enough about the quirks of each rebel group to persuade them to lay down their differences—and their guns—long enough to come to the bargaining table. Two other young Lebanese fighters, Samir and Hassan, also went with us.

The Soviets were murdering our brothers and sisters by the thousands. We went to help the *mujahadeen* repel the Communist invaders. But as they say, war makes strange bedfellows. We loved the idea that the hated Americans were on our side in this war, though for different reasons, and that the Saudis, whom we also hated, were financing our operation.

We were not the only Muslim group to lend assistance to the Afghan *mujahadeen*. Hezb-e-Islamie-i-Gulbuddin, a radical Islamist party that recruited from Muslim religious schools, helped the Afghans, bolstered by aid from the United States and Pakistan. Another Islamist group, Jamiat-i-Islami, infiltrated northern Afghanistan from Pakistan. The Islamic Union for the Liberation of Afghanistan, which promoted *jihad* among Arab youth, was funded by Saudi Wahhabists. Abdullah Yusuf Azzam, a radical university professor who had been in Saudi at the same time as I, even issued a *fatwa*, or religious decree: "Defense of the Muslim Lands, the First Obligation after Faith." In this document, Azzam declared that, like the Palestinian struggle I had known all my life, the Afghan rebellion was a *jihad* that required all Muslims to rise up and kill foreign occupiers. Saudi's grand mufti, Abd al-Aziz Bin Bazz, agreed with the edict. Now, my friend Sheikh Fahim had no need to keep his contributions secret.

For us, the PLO, Saddam Hussein, and the Muslim Brotherhood provided logistical aid. The Syrians (against their will, of course) provided our main weapons. And Sheikh Fahim had lined the purse of a rogue Pakistani general named Hafiz, who agreed to provide us with safe passage from the Turbat region of his country through the mountains of Afghanistan.

When our ship pulled in from Iraq, the Pakistani convoy was waiting near the wharf. Using a small forklift, the ship's crew loaded the drab olive crates into a pair of Russian-made trucks—ironic, since we meant to go blow up some Russians. Our convoy of trucks and Jeeps rumbled through the ancient wasteland of Turbat, across the Afghanistan border and up into the arid mountains that would lead us to Kandahar. The climb up the mountain roads was treacherous. The trucks were wide and the trails narrow. Our tires bounced dangerously close to the rim of plunging gorges. Many times, the driver came to a complete stop on a steep grade, shifted into the lowest gear, and still could barely get the truck moving again.

Finally, the skinny roads narrowed to what could be called no more than goat paths. At that point, the Pakistanis handed us off to a band of Pashtuns, the dominant Sunni tribe in Afghanistan. The Pakistanis helped us move the rockets from the trucks to mules the Pashtuns had brought. The Pashtuns were mostly farmers and goatherds, but the Soviets had forced many of them to become guerrillas as well. Still, with their wild beards, flowing pants, and tunics, they looked fierce and had a reputation for being experts with knives.

The Pashtuns had brought with them nearly twenty mules and donkeys, the pack animals they still used to transport fruits, grains, and produce to market. But since the beginning of the war, the tribes had begun using them to carry a different kind of cargo—weapons. Aassun and Zeid climbed into the back of a truck and began cracking open the green crates. Inside were smaller boxes, each containing four rockets. With expert speed, the Pashtuns wrapped each rocket box in thick canvas and secured the bundle with rope. They then placed each box in an empty canvas sack, lashing two sacks to each animal so that they hung down, one on each side, secured across the creature's back by canvas straps. To conceal the swaddled rockets, the tribesmen placed in some of the canvas bags large cloth sacks labeled *roz*—rice. Other bags they stuffed with blankets and hay, feed for the donkeys and mules. All this was designed to fool the Soviets, who often buzzed legitimate mule trains in search of *mujahadeen*.

We were only able to transfer one hundred of the rockets to the pack animals and were forced to leave the rest with the convoy. I went and found the Pakistani captain in charge. "Please remind General Hafiz that Sheikh Fahim will be very keen to see us return with a second load of rockets. Tell him to take good care of the sheikh's property."

As the convoy rumbled away, Aziz, the Pashtun leader, gave us each a set of Afghan clothing: Flowing pants, tied at the waist and gathered at the ankles, that had once been white but had yellowed to ivory and were covered with stains; a same-colored tunic to the knees; a brown woolen vest and a wool cap. They also handed us each a long beige scarf; I noticed some of the Pashtun wore a similar cloth wrapped completely around their face and neck, revealing only their eyes. I wrapped mine in the same fashion and put on my sunglasses to knock out the glare.

The Pashtuns didn't talk much, except to each other in their native Beluchi tongue from which I could catch a sprinkling of Arabic. One of the tribesmen, Rafuq, did speak a little more Arabic than the others so I talked with him about the journey ahead, a four-day trek to our rendezvous with an Afghan warlord named Abu Haifem. As we advanced, I kept a wary eye on the narrow path; if you wavered to the right or the left, you would likely fall into a gorge. Looking below, I could see the thread of a small river or stream snaking through the floor of the abyss.

Down there, green trees and shrubs flanked the water's edge. Where we were, only a bland, endless palette of dirt and stone jutted up into a hard blue sky.

The journey was much worse than I expected and grew worse as we went along. Along the lower trails, the desert sun scorched our skin. As we climbed higher, harsh range winds beat us constantly, carrying so much grit that I felt like I was eating breakfast right from the air, even through the scarf that covered my face. As we tramped along with the pack animals, we dodged steaming piles of dung about every twenty feet.

As we gained elevation, the air turned brutally cold. Near the end of the first day, I began to notice Russian helicopters below our altitude patrolling for *mujahadeen*. On the second day, as we ascended narrow rugged trails, I watched the eastern sky turn a smoky red as a Soviet bomber pummeled an Afghan village.

"Sikhoi," said Aziz, naming the bomber, which appeared as a long silver tube in the distance. "They are like flying death. When the villagers see them coming, there is nothing they can do but hide and pray."

I had heard stories of hundreds of mud-walled huts smashed into jagged ruins, thousands of Muslims killed. I stared out at the fiery horizon. "We are here to change that."

Our rockets represented a chance to liberate the valley villages, temporarily at least, from Soviet air attacks. The villagers were mostly farmers and herders, tied to the land by their crops, their animals, their water supply. Most of the *mujahadeen* were part-time fighters with responsibilities at home. For too long they had had to leave their villages and livelihoods in the care of women, children, and old men in order to escape the Soviets' systematic attempts to purge the villages of rebel fighters. Now, if the *mujahadeen* could control access to the valley with the rockets, they might have time to regroup.

By mid-afternoon, we arrived at a cave system called *al-qa'idah*, or "the base," a *mujahadeen* stronghold secreted deep inside a labyrinth of jagged gorges. Abu Haifem met us at the main entrance and introduced himself.

"Welcome, welcome," he said, greeting us with firm handshakes and a clasping of our wrists that signaled our warrior brotherhood. "Before we go in, I want to tell you that there are rules here. I am the liaison for all things. Anything you want to do, you must go through me."

I nodded my understanding.

Abu Haifem stepped aside so that I could see deeper in the cave. I had expected a primitive setting with a few *mujahadeen*. Instead, I saw a fully operational military base thrumming with the low conversation of at least two hundred warriors.

In one area, I saw stacks of supplies—bags of rice and crates of what appeared to be military food rations. In another corner, two *mujahadeen* guarded an arsenal of AK–47s, RPGs, and an assortment of ammo boxes. I saw a sleeping area and to the left several *mujahadeen* were gathered, each holding a Koran, in a circle with a man who appeared to be an imam.

The biggest surprise: an entire corner devoted to what appeared to be a communications and surveillance station. Radar and radio equipment, and at least six men in Afghan dress and *keffiyeh* who were clearly not Afghans. It was instantly clear that the *mujahadeen* gave that area a wide berth, as if it were surrounded by some kind of force field. Or it might have been the huge, grim-looking man standing at the edge of the equipment holding a grenade-tipped weapon. His forearms were as big as my neck.

Abu Haifem saw me staring. "They are Americans. Don't cross to that side."

Americans. Instantly, I was on guard.

Abu Haifem then led us toward the rear of the cave. Stalactites hung from the ceiling, dripping water into stone pools. When we passed the Americans on the right, I could see that their station was elevated on a kind of natural rock platform. The man guarding it kept a close eye on us as we passed, and I him. These were not regular military. Those I would have faced head on. But not these men. I could tell from the way they held themselves, like tigers coiled to spring, that they were Special Forces of some kind, or perhaps CIA. From the platform, I heard snippets of three languages: English, Arabic, and Russian. In spite of the testosterone of my twenty years, in spite of my time at war in Beirut, in spite of thirteen years of training, I knew instantly I was outmatched. In fact, it was possible these half-dozen men could take on the entire force of *mujahadeen* assembled in the cave. That was the signal they sent off. I could smell it.

Abu Haifem then led us through a passageway to a sandpit, a kind of cave within a cave.

"You can store the rockets here," he said. "I will post guards."

That evening, Aassun, Zeid and I sat with Abu Haifem and made a simple dinner of meat and rice. We gathered around a tiny fire built in a stone pit in the corner of the cave opposite the Americans.

"Tell me about them," I said.

"Advisers," he said. "They arrived a few weeks ago. Strategy, tactics. That is their game."

"And the radar?"

"The Americans monitor the Soviet air traffic. It helps the *mujahadeen* stay clear of Soviet patrols. We can get to and from cover and from our base camps without detection."

By base camps he meant the cave systems. Despite the Soviet's superior technology and firepower, the *mujahadeen* had been able to hide in networks of natural mountain caves, staging small-arms and RPG attacks that bruised the Communist invaders. Some of the caves, such as the one we sat in now, were concealed behind rock formations and intricate gorge systems impassable even to the Soviet helicopters. Further, enough *mujahadeen* lived in the villages to prevent the Soviets from concentrating their forces on extended sieges on the Afghans' mountain positions.

"Who is in charge?" Zeid wanted to know.

Abu Haifem nodded toward the raised rock platform. "See the big man talking on the radio phone? It's him. He calls himself 'Rick.' We call him 'Abu Fox.' "

In the dim light with his face covered, I could not tell much about the man. But when daylight came, I wanted to know who I would be dealing with, which American might have the most influence over what happened to our rockets.

"How will I know this 'Rick' tomorrow?" I said.

Abu Haifem peered at me across the flickering fire. "Look for the man with eyes like ice."

4

I awoke the following day to the distant pounding of Soviet bombs and the low chop of rotor blades bouncing off the mountains as Mi-24 Hind helicopter gunships combed the valley floors for rebels. With their gun pods, rockets, and 100-kilo iron bombs, the Hinds were both fearsome and persistent. Unlike the bombers, which had to frequently return to base to refuel, the Hinds could hunt their prey for hours.

"We move mostly at night," an Afghan fighter named Tariq told us over a breakfast of rice and goat. "The helicopters hunt in pairs and packs. We are sometimes able to bring them down with RPGs. But still, they rain death upon the *mujahadeen* and the villages. We call the choppers *Shaitan-Arba.*"

Satan's Chariots.

That evening near sunset, Abu Haifem rallied a reconnaissance party: my five *fedayeen*, several *mujahadeen*, and four of the Americans, including Abu Fox. The Afghans meant to lead us to an area from which we might launch the SAMs at the Soviets. Range was an issue. The rockets we stole had a maximum range of just over four kilometers—only two miles. To fire at Soviet aircraft, particularly Satan's Chariots, at so close a range—and to miss—would likely mean instant detection and certain death.

Outside the cave, the sky had taken on the colors of fire, but the frigid mountain air bit at my face and hands. Again, we had all dressed in Afghan clothing, every one of us with his face covered. In fact, because of the Americans, I had not uncovered mine since we arrived. I and my *fedayeen* had brought 9 mm handguns with us from Lebanon, but Abu Haifem issued us each an AK–47. I slung mine from my shoulder. Looking around at the recon group, I could see that the *mujahadeen* were similarly armed. Tariq was among them and had brought with him an RPG–7. The Americans also carried various assault rifles and, under their tunics, who knew what else.

As I observed all this, I felt the bore of someone's eyes and looked up to see Rick, the American leader, standing just a couple of meters away, gazing steadily at me over the shield of his white *keffiyeh*. Even at this distance, I could see that his eyes were the crystalline blue of a glacier, rimmed in thick red lashes. Something in his gaze bothered me. It was not aggression or defiance, but more like . . . *knowing*. Knowing more than he should. I held his stare for a moment then glanced away as Abu Haifem gave a signal to move out.

Our trek took us farther along the same goat trail that had deposited us at *al-qa'idah* the night before. I walked with Aassun and Abu Haifem, just behind the Americans. When the rock formations that concealed the main cave gave way to more open space, I saw a vast valley spreading below us, ringed on the opposite side by more jagged and barren mountains that speared the sky, their peaks frosted in snow. I wondered how the *mujahadeen* planned to take us through these trails without exposing us to the Soviets. Their primitive genius soon became clear.

Over the centuries, underground springs and the runoff from melting snow had carved narrow waterways into the mountain stone. Many of these had gone dry or mostly dry and, where the water still ran underground, had developed a sparse cover of desert scrub and bushes. Cleverly, the *mujahadeen* had dug a meter or two deeper into these natural cuts in the earth, creating "grooves"—pathways beneath the foliage under which a man could walk upright without being seen from the air.

"Pathways like this one connect many of our mountain bases," Abu Haifem told us as we entered the first groove under a canopy of wormwood and camel-thorn. "They are almost as good as the U.S. interstate system, yes, Abu Fox?"

The American glanced back over his shoulder, an enigmatic smile in his eyes. "Better," he said.

The man unnerved me. I definitely did not trust him and suspected he wanted to take control of the rockets, or at least control what we did with them. As Redding had demonstrated perfectly, Americans never enter a situation unless they want to be in charge. There was no way I would let this American take charge of us.

Still, his watching manner pricked my curiosity. How did he see us? I wondered. What did he make of this small band of men who came all the way from Lebanon through Pakistan to help the Afghans with rockets stolen from Syria?

For a solid thirty minutes, we walked in the cover of the grooves, the light seeping slowly away. It was not yet full dark when we reached an outcropping from which we could see a wide *madiq*, a mountain pass, at least twenty kilometers away. I saw a dozen helicopters flying through the "V" away from us, insect-small in the distance, backlit by the fiery last light of the day.

"There is a Russian base on the other side of the pass," Abu Haifem said. "The Sikhoi and the choppers—they all come into this valley from that direction. The MiG fighter jets are more unpredictable. They can come from anywhere."

Aassun and Zeid emerged from the groove and joined us, gazing out across the sprawling valley. "The *madiq* is far out of SAM range," Aassun said. "We will have to advance at least fifteen kilometers in the open."

"The Soviets fly in groups," Zeid said. "As soon as they pinpoint our firing position they will kill us."

Abu Fox and his men, along with Tariq and the other *mujahadeen*, joined us at the valley rim. I delivered my battle plan to Abu Haifem. "We will take our *fedayeen*, plus two of your men, and five to seven rockets. The *mujahadeen* can carry a *doctoryov* and RPGs. We will advance outside the grooves toward the *madiq* until we are well inside the SAM range. We will fire on the Soviets, bring down as many aircraft as we can, then fight our way back."

It was a bold plan, and I delivered it proudly, knowing it meant near-certain death for us and whoever went with us. In my view, the Afghans were my Muslim brothers. If this mission was my appointed time to die, so be it.

"That is brilliant," Tariq said. "I will go with you. Who else will come?"

But before anyone could speak, Abu Fox quietly raised his right hand. He then turned to me and dipped his chin slightly, a gesture of respect. "Your plan is a courageous one," he said. "But why do you want to throw a rock at someone who is bigger than you, then run away and hope everything will be alright?"

My skin bristled but I remained silent. *I knew it. I knew he would try to be in control.*

A chill wind ruffled my *keffiyeh* as I wrestled down my pride and resolved to hear this infidel out. I had learned that listening to your adversary gives at least the appearance of wisdom. You can always shoot his ideas full of holes once he has spoken.

Abu Fox smiled at me with his eyes, then laid out a plan in which my *fedayeen* would advance within SAM range as I had suggested, but in two teams—one with two men and one with three, five rockets split between us. Meanwhile, a large *mujahadeen* force would establish three antiaircraft artillery emplacements, setting a multisided trap. This had been tried before and easily defeated by the Soviets, who could simply pick off triple-A gunners from their superior range. But now the *mujahadeen* had rockets. When the Soviets saw their own aircraft tumbling from the sky in flames, Abu Fox theorized, their reaction would be panic.

"The Soviets always come first with helos acting as scouts, taking out any *mujahadeen* that fire on them," he continued. "They believe they know the range of all weapons currently in use by the *mujahadeen*. They believe they can come within three hundred meters without fear and hold an area. This time, we will let them come."

According to Abu Fox's plan, my *fedayeen* would let the choppers pass, allowing them to advance close to the mountains where the *mujahadeen* would lie in wait, holding their fire. While the Soviets grew comfortable that no attack was coming, we would wait for other, larger prey to fly into the valley.

"When the bomber comes, the *fedayeen* will let it advance past the SAM positions, then fire their rockets," the American continued. "Take out the first aircraft in range and the last, then take out one more. The second the helos try to return fire, the *mujahadeen* will hit them with DShKs and Quad 50 to create a diversion allowing the *fedayeen* to withdraw before the Soviets detect their positions."

Abu Fox then turned and addressed me directly. "Again, your plan is very courageous. But let us consider this plan, in which our enemies are the only ones to die."

5

The American's logic hit me in the face like a brick, demolishing everything I had ever learned. It was my first encounter with western military strategy, and I instantly saw a stark difference:

The jihadist thinks "me." A man used to liberty thinks "us."

The jihadist thinks about avenging a village. A man used to liberty thinks about saving a country.

The jihadist counts his own death as a given, even as an integral part of the plan. The western strategist plans to kill the other guy, then go home and smoke a cigar.

I could not argue with this thinking. Still, my testosterone screamed at me to trump the American's plan with a better one. But as Abu Fox regarded me over his *keffiyeh*, I thought for a moment that I saw in his eyes an olive branch.

Using blue flashlights to illuminate the grooves beneath the wormwood, the recon group made its way back to the cave. Night sounds now skittered and whispered along our path. In the distance, the yip and whine of some kind of wild dog. The wind felt pregnant with snow, but I ignored the cold and trudged silently along behind Aassun and Zeid. Alternately, I berated myself for not having topped Abu Fox's plan—and for having shown myself such a small thinker and poor tactician.

Soon, the cave came into view, but as I walked toward it, I felt an arm fall across my shoulder.

"I need to talk to you." It was Abu Fox.

I stiffened, instantly on guard. "What about?"

Aassun and Zeid stopped and turned around, but I could not see their eyes in the thick darkness.

"Let's walk over here," he said, indicating a high stone outcropping that overlooked the valley. "It will be more private."

I stepped away from Abu Fox and toward Aassun, placing my left hand on his left shoulder. "Wait here," I said, hoping he would catch my serious tone even though he could not see my eyes. Then, keeping my right hand poised near my knife sheath, I walked with Abu Fox into the winter darkness.

The American lit our path with a blue beam. We reached the edge of a cliff fortified by tall, vertical rock formations that stood like stone sentinels. Abu Fox stopped abruptly, turned, and sat down on the ground in front of me. It was a gesture of submission and it surprised me. Warily, I lowered myself into a squat—not sitting, ready to spring in any direction. Then Abu Fox surprised me again: he laid the flashlight on the dirt between us, lifted his right hand, and uncovered his face.

In the Muslim world, if a woman unveils her face to a man, it is an invitation to greater intimacy. Among warriors, if a man unveils his face, it is either a step toward mutual trust or he is showing he is not afraid of you.

Which is this?

A sharp wind whistled around the rock formations, blowing Abu Fox's *keffiyeh* forward so that it framed his face. In the blue light, I could not see much except that he wore a moustache and beard—and that he was smiling.

I did not return the favor. "What do you want?"

"How deep are you stuck in all this?" he said.

My mind flipped through possible meanings of *all this*: The Afghans. Armed struggle. *Jihad.* It did not matter; the answer to all was the same.

"All the way," I said.

In the darkness, Abu Fox peered at me for a long moment. "Are you sure about that?"

It was as though this American had somehow seen into my heart to the moments of weakness when I wished I could lay *all this* down. Quickly I looked away at the wind-whipped chasm below us, afraid that if I kept looking at this man, he could somehow pull my secrets out through my eyes.

"There is a life out there for a man like you," the American said. "You are so young. You haven't even tasted life yet. In my country, people like you are highly regarded. You speak many languages, understand many cultures. You bring something that people born in America don't have—something my government would pay well for."

Looking away into the valley, I kept my face perfectly still. But my heart took up a terrible pounding. This infidel was proposing the outrageous, asking me to cross over. I would be an apostate, on every faction's most wanted list. I would lose my home, my country, my safety.

And yet, I was seized by a searing, overwhelming desire to say yes.

It was a secret longing and not just of mine, but of many young Middle Eastern men. To stretch toward freedom, to enjoy life outside the suffocating bondage of government and rules and family taboos. To pursue a career. Learn for learning's sake. Take a woman to dinner.

I had done all these things, but not in pureness of heart. Always with an agenda: my jobs were a front. I learned but only to advance *jihad*. Except for Fatima, I lured women so that I could later use them as party favors. I had been raised to hate America and had hated her all my life. But I had also seen the freedom Americans enjoyed and now burned to taste it.

Abu Fox did not move or speak. If he could see into my mind enough to be so bold, I wondered, could he now see the battle raging inside me?

I opened my mouth to speak, but closed it again as, suddenly, the teaching I was weaned on rose up inside me like a cyclone. The pull of Islam was stronger than my storm of desire, purer than the lure of freedom. Since my boyhood, I had breathed it, drunk it, dreamed it. My faith was all I knew, and I also knew I was naked without it. A hundred *sura* now exploded through my mind, filling every secret niche of doubt, cutting off my shameful desire as though shearing off a rotting limb.

Abruptly, I stood and looked down at Abu Fox. "This conversation is over. I have nothing to say to you."

The American gazed up at me. "I understand," he said, his eyes glinting faintly in the blue light. "Maybe before you leave this place, you'll let me know what you really want in life."

I turned my back on him and walked toward *al-qa'idah*.

6

That night, I lied to my men about Abu Fox, saying the American only wanted to make clear his country's commitment to aiding the *mujahadeen*. If they knew the American sensed in me someone who might be turned, they themselves might begin to doubt me.

The next morning, we gathered in the cave and finalized the plan. The *mujahadeen* would carry the rockets and other weapons in the grooves. From that point on, we would have to carry them by ourselves in the open. Aassun, Samir, Zeid, Hassan, and I would travel by night to set up the rocket positions, guided by an American team who would monitor us with long-range night vision devices and, with their bird's eye view into the valley, guide our progress with voiceless radio signals. Finger-tapping meant "keep moving." Whistling meant "stop." Scratching noises in the transmitter meant "hold your position until advised."

We would make most of the trek to the rocket positions through the night, then stop and make camp, before completing the final leg of the journey before first light. Meanwhile, the *mujahadeen* would receive separate guidance to set up their triple-A positions around the pass. From *al-qa'idah*, the Americans would monitor incoming Soviet aircraft and coordinate the attack by radio.

Our action signals during the attack would be verses recited aloud from the Koran:

> *We made behind them a dam and before them a dam:* Incoming
> aircraft. Stand by.

We have given you the victory: Fire.
He crossed his eyes and retreated: Retreat.

As the day progressed, my anticipation grew. In Lebanon, the swamp of the civil war had obscured my objective—*jihad* and the global advancement of Islam. Here the lines of battle were clear-cut. The Communist infidels were murdering Muslims, marauding over Muslim lands. Despite Abu Fox's western cigar strategy, I was again ready to die. I was not alone. Near sunset, Aassun, Zeid, and our other men gathered in a corner of the cave and we submitted ourselves to Allah. Because the *mujahadeen's* water supply was limited and precious, we performed the ritual cleansing for *al-shaheed,* the martyrs, with sand, as prescribed by Muhammad in the *hadith.* Then we knelt facing east and recited the *salat al-akhra,* the final prayer.

When I finished, I felt again the bore of eyes and glanced up to see Abu Fox atop the radar platform, looking at me and shaking his head.

Soon after, the sun slipped behind the mountains and its light bled away, leaving an indigo twilight. Loaded with five rockets and three launchers, my *fedayeen* and a *mujahadeen* support unit of five men stepped out of *al-qa'idah,* along with two of the Americans. This time, we were dressed in black clothing and *keffiyeh,* the better to melt into the night. An hour later, we had retraced our route through the grooves, emerged beyond their safety, and begun our slow descent into the valley.

Four hours later, we made camp, sleeping in the open, crowded around a mimosa tree. We lit no light or fire of any kind that might give away our position. During the long night, we rotated guard shifts, always with two men staying awake and three men sleeping. Our sleep was interrupted, however: late into the night, *mujahadeen* in the villages set off several explosions—bait for the Soviets to investigate the next day.

Two hours before dawn, we heard finger-tapping on the radio: *Move out.*

Two hours after that, the scratching came: *Stop, this is your position.*

The sun rose, flooding the valley with light. In the distance, beyond the pass, we heard the thudding beat of the Hinds. We lay low, eyes on the pass, until a chopper formation appeared over the peaks on our right, painted in camouflage, bristling with rockets. The Hinds overflew us, sniffing the valley for *mujahadeen.*

The Americans kept absolute radio silence.

Next, a MiG fighter seared in over the mountains and took up a high racetrack pattern, circling like a hawk. Minutes later, the target appeared: a Sikhoi bomber.

The choppers had roamed to the other end of the valley. And now a fire rose inside me, the fire of victory before victory has happened. As I rose from my cover, I felt as if the whole world was watching me, even Allah, cheering me on from *jannah.*

The signal came: *We have given you the victory.*

Adrenaline charged through my veins. I felt as if I alone could cut down an entire Soviet battalion. The Sikhoi flew directly toward me, then banked slightly right, creating a wider target. I shouldered my SAM launcher, took aim, fired, and dove for cover again.

The missile locked instantly onto the Sikhoi's heat. It streaked up through the sky and pierced the plane where its left wing joined the fuselage. The SAM exploded, severing the bomber's wing, launching it up and back, away from the aircraft. The Sikhoi then detonated in a series of rapid booms, fire ripping forward and aft through the fuselage as the bomber continued in forward flight. As I watched, the Sikhoi's right wing spiraled away, then the plane disintegrated, debris bursting out across the valley.

A single Hind helicopter came roaring back, but Aassun rose beside me and blew it out of the sky. From two hundred meters away, Zeid's position, I saw another missile rocket skyward, narrowly missing the circling MiG. Now I heard triple-A fire erupt from *mujahadeen* ground positions, the sound echoing in the gorge like thunder.

As Abu Fox had predicted, the Soviets blazed out of the valley in a hasty retreat. At that sight, my mind and body soared to a place I had never been in my life. It was the highest point of ecstasy, as though I had entered paradise.

7

After we struck the Soviets in Afghanistan, my team withdrew through Pakistan. Sheikh Fahim connected with a powerful sheikh in Kandahar who applied pressure to General Hafiz, the Pakistani general with whom we had left the remaining SAMs, to ensure that the missiles were distributed to the Afghan *mujahadeen*. Sheikh Fahim also sent a private boat to pick us up in Pakistan and carry us back to Iraq, where I caught a flight to London, then to the U.A.E.

During that journey, I had much time to think about what Abu Fox had said. That there was a life in America for someone like me. Many of the *fedayeen*, as well as fighters from other factions, fantasized about going there to wage what we called "cultural *jihad*": converting infidels to Islam while slowly, incrementally changing the institutions of American society—its schools, its laws, the government itself. A lot of university students were already there to begin this *jihad*, but they were not strong or well organized, Sheikh Fahim said. They were not jihadists. Also, they had begun to get soft, taking the Saudi money and buying Mercedeses, women, even their educations. A well-placed gift with this professor or that one, and they had an A in every class. Sheikh Fahim felt I might be able to renew their fire, put them back to work.

I was anxious for the assignment. A lot of jihadists like me, if we did not attach ourselves firmly to a Gaddafi or a Hussein or an Arafat, would likely wind up dead. Sooner or later one of the groups would turn on us like a black widow. To be assassinated was a real possibility. So with the blessing of Sheikh Fahim and other Saudis, I decided to go to America as Abu Fox had suggested—but not to work for her.

Instead, I was going to infiltrate, to poison, to destroy.

Southwestern United States
2008

In February, Zak, Walid, and I were scheduled to speak at a conference on terrorism at the Air Force Academy in Colorado Springs. A week long, the event featured many speakers, as well as guests from universities and think tanks around the world. The conference was supposed to result in a report to Congress recommending next steps in the war on terror.

Two days before the conference, my phone rang. It was Keith, our manager. "Have you heard from Zak?" he said.

"No, not yet. Is he supposed to be back from Finland?"

"On his way. He should have called me from Heathrow, in London."

Since our first meeting, Zak and I had become fast friends. We spoke at least once a week, with my calling him at his home in Canada. My heart had been whispering to my brain to call him, but I had been so busy. Now I called his cell. He was probably still en route from Finland. No answer. Next I called his home. No answer.

I tried each number several times. It was not like Zak not to check in.

That same day, a newspaper called *The Gazette* ran the following headline: "Factious choice in speakers." The article itself began by calling us liars:

The Air Force Academy will host three "former terrorists" as speak-ers Wednesday to the cadet wing, despite warnings that at least one of them has fabricated portions of his past and protests that the pur-pose is to promote Christianity. Critics say the speakers, who have converted to Christianity, were invited to profess evangelical beliefs, inappropriate in a government academic setting.[14]

I was stunned. "Former terrorists"? In quotes? And who among us had fabricated our stories?

The writer went on to quote a member of the Military Religious Free-dom Foundation who, very simply, lied: " 'Despite the speakers' self-described knowledge of radical Islam, the goal of the seminar isn't to enlighten cadets to other belief systems,' said David Antoon, a 1970 academy graduate and a member of a group that has accused the acad-emy of encouraging Christian proselytizing."

In fact, we were going to the Air Force Academy *specifically* to "en-lighten cadets to other belief systems"—the belief systems that had re-sulted in the bombing of the Marine Corps barracks in Beirut, the World Trade Center bombing, the attack on the USS *Cole* in Yemen, 9/11, and more recently, suicide bombings and the daily slaughter of ci-vilian women and children around the world.

We *knew*. We had fought on that side. Now this man, Antoon, sitting in his "safe" country, where since 9/11 federal agencies had halted at least fourteen domestic attacks, pretended to know better than us?

I was incensed. These people did not interview me. They did not in-terview Zak or Walid. I had seen fairer reporting from *al-Jazeera*.

The next morning, early, Keith called me again. "Have you heard from Zak?"

"No. Not a word."

Now my heart was troubled. Could something have happened to him? I thought of his frailty, his diabetes, his heart. Could illness have struck him in Finland? Then a worse thought: What if he had encoun-tered hostility to his message in Europe, where radical Islam is strong?

Again, I tried each number several times, then called Keith. "He could be dead in a hotel room somewhere," Keith said, real concern lacing his voice. Then he echoed my earlier thoughts: "Or someone could have gotten to him."

Keith decided to call Zak's church in Canada. "I'll have them go to his home and check to see if he's there. If he doesn't show up by this afternoon, I'll tell them to call the police and have them break down the door."

The next day, another media attack, this one from the *New York Times*:

> *Muslim organizations objected to the fact that no other perspective about Islam was offered, saying that the three speakers—Mr. Anani, Kamal Saleem and Walid Shoebat—habitually paint Muslims as inherently violent. All were born in the Middle East, but Mr. Saleem and Mr. Shoebat are now American citizens, while Mr. Anani has Canadian citizenship.*
>
> *"Their entire world view is based on the idea that Islam is evil," said Ibrahim Hooper, a spokesman for the Council on Islamic American Relations. "We want to provide a balancing perspective to their hate speech."* [15]

The Council on Islamic American Relations (CAIR) has been linked with terrorists—both by their own words and by federal prosecutors—for years. And the *New York Times*, a respected nationally read newspaper, quotes their spokesman on *our* credibility?

As CAIR noted in its 1996 report, "The Price of Ignorance," the group considers it "hate" when U.S. law enforcement agencies arrest top terrorist officials. CAIR founders Nihad Awad and Omar Ahmad in 1993 reportedly attended a three-day conference aimed at derailing the Olso Peace Accords because of fear the accords would isolate the Islamist Hamas movement. [16] The following year, Nihad Awad declared, "I am in support of the Hamas movement."

In 2007, CAIR was named an "unindicted co-conspirator" in a case that linked the Holy Land Foundation, an Islamic charity, with terror groups. The case ended in a mistrial. But in a federal court filing, prosecutors described CAIR as "having conspired with other affiliates of the

Muslim Brotherhood to support terrorists." To top it off, four CAIR officials have either been convicted of terrorism-related offenses or deported because of terrorist ties.

So when I read in the *New York Times* that CAIR's Ibrahim Hooper accused Zak, Walid, and me of "hate speech," I did not know whether to laugh or run the newspaper through my shredder. Maybe both.

America
1981–1985

1

How can a terrorist penetrate America? What does it take? The answer is simple: it takes a rope from the outside and a rope from the inside. Money and documents are the outside rope. America's own institutions, particularly our universities, are the rope within.

In the 1970s, a new kind of bad guy burst into view: the international terrorist. Wielding a machine gun, his face was sheathed in a black *balaclava*, meant both to conceal his identity and inspire fear. The radical Muslim began to show himself all over the world on a regular basis: Entebbe, Mogadishu, Germany. But in those days, no one thought radical Muslims would come to the United States. It happened while America slept. And it continues today. Muslims crossed the Canadian border, forming a network all the way through the United States. I was one of them. We became termites in the wall of the Great Satan. The wall looked sound from the outside. But inside the wall, funded by the Muslim Brotherhood, the Saudis, and the United Arab Emirates, we ate away at the foundations of this country.

I was twenty-three years old when I arrived here in 1981, bearing a temporary visa I obtained in Abu Dhabi and thirty-five thousand dollars in my bank account, given to me by an Islamist sheikh whom I had introduced to three very accommodating French girls. I remained wired into the Muslim Brotherhood and other groups wielding heavy sticks. I first set up in Wassau, Wisconsin, where I freelanced as I had in Europe, speaking in poor neighborhoods and on university campuses about the virtues of Islam. I also networked quickly with Muslim student groups already established in America, such as the Muslim Students Association (MSA) and the Muslim Arab Youth Association (MAYA). I attended their conferences to hear Islamist speakers exercise their first-amendment right to hate America and the rest of the evil West.

Less than a year later, I moved to a major southern city for one reason only: it was smack in the middle of the Bible belt, the center of Christianity in the United States. If I was going to target America, I thought, I might as well aim at her heart.

The city where I settled already harbored a significant group of young Muslim radicals, already hard at work in an apartment mosque. Several men concentrated on collecting information. Some specialized in "mapping." Where do the Jews live? Put it on a map. Which city officials are Jews? Put them on a map. These brothers also mapped the Muslim community, which was much smaller then than it is today. Another brother worked for the city and was able to get us blueprints of key buildings. We made copies and mailed them to associates in Saudi Arabia and New York.

One of the brothers, Hamza, worked at the DMV and was able to procure names and addresses. He carefully catalogued which Muslims were peaceful and who, therefore, could not be trusted.

Another brother, Hamer, a Saudi from a high family in Riyadh, was a professional student who used his father's money to keep himself constantly enrolled at the city's major state university. Introducing himself around campus as Marco, he affected the image of a friendly, wide-eyed foreigner who found America charming. But behind Hamer's smile lay a calculating mind as sharp as a razor. While I knew him, he finished two degrees, all the while using oil money to buy small grocery stores and gas stations, which we used to launder money made selling illegal cigarettes.

All over the city, then linking up with other cities around the south, we established small sleeper cells in apartment mosques. In addition to the Koran and other religious literature, we kept radical pamphlets published by the Arab student groups, books on *jihad,* and a series of crude VHS tapes that were like a mini video boot camp: lessons on hand-to-hand combat, mixing chemicals, and the proper use and care of the AK–47.

As in Europe, my job was recruitment. When I was not preaching Islam, I affected a Parisian accent, passing myself off as a light-skinned, blue-eyed Frenchman. But while evangelizing, I revealed my Middle Eastern background as I canvassed neighborhoods ripe for a message of power, discipline, and success. I spent my days opening the eyes of many to the glory of Allah and opening the eyes of a select few to the teaching of *jihad.*

It was very easy: all I had to do was knock on doors.

"Hello, I am Kamal Saleem," I would say. "I am just in your neighborhood looking to see who is hungry or has need of financial help."

You would not believe how many people in these Bible belt neighborhoods simply wanted something to eat. Whenever I found such a family, I went to a grocery store and bought big sacks of beans, rice, flour, and canned goods. Then I delivered the food, saying, "This is a gift from Allah. Allah sent me here as a messenger." Most people, especially grateful mothers on welfare and food stamps, thanked me. Some raised a skeptical eyebrow, and some choked back tears. But none of them turned away the food.

I simply blessed them and went on my way. No pressure. But I would visit again.

I knew very well that a mother was the key to a house. The next week, I would show up at her front door with a paper sack brimming with more groceries. Only this time, I tucked in a package of meat. When I put meat in the grocery bags, the American poor loved me.

"A gift from Allah," I explained. "He sent me to bless you."

On the third visit, I would bring a half gallon of milk. Meat and milk, these are the expensive things. And the next time I came, many mothers would welcome me in. These women were not only the key to their own homes, but to whole neighborhoods. By this time, I had served them. I had shown them kindness. And now they wanted to know why.

I remember one woman, Maria. I met her on a day when her baby had had no milk or formula for three days because she had no money to buy any. I rushed to a grocery store nearby and quickly returned with a gallon of milk.

"God bless you!" she said, standing in the doorway, holding her baby girl, a tiny smudge of a child with thick lashes fringing wide, dark eyes. Maria was a tiny Hispanic woman in her twenties with dark hair she wore swept back into a loose ponytail. The baby burrowed and sniffled at her neck. "I have been praying and praying that God would send someone to help us."

"He has sent me to help you," I said.

Behind her I saw a bare floor and a worn sofa. A toddler played on the floor with some kind of wooden dog with wheels instead of legs. "I am a Muslim. Like you, a person of the Book, the Scriptures."

Most of the Hispanics I visited were Catholics, and, I had learned, many of the African Americans came from the Christian denomination called Baptist. My line was, "The Jews and the Christians and the Muslims are all people of the Book. You practice Christianity. I practice Islam."

I knew it wasn't true. I knew Jesus Christ had been a Muslim. All the true prophets were Muslims, but the Christians and Jews, down through history, had perverted the truth on this point. Still, I was practicing *al-toqiah*. It was okay to lie as long as I was lying in order to serve Allah.

Maria invited me in. I sat on the sofa while she stood on the other side of a small counter that formed a tiny eat-in kitchen, pouring some of the fresh milk into a baby bottle.

"What is Islam?" she said.

"It means peace. To come to peace with God." Another lie. "Islam" means "submission."

"You know, we serve the same God," I continued. "It is just that Muslims call him Allah."

Her toddler, a boy of about two, abandoned his toy dog and pulled himself up on my knee. "What does your husband do?" I asked Maria.

"He is a janitor," she said. "He works at the elementary school."

"Ah, a hardworking man," I said. "You would make the perfect Muslim family."

She laughed and emerged from the kitchen holding the bottle in her right hand. In her left arm, the baby whined and reached for it. "Why? Why would we make a good Muslim family?"

"Islam is a religion of discipline," I said. "Already, your husband is working hard to provide for you. Muslim families band together to help each other. For the Muslim, God empowers and makes positive changes in your life. And it's a proven statistic that Muslim children stay out of trouble and do better in school."

I knew no such statistic, but I made it up right on the spot. I was selling Maria what I sold in every house: hope. I sold them a future they could dream about. And I did not tell Maria that if she and her husband converted to Islam, if he so chose, she would become his doormat.

2

Some of the most fruitful neighborhoods were inhabited by poor African Americans. In the South, prejudice was still very much alive. Many of the men were unemployed, living on welfare and food stamps, and they were angry. They felt downtrodden and exploited.

Perfect.

One day in 1983, I drove down to a fringy ghetto neighborhood on the northeastern edge of the city. A mix of businesses and homes lined cracked, narrow streets, with tiny clapboard houses jammed between shabby office buildings and liquor stores offering to cash your government check. Cruising the streets slowly, I saw such a store on a corner, its windows shielded with metal bars. Next to a newspaper stand that was chained to the ground, a black man in his early twenties leaned against the wall, wearing a black stretch cap and trying to smoke a cigarette.

I parked on the street and walked up as if to buy something in the store. The young man attempted a tough stare. Inside, I laughed. *Would he stare that way if he knew who I was?*

I smiled at him and nodded toward the bars on the store windows. "This place looks like a fortress. Are they afraid?"

The tough stare dissolved immediately, replaced by a war-weary look I had often seen among Lebanese civilians. "Yeah. Couple people 'round here like to hit the place when they run short on money."

I looked at the boy's jeans, not washed in a week. Adidas tennis shoes, worn and out of date: Nike was the cool brand now. Only his shirt, a plain yellow T, seemed new. From his clothes and his manner, I suspected this boy was not a criminal, just jobless and lonely.

I took a few steps closer, extending my hand. "My name is Kamal Saleem. It is nice to see a friendly face here."

"Antonio," he said, shaking my hand. "That's some kinda name. Where you from?"

I had perfected the art of finding something in common with those I hoped to convert: poverty, family breakup, illiteracy. I became like a fortune teller, gauging reactions, playing with feelings, finding the "tell" and moving in.

"The Middle East," I said. "From a neighborhood like this one."

In my country, I told him, there were Bedouin tribes who lived in the desert and were even poorer than the people in Antonio's and my neighborhoods.

"The Bedouins have nothing," I said, leaving out the part about the wealthy sheikhs. "But there was one Bedouin boy who rose to become very famous. His mother died, then his father. After that, his grandfather raised him. Then his grandfather died and the boy went to live with his uncle, who had no idea what to do with the boy, who did not even know how to read."

Antonio took a pull on his cigarette. "Yeah, there's a lot of that around here."

"Those aren't really good for you, you know," I said, gesturing toward his smoke.

Antonio looked at me with mild surprise. "Why should you care?"

"This boy I told you about, he grew into a man who cared for a lot of people. After he left his uncle's tent, he lived in a cave and God sent an angel to visit him—Gabriel, the greatest of all angels. And this man, whom no one cared about, God made him a prophet."

I checked Antonio's face. He was listening. A story will do that—hook a person's interest in a way even the best argument cannot.

"Much slavery was taking place in that country," I went on. "The light-skinned people were the wealthy ones, and the dark-skinned people were made slaves. This prophet reached out to people and told them that slavery was wrong."

Another lie. Muhammad himself had slaves.

"As a matter of fact, this prophet's right-hand man was a former slave, a black man named Belal, with a voice so beautiful that the prophet used his own money to free him."

"You keep sayin' 'prophet,' " Antonio said. "This prophet got a name?"

"He was a Muslim prophet and as Muslims, we refer to him as Muhammad. Like Christians and Jews, we are people of the Book. We all worship the same God."

"Then how come I ain't never hearda no Muhammad?"

I allowed my eyes to light up. "Ah, because God is so *wise!* First, he gave us Judaism. You've heard of Moses, right?"

Antonio nodded.

"Then he gave us Christianity. Jesus was the most important prophet."

Antonio dropped his cigarette and ground it out with his shoe. "Yeah, my grandmama try all the time to tell me about Jesus. *Jesus* this and *Jesus* that and *praise Jesus!*" He chuckled and shook his head.

Instantly, I noted that he was not a Christian. This was good. I went for the bullseye: "But when the Christians started killing people all over the world, God got fed up with them. Then he brought Islam, the final religion."

"So what about the Jews and the Christians?" Antonio asked. I sensed he wanted to add, "and my grandma?" but he didn't.

"Allah will have to judge them about what he told them to do. Listen, I am thirsty. Are you?"

I went inside the store and returned with two Pepsis in glass bottles. Antonio and I sat down on the curb side by side, drinking and talking. Now he was asking all kinds of questions, and I knew the hook was in his mouth.

In the days that followed, I gave Antonio "the treatment" I gave every convert. I introduced him to the brothers at the apartment mosque, discreetly slipping in the term *al-mani*, our code for someone who is still on the "other side." No matter how much Jew-mapping and combat tape watching might have been going on in the apartment *before* I walked through the door, this introduction prompted an outpouring of kindness sweet enough to rot teeth.

Because all my new converts were American and had lived all their lives in sin, I did not hit them hard with the rules of Islam. Instead, I directed them little by little—how to pray, how to wash, how to read the Koran.

At first, I saw Antonio every day, always building him up, telling him I was impressed with his progress in the faith. After a couple of weeks, I began teaching a few do's and don'ts of Islam—no ham, no bacon, that sort of thing. But it was still too early for the higher rules: Do not drink alcohol. Do not use your right hand in the bathroom. Do not look upon women. Do not tolerate a disrespectful woman. Do not tolerate your grandma's Christianity.

When I learned Antonio had a girlfriend he was sleeping with, I went to her apartment and, towering over her in her doorway, commanded her to break off the relationship completely. "And if I find out you have been calling him, remember, I know where you live."

Then, to make up for the new lack of sex in his life, I lied to Antonio about how many virgins he would receive in *jannah* for picking up trash at the mosque.

Not every recruit was as easy to harvest as Antonio. But sometimes the difficult ones yielded the sweetest fruit. One evening in 1983, while canvassing city streets, I met a black gang-banger named Solomon. Two-hundred-seventy pounds of solid muscle, he wore a black bandanna like a headband and traveled with a posse. Over a period of months, I learned his reputation as a drug-dealing street king who loved the ladies and ruled his little corner of the city.

Solomon regarded me as a religious man and had apparently told his men not to hassle me when they saw me on the streets. Whenever I ran into Solomon himself, I never failed to invite him to mosque.

Surrounded by his posse, he always listened to my pitch politely, but then laughed it off. "Why would I want Islam, man? I got everything I need. Dope. Money. And all the women I want."

Laughter, high fives all around.

But later that year, Solomon was busted for dealing cocaine after his laughing friends ratted him out to the police. And just like that, prison. No ladies, no money, no dope. But I knew he did not need those things any longer. What Solomon needed now was power. I went to visit him in jail before they shipped him off to the penitentiary.

We sat together in a dirty dayroom at a table topped with chipped orange Formica. "Now you are going to prison," I said. "You are young. You will be fresh meat."

Solomon stuck out his chin and scowled. "I can take care of myself."

"What if I told you I know someone on the inside who can help? Someone who helped me once?"

Then I told Solomon about the Muslim Brotherhood.

At the state prison, the brothers gave Solomon a new name: Mustafa. And when he was released from prison two years later, my cell sent Mustafa to a terror camp in Pakistan.

3

A couple of months after putting Mustafa on a plane, I sped down a main city artery with the wind in my hair and the bright urban sun beaming down through my open T-top. The car, a nearly new red Mazda RX-7 had only a little over three thousand miles on it when I bought it through Muslim connections to an American car theft ring.

After a morning at the apartment mosque, I had stopped off at my own apartment to change clothes. I had just leased the apartment in another area of the city, near a college I wanted to penetrate. I was meeting some Moroccans for an early dinner at a Jordanian restaurant and wanted to make a good impression. Since I was still living out of boxes, I bought a new shirt at Dillards and stopped in at the apartment to put it on. Now, flying south down the expressway, my left hand on the steering wheel, my right hand on the shifter, a sense of blessedness thrummed through my bones. New clothes, hot car, power. I had worked hard in America and made many influential connections. I had a good cover job, women at my whim, and an unending supply of money, all the while advancing the cause of Islam and bringing glory to Allah.

Ahead of me, a black sedan slowed. I downshifted, then nudged the steering wheel left and switched lanes. I hit the accelerator and flashed by the sedan, hugging the grass median strip on my left.

My thoughts drifted back to the Moroccans, a golden opportunity. They were newcomers to the city and, my sources told me, Muslim zealots. I would tell them about the advance of Islam in America. Mentally, I rehearsed the complete speech I had prepared for them. Buy them dinner and the best wine. Hint at the financial backing I could bring. Invite them to join us for prayers. It would be an achievement to add another nation to our growing network. As the RX-7 ate up the black ribbon going south, I mused over my four years here: the Islamic converts I had made, how many I had wooed into the finer parts of the faith, into *jihad* itself. The mapping, the false documents, the money laundering fronts.

And the money—the money. My group had been the conduit for millions of dollars coming into America for the specific purpose of slowly, carefully eating away at America's infidel Zionist faith, preparing it for the Day of Islam.

My heart danced. *Surely, Allah is pleased with me.*

I pressed the accelerator past the forty-mile-per-hour speed limit. I wanted to be a bit early so I could order drinks and hors d'oeuvres before the Moroccans arrived.

On my right I noticed the black sedan again, passing me but drifting left as though the driver did not see me. Then the car veered sharply, sweeping into my path, the driver's-side door no more than ten feet ahead.

I braked hard and steered left. But the road curved to the right and my tire bit the median curb, lifting me up over the grass.

I was airborne.

"Allah!" I cried.

Reflexively, I jammed both feet into the brake pedal. The car landed hard in the grass and spun clockwise. I squeezed the steering wheel in a death grip and watched, amazed, as time seemed to slow down.

Tick: I watched the lane I had just been in spin by—

Tock: Still spinning, now facing the opposite direction—

Tick: My front end pointed at the northbound lanes, sliding toward heavy oncoming traffic—

Tock: A dirt construction site on the far side of the lanes. Hope flickered—if I could just slip through between cars. . . .

My car was pointed southeast when I slid into the northbound lanes and the grille of a trash truck blocked out the sun.

Colorado Springs
2008

The 3 Ex-Terrorists were scheduled to speak together at the Air Force Academy in less than eighteen hours, and Zak had been missing for the better part of two days. As the minutes ticked past, my anxiety notched higher and higher. Most people, when a loved one is missing, reasonably hope for the best and imagine the worst. We had good reasons to feel certain of the worst.

Since Zak had been speaking out against radical Islam, jihadists had set fire to his home and his car, and physically attacked both him and his family.

It was part of the risk we all took, a risk that some Americans threw back in our faces with abandon. The day before the AFA event, *The Gazette* published a second story that attempted to discredit us, this time quoting a college professor who specifically called me a "fraud." Again, the reporter did not bother to ask me my side of the story.

I had just finished reading the story when my phone rang. It was Keith. Zak had called and was okay. "You're not going to believe what happened," Keith told me. Zak had decided to fly straight from London through Chicago to Colorado Springs to meet us for the AFA event, instead of stopping off first at his home in Canada. But at O'Hare, his blood sugar had dropped so low that he nearly fell into a diabetic coma.

Airline personnel were able to retrieve his medication from his bags, but the episode left Zak so weak that it was all he could do to dial the phone to let Keith know where he was.

Relief showered my soul. This frail man had carved a special place in my life. He was a kindred soul, a man who like me had thrown down his arms, a brother who understood me exactly. I did not think I could bear it if he were harmed.

The next morning, Walid, Zak, Keith, and I rendezvoused at a hotel in Colorado Springs. By then we had a new problem: During the night, someone had broken through the tinted rear window of Keith's rented SUV and snatched Zak's luggage. In a packed hotel parking lot, it was the only vehicle touched.

We did not have time to contemplate whether this was a crime of opportunity or Zak was the specific target: We were scheduled to do an interview on a local CBS morning show. Keith quickly arranged alternate transportation, and we crowded in for the ride to the television studio. Zak was forced to wear the rumpled suit he'd been flying in for two days.

We passed quickly through makeup and waited only moments in the green room until a production assistant ushered us before the cameras and hot lights of the set. The female host ran through introductions, then asked, "How are terrorists getting into the United States?"

I am so glad you asked that question, I thought.

"Jihadists today do not have to import terrorists," I said. "The majority of the jihadists in the United States are recruited here from poor neighborhoods, universities, and jails. The Muslim Students Association and other groups operate in hundreds of colleges and universities in the United States. Their members are not all radicals, but the radicals among them are busy recruiting new members."

We'd entered the CBS studio before sunrise. After the interview, we stepped out into chilly sunshine. Less than thirty minutes later, we arrived at the Air Force Academy. Pine-covered foothills sloped up into higher peaks capped in blankets of snow. Military police had configured the academy entrances for heightened security, with concrete barriers forming an S-shaped gauntlet meant to frustrate would-be car bombers. We snaked through with the rest of the traffic. At the guard house, armed MPs arranged for a public affairs officer to escort us into the heart of the institution.

Our first stop was a briefing room where a general laid out the ground rules for our talk. We were prohibited, he said, from talking about Christianity and party politics.

I asked a question. "Can I talk about how I came to leave *jihad?* That story involves my conversion from Islam to Christianity."

"I don't have a problem with you telling your own personal story," the general said. It was proselytizing he didn't want.

Which was fine with us, because that's not what we wanted either. We only wanted to warn Americans that vipers were living among them—and that the vipers were laughing.

America
1985

1

As the image of the truck grille filled my window, events sped up, then flashed past like scenes in a movie trailer: the truck's right headlight exploded through my passenger window, showering me with glass. My body slammed up and forward, tearing the seatbelt loose. The impact ejected me from my seat even as the truck still pushed the RX-7 north. My ribs, then thighs, then knees, ripped over the steering wheel as I catapulted up through the open T-top.

I don't remember flying through the air. I only remember plunging head first into a mud hole, the weight of my body hammering my head into the ground like the point of a stake. Pain slashed into my neck. Then, like the falling tower, my body arced all the way over and my back smashed on the ground. Bright flecks of light swam in my vision, but I did not lose consciousness.

I tried to get up, but could not move.

Allah, where are you!

From my bizarre position, I could see legs running toward me.

Allah, I have done mighty things for you! Do not abandon me now!

One set of legs turned into a face as a man in a blue T-shirt knelt beside me, using his body to shield my face from the sun.

"Everything is going to be all right," the man said in a gentle southern accent, his blond hair backlit by the sun. "We're going to take care of you."

Through bleary eyes, I saw that the man's eyes were the bright blue of an autumn sky. He smiled at me. Angry at my own helplessness, I wanted to hit him.

Then a crushing thought: *the Moroccans! I have lost the Moroccans.*

I would not have another chance to impress them. My neck was probably broken, but I was more concerned about losing the opportunity to add zealots to our network.

The man with the gentle voice continued to annoy me with his irritating smile. "My name is Brian," he said.

Again, I tried to pull away, but pain pierced my neck like stabs from a dagger. I found I could not move my extremities at all. Fear roared in like a dragon, fear such as I had not known since the Golan Heights. Brian must have sensed my distress because he said, "Don't try to move. Somebody's already called an ambulance. We don't want to move you because you might have a neck injury. Everything's going to be all right. We're going to take care of you."

Silently, I vowed to break *his* neck if he said that again. Mud crept into the corner of my eye, stinging, blurring my vision. Instantly, the man stood, stripped off his T-shirt and knelt to clean my face with it. The dagger sawing into my neck now sprouted a second blade and attacked my brain. Blood thumped in my ears, and the drumbeat was excruciating, maddening. Slowly I realized I could no longer feel my arms and legs. What could I have done to make Allah so angry with me?

I am your great warrior! I have done mighty works for you!

Dimly, as I heard the high, faint thread of a siren somewhere far away, I began to whisper the sacred writings: "In the name of Allah, Most Gracious, Most Merciful, have we not expanded thee thy breast and removed from thy burden they which did gall thy back? And raised high the esteem in which Thou art held? So, verily, with every difficulty, there is relief."

Allah! Where is my relief?

My memories of the next hour are like a packet of snapshots tossed one by one on a tabletop:

... An ambulance ride, some medication for pain

... Questions, questions: "Do you know your name? Do you know what day it is?

... Are you allergic to any medications? Do you have any metal plates in your body?

... The squeak of gurney wheels rolling into an emergency room

... Bright lights, strange faces, the smell of alcohol

My first clear memory is of a dark-haired physician with a widow's peak and a face that appeared to be smiling even when he was not. "I'm Dr. David," he said. "I'm an orthopedic surgeon. The ambulance atten- dants tell me you're a Frenchman? Do you speak English?"

Looking up at him, I nodded.

Only yes or no answers. Don't give too much information.

"You've got some pretty significant injuries here, but it doesn't look like anything life-threatening," Dr. David said. "Is there anyone we should notify? Any family? Friends?"

I could not give out the names or telephone numbers of my brothers. Many were in the country illegally. What if the hospital sent the police to the apartment mosque? The videotapes and literature alone were enough to tell our story.

I shook my head: *No. There is no one to call.*

"And I see here that you don't carry health insurance," the doctor said, tapping a clipboard. Then he looked up at me and smiled. "That's okay. Everything's going to be all right. We're going to take care of you."

Exactly what the irritating blue-eyed man had said at the scene of my accident. What was *wrong* with these idiots? Everything was *not* going to be all right. I could not move my legs or arms. The pain medication had only slightly dulled the searing pain in my neck. And now my head continued its violent throbbing, the pressure in my skull so intense it squeezed water out of my eyes.

On the ceiling, long, white fluorescent lights marched away like high- way stripes leading toward some hated destination. Suddenly, they grew unbearably bright.

"My head," I whispered, and I saw a nurse with teddy bears on her shirt coming toward me with a needle.

2

My eyes flickered open in a dim room, and for a moment I could not get my bearings. But as my head cleared, images of the accident, the ambulance, the emergency room came flooding back. I did not move, but slid my eyes slowly left, then right.

I am alone.

Looking toward the foot of the bed, I could see that most of my body was immobilized, my legs and hips strapped to some kind of boards. Even on the battlefields, I had never been this helpless. Even when Abu Zayed shot me, I got up and limped away.

Allah, why have you allowed me now to be at the mercy of infidels!

I heard the whisper of a door opening, footsteps, and a cheery voice: "Ah, good to see you've rejoined the land of the living!"

I turned my head slightly to the right and saw a white-coated man smiling down at me. "I'm Dr. James, head of physical therapy. How are you feeling this morning?"

I'm lying in a hospital unable to move. How do you think I'm feeling?

"A little pain," I said.

"A little, huh? Well, I'd say that's good news considering what you've been through." He moved to the foot of my bed, retrieved the chart, and returned to stand by my head. "Mind if I raise your bed a bit so we can chat?"

I shook my head, and a moment later a buzzing set in as the top half of the bed rose to a slight angle.

"I just want to let you know what's going on, what the prognosis is," Dr. James said, his face full of calm assurance. "You have chipped posterior fractures of the C-5 and C-6 cervical spine. In English, that means you broke a couple of vertebrae in your neck. But not badly, nothing permanently debilitating."

Dr. James reviewed my chart aloud: referred pain through the right arm and hand with numbness radiating out into the right thumb. Severe contusion of the right shoulder, limited movement of the right arm. Similar symptoms in the left arm. Lower extremity pain, respiratory difficulty, blurred vision in both eyes.

"None of these things are life-threatening, but I'll tell you what, to look at you, looks like you've been through a war." Dr. James ended with a chuckle. "Do you have any questions?"

"No."

"Okay, then, not to worry," he said with a smile. "Everything's going to be all right. We're going to take care of you."

What?

Brian, Dr. David, now this man. They were all saying the exact same words. Like a chant, a spell, an evil mantra. I began to seriously wonder if the *jin,* the demons of *Gahenna,* were alive in these smiling infidels, conspiring against me.

Later that morning, Dr. David stopped in. "Are you sure there's no one we can call?" he said.

"No. No one," I said, pouring on the Parisian. "My family lives in France."

On my fifth day in the ward, the door opened and in walked Brian, the blue-eyed man from the accident scene, arms full, smiling his infernal smile. "Hey, Kamal. How're you feeling?"

He spoke as though we were old friends. I wanted to rip his throat out.

Wearing a brown blazer over a blue polo shirt, Brian crossed the room and unloaded his cargo of cut flowers, mixed nuts, and homemade cookies in an orange-lidded Tupperware container.

The door opened again, Dr. David walked in, and a smile lit his face. "Well, good morning, Brian. What are you doing here?"

"Me? What are *you* doing here, John?" Then Brian gestured toward me. "This is the man I was telling you about, the one I helped at the accident."

"You're kidding," Dr. David said, wrapping Brian in a back-slapping hug. "This is the man I told *you* about, the Frenchman."

Oh, no, I thought. *Born-again Christians. Only foo-foo Christian men hug each other like that.*

The door opened again and in walked Dr. James. "Well, hey Brian, what in the world are you doing here?"

Brian jerked his head at Dr. David and laughed. "Mark!" he said, walking and embracing the doctor. "Dr. David and I just had the same conversation. Kamal, here, is the guy I was telling you about, the one from the wreck."

Dr. James chuckled. "Wait a minute. I told you about him first, at my house the other night, remember?"

What is this, a competition?

Brian and the two doctors chatted quietly a while longer, completely ignoring me. Now my radar was on full alert. All *three* of these men had been telling each other about me? Why? What did they know? Who else was at Dr. James' house during this conversation? Police?

Suddenly, the conversation stopped and all three men approached my bedside. Dr. David spoke first. "Listen, Kamal, here's the problem. Your medical bills are already very high. Between the ambulance run, the emergency room, and the medication, plus five days laid up in this room, you're already in the high five-figure range. Problem is, you don't have any health insurance, and if you stay here much longer, the folks down in billing are going to be after you for the rest of your natural-born life."

I thought of home, Lebanon. There, if you did not pay your medical bills, they sent you to a free hospital known for its butchery. I did not want to go to a place like that. And if the Americans came after me for money, if they got the authorities involved—lawyers, courts—what would they find? A bank account that grew fat then thin then fat again with large cash deposits, while I worked only odd jobs? Would the network be discovered? My American residency revoked?

What about the sheikh? I could call Sheikh Fahim. My bills would be nothing to him.

These thoughts flashed through my mind in seconds as Dr. David continued: "At this point, the reality is you're in the mending stage.

There's nothing wrong with you that time won't heal. But you don't need to be lying here in the hospital racking up more bills day by day. On the other hand, you don't have anyone—any friends or family—who can take you home to recover. And in your condition, you certainly can't take care of yourself."

He was right about that. No one in my network would be able to stay with me twenty-four hours a day, seven days a week for what could be months.

Now Dr. David paused and glanced at the other two men, who both nodded their encouragement. "So here's what we're thinking," Dr. David said. "My wife, Theresa, is a registered nurse, but she's a stay-at-home mom right now. She and I would like to open our home to you. We have a comfortable room you could have to yourself."

Instantly, I was suspicious. I felt my eyes narrow to slits.

Dr. David saw my expression, but plunged on. "Theresa could take care of you during the day. I could do regular ortho exams right there at the house, free of charge, even drive you back here for your follow-ups. None of this would cost you a dime."

Now Smiling Brian piped up. "And the three of us also know some folks who just might be able to help you out with your medical bills.

Why? Why would they do this?

When Dr. James spoke next, it was as if he had read my mind. "Kamal, there's no catch here. No catch at all. We just want to show you the love of God."

3

John and Theresa David lived in the middle of a pine forest. A long driveway led through a stand of fir and spruce to a grand brick house with high windows of leaded glass and fancy double doors with brass ornaments.

I had considered the Davids' offer and my alternatives. The medical bills would not be a problem; I was certain Sheikh Fahim would take care of them. But that would require getting alone with a telephone and explaining a long distance call to Saudi Arabia. This would also mean revealing my connection to that country. And even if the sheikh were to send the funds, I could not get out of bed to make the deposit, which would mean one of the brothers would have to do it. And I was not about to reveal Sheikh Fahim as my golden goose.

Looking back, I realize that my own ignorance of American health-care and finance finally pushed me to the Davids' house. I did not know Americans often take months or even years to pay off their medical bills and that hospitals cannot do much about it. I also did not know that hospitals are required to render care even if a person cannot pay. I thought if I did not cough up seventy or eighty thousand dollars imme-diately, the bill collectors would pounce on my head, bringing the au-thorities with them.

But even beyond the money, I realized with a sudden pang how alone I really was. Dr. David was right: I had no one to take care of me. I thought of my mother, my sisters, how they would fuss over me if they could see me broken this way. My heart squeezed tight in my chest. The truth was, I had many "brothers" in *jihad*, but no friends. To make a friend would mean letting someone get close, and I had learned long before that close friends die. They also provide a way for the authorities to trace you.

And so, I accepted the Davids' offer.

If these Christians want to be fools, let them, I thought, lying in the hospital room the night Dr. David had offered his hospitality. *I will take advantage of their generosity. Then, when I can walk again, I will disap-pear into the night.*

That had been two days before. Now, Dr. David guided my wheel-chair up his front walk, flipped an expert reverse, then gently rolled me up the front steps, one at a time. Inside his spacious home, he intro-duced me to his wife, Theresa, a strawberry blond dynamo who imme-diately began to chatter as if she had known me since nursery school.

"Kamal, I have been looking *so* forward to having you here," she said, laying her hand on my arm. "You are absolutely welcome to anything in our home. And I am going to be right here to help you with anything you need."

The first thing I need, infidel woman, is for you to stop touching me, I thought. *Then: stop talking.*

But outside, I offered a pained smile. If I was going to go through with this, I had to pretend to be grateful—at least long enough to make my escape.

Dr. David wheeled me into a downstairs bedroom large enough to please a Saudi prince, and with four tall windows looking into the pine forest. A four-poster bed dressed in lacy white quilts dominated the center of the room. There were enough foo-foo pillows on it to please a queen.

Theresa saw me staring. "There's a feather bed on top of the regular mattress. And the pillows are down-filled. Very comfortable. But if you would prefer foam pillows, I can get you some of those, no trouble. No trouble at all. Whatever you need, just say the word."

I began to suspect that if this woman took a breath, she could talk for thirty minutes before taking another. I was now certain I had somehow angered Allah and he had sent this woman to torment me.

At that moment, Allah sent more torment: Three young children, two boys and a girl, swept into the room like tiny tornadoes.

"Kamal, these are our kids," Theresa said. "Elizabeth, Jacob, and Caleb."

Elizabeth, about six years old, was a carbon copy of her mother, strawberry blond with bright blue eyes. Jacob, about eight, had the same blue eyes and white-blond hair, while his brother Caleb, about two years older, had his father's dark coloring.

"Hi, Uncle Kamal!" Elizabeth squeaked.

Uncle Kamal? Allah, help me!

Together, the doctor and his nurse-wife helped me into the bed. I sank into the feathery top and decided instantly that it was the softest, most comfortable spot I had ever laid in my life. Inexplicably, a sense of peace and security settled over me, followed immediately by a wave of guilt.

No! I would not be seduced and defiled by these people. Their kindness was a means to an end. Nothing more.

"Kids, you keep Uncle Kamal company while we run and get him some dinner," Dr. David said. Then he and Theresa disappeared through the bedroom door. Like troopers mounting an island invasion, the three children hopped up on the bed, bouncing on their knees, Elizabeth and Caleb on my left side and Jacob on my right.

"Uncle Kamal! Uncle Kamal!" they sang in unison.

Can you not see I am injured?

I did not want the Davids to hear me being unkind to their children, but this I could not tolerate. "I am *not* your uncle!" I whisper-shouted, stealing glances at the bedroom door.

The children ignored me, bouncing softly, chanting, "Uncle Kamal! Uncle Kamal!"

"Stop calling me that! Get off the bed, you monkeys!"

"Look at all his *Band-Aids*," Elizabeth said to Caleb, wide-eyed. "I never saw that many Band-Aids before."

"I *know*," Jacob said. "Let's pray for him!"

And with that, all three children reached for me.

I froze, stiff as a fallen tree. Glancing down, I saw their six tiny hands, pale as snowflakes, lying against my broken body. And all three children bowed their heads, closed their eyes, and began to pray that Uncle Kamal would be healed.

I was *livid*. Like a volcano on the verge. But I could not move from under the hands of these tiny infidels praying to their Christian god.

"Stop it!" I whispered. "Stop it!"

But they did not stop. I looked at Elizabeth's face and saw a tiny smile. She seemed in rapture, floating off to her alien heaven to make an inquiry on my behalf. Jacob and Caleb had their eyes screwed shut, and their lips moved earnestly, fervently. And without warning, a word filtered through my anger like springwater through cracks in a stone wall: purity.

I flashed back to the rooftop prayer of my childhood when I had come naked before Allah under the tea saucer stars, petitioning heaven with my whole heart. A child's heart. A heart without vanity. Without treachery or deceit. A heart that wanted only to please the object of my worship.

In these children's faces, I saw that boy I used to be and, for a moment, mourned. That boy was gone. The man who had replaced him was trained only to deceive, to fight, to kill. But now, through the hands of the innocent, a force washed over me that I had not been trained to resist: love. This love was huge and overpowering, but it did not require of me my blood or my strength or my hatred. It required only my surrender.

And from the mouths of these little children, I heard that this love had a name: Jesus.

4

When I accepted the Davids' invitation, I expected their house to be crawling with the spirit of the *jin*. I pictured myself lying in some kind of sickroom, tolerating their kindness and warding off their darkness while counting the days until I could return to my brothers. But from that first day, the Davids' house seemed full of light. Not a light I could see, but a light I could feel.

I did not like it at all.

The children's prayer had only hit me at a weak moment, I reasoned. My body was broken; perhaps my spirit had sustained damage as well. Besides, they were cute kids. Anyone can be lulled by cuteness, which is why jihadists sometimes used children to carry bombs.

Then the Davids hit me with another weapon: Southern hospitality. Theresa cooked like a woman possessed by Betty Crocker's ghost. Everything from stroganoff to exotic goulashes to fried chicken with mashed potatoes and gravy. Theresa and the kids served me three meals a day in bed. I had not eaten so well since my mother's *yaknah*.

After a couple of weeks, I was able to sit comfortably in my wheelchair without putting too much strain on my neck. Many evenings Theresa or Dr. David would wheel me into the living room and the whole family would sit down to watch TV. The room was huge, but warm, with a big stone fireplace and a grand piano, which little Elizabeth could already play. I listened as the family talked about family things. Jacob was a champion swimmer in his age group, so there were lots of ribbons and trophies to discuss. Caleb was a ball-sport man—soccer, baseball— and there in the living room, the family relived the best moments of his games.

All the while, I watched them, calculating. And I became very confused. All my life, I had been taught that Christians were thieving dogs. But these people had not stolen from me; they had taken me in and cared for me. I had taken people in, too. Hundreds of people like Antonio. But I had lied to them in order to win them to Islam and with an agenda to turn them against their own people, even their own families.

Sitting in the Davids' living room night after night, I questioned for the first time in my life the teaching I heard sitting at my mother's kitchen table, and at *Masjid al Bakar* at the feet of Abdul Rahman. This Christian family did not match the picture my childhood tutors had painted of sinners and whoremongers, of greedy zealots interested only in the conquest of Muslim lands. Instead, they became a living testimony, people who loved to laugh, who cried at sad movies, who were goodhearted enough to risk everything they had to help a stranger. In fact, the more I was with the Davids, the more I came to see that Abdul Rahman and Abu Yousef fit the enemy image burned in my brain more than did these people did.

If that weren't enough, once a week a group of about forty men came to the house for a meeting. It was a chapter of a larger group, Dr. David told me, called Christian Businessmen. I was invited to sit in on some of the meetings. The men talked about their business successes and struggles, offering each other tips and strate-gies. At the end of each meeting, they always spent a lengthy time praying for one another. And each time I joined the meeting, they prayed for me.

These men actually stood, joined hands, and gathered around me in a circle. I wanted to believe that they were sincere. But that would go against every teaching held dear, everything I believed to be true about this life and the next.

Do you not know I hate everything about you? my heart screamed reflexively. *Do you not know that I especially hate it when you smile at the name of Christ?*

As they prayed that my neck would be healed, I prayed silent curses upon them. It was what I had done all my life. It was the very *purpose* of my life.

But lying in the high four-poster bed at night, I thought of the prayer meetings I had attended at radical mosques around the world. We never prayed that our enemies would be healed. We cried out to Allah to hand us victory over them, that he would give us their land, their wealth, their women. At Sabra and in other camps, we cursed the Jews, the Christians, and the Americans, and prayed fervently that Allah would allow us to cover our hands in their very blood.

But these Christian men did not care whether I was from Tanzania or India or Boise. And never once did they try to force their religion on me, as I had forced mine on others, sometimes at the point of a gun.

They never said, "You are Muslim. You are a foreigner. You are different from us and don't deserve to live." Instead, every time they came to visit, each one of them wrote a check or left an envelope with cash. And within three months, my medical bill was completely paid. I did not understand any of this. I could not make these contradictions add up in my mind.

Colorado Springs
2008

The Air Force Academy lecture hall was a huge amphitheater with seats rising in semicircular rows from a ground-level stage. The room was modern, with booths for electronics and projection equipment near the top rows of seats. I did not know it then, but organizers had switched the venue at the last minute to ensure better security. As conference attendees filed in and filled in the rows, I noticed at least a dozen armed guards posted along the outermost walls, and at intervals along the steps that led from the bottom to the top of the hall. Some wore handguns in holsters; others carried rifles.

Zak was scheduled to speak first. But he was so weakened by his diabetic episode the day before that his knees buckled twice on the way to the podium. During his talk, he gripped its edges to support himself and kept cutting glances my way. His hooded eyes transmitted to me a clear message: *I am not going to last long up here.*

It was true. Fifteen minutes into his talk, he thanked the audience for their attention and shuffled off the stage. Now it was my turn. As I took the podium to polite applause, I looked up into the auditorium. Uniformed cadets and officers filled most of the seats. Sprinkled in between were international guests—students from overseas universities, including schools in the Middle East.

The night before, I had stayed up until 1 A.M. going over my speech. I wanted to make clear to the audience how a boy could be raised a killer. I wanted to share some of the things my mother had taught me, like the time she told me, "If you kill a Jew, your right hand will light up before the throne of Allah, and you will go straight to heaven."

Also, she taught me that to kill a Christian you must have a reason. "If he spits on your hand, you can retaliate," she said. "Kill him in self-defense. But for a Jew, you do not need a reason. That he is a Jew is enough."

When your mother loves and cares for you, when she is hardworking and devout, when the people in the neighborhood straighten up in her presence, then you believe whatever she teaches you in the family kitchen. I never doubted her. Not once.

The night before the AFA event, these scenes replayed themselves in my mind, accompanied as always by the ghost-senses, the smell of baking baklava, the scent of olive oil, the sound of the berry tree scratching on the window.

Now I took the podium and began to tell my story. *My* story. Not the false one that the newspapers had attributed to me.

I told of growing up in Lebanon, tutored in the ways of *al-shaheed,* the martyrs for Allah . . .

. . . of dreaming at age six that I caused Allah, a rigid, stone-faced god, to laugh with delight as I lopped off the heads of infidels with my mighty sword . . .

. . . of being recruited by the Muslim Brotherhood and introduced to the PLO at age seven . . .

. . . of carrying small arms and ammunition into Israel, carrying a knapsack and disguised as a Bedouin boy . . .

. . . of undertaking a life whose central pulse was the hatred of Jews and Americans . . .

. . . of coming to America to destroy her from the inside out.

"I loved Allah with all my heart," I told the AFA audience.

I shared from the Koran the *sura* that says that if Muslims refuse the call of *jihad,* Allah will replace them with better Muslims; and another *sura* in which even the stones and trees say, "There is a Jew behind me. Come and kill him!"

During my talks, I always watch my audience. I can tell immediately who is with me and who is not. At the academy that day, I heard whispering from the gallery. Low in the amphitheater, I saw two Middle Eastern men, and next to them, two women who could have been Middle Eastern, but might also have been Pakistani. All four glared at me and whispered loudly among themselves. High in the amphitheater, I saw two slim blond men dressed in civilian clothes. They were doing the same thing.

I pressed on: "At the assault camp, I learned to hate the Great Satan. The PLO showed us propaganda movies in which Christians and Jews acquired Muslim blood to use in their religious ceremonies. These films told us that the Americans were poisoning our water and air in order to destroy our world. We watched sex movies and were told these were made by the Americans and Hollywood Jews to corrupt the holiness of Islam, to take our women, and to introduce into our world every kind of evil."

The Middle Eastern group began shaking their heads. Their whispering grew louder.

"We sang hate songs calling for the destruction of the infidels. Part of the lyrics talked about building a ladder to glory out of the skulls of Americans and Jews," I continued. "And every Friday at the noon prayers, we cast violent curses against America, her leaders, and their seed and called for the spilling of their blood, that they would die by the sword."

The hall became quiet as now it seemed that even my critics were in shock at what I was sharing. I told them how groups like the Islamic Thinkers Society, which has some common ideology with al-Qaeda, supported *al-Muhajiroun*, demonstrated on a New York street corner in exercise of their "free-speech rights." While stomping on and tearing up an American flag, they publicly laughed at Americans for being stupid while they used their constitutional rights to argue that the Constitution should be replaced with Sharia law and the country ruled by a new Islamic caliphate.

I told them how Omar Ahmad, founder of the "moderate" Council on American-Islamic Relations (CAIR) said, "Islam isn't in America to be equal to any other faith . . . [but] should be the highest authority in America, and Islam the only accepted religion on earth."

I heard whispering again and looked up to see the blond men with their heads together. Glancing to my right, I saw an MP staring hard at them.

Next, I shared how I came to America and preyed on the weak and the poor, speaking in various mosques and universities, raising funds for the cause of *jihad*. And then I spoke more from the Koran itself, the holy book where I learned my deadly philosophy:

Sura 2:191—"Kill the disbelievers wherever you find them."
Sura 9:123—"Murder them and treat them harshly."
Sura 9:5—"Fight and slay the pagans, seize them, harass them,
 and lie in wait for them with every trick."
Sura 8:12—"I will cast terror into the hearts of those who disbe-
 lieve. Therefore strike off their heads."

Now I addressed the audience with force: "Wake up, America! You must arise! You must wake up to the issue of radical terrorism."

A brief shower of applause rolled over the whispering like a wave.

"In the mid-1980s," I continued, "I had an accident and met three American men who loved me and showed me kindness that completely changed my life. Today, I wish to expose the hatred and evil from which I came so that I can make Americans and the West truly understand the threats that face our great nation and the free world. When Walid, Zak, and I believed and fought for Islamic fundamentalism, we were willing to die for the prize of *jihad*. Today, we come with a new truth. Now we love this country and live for her, standing and fighting for America as Americans."

We ate a buffet-style lunch with the cadets that day, served in an-other building a short walk from the auditorium. Afterward, I walked back through an open breezeway with Zak, the chilly sunshine pushing against the edge of the shade. The walkway was filled with conference attendees headed back to hear the next speaker, who was scheduled to begin in minutes.

Even in the throng, I could feel someone crowding me from be-hind. Then a man was at my right ear, his left shoulder pressing into my right one.

"Hello." His breath was on my neck. Cadets and officers pushed past us.

I turned slightly to see an unsmiling face.

His eyes, I thought. *Palestinian.*

"You call yourselves Arabs," the man said. "Then you must speak Arabic."

On my left, Zak laughed. "Of course, we speak Arabic. What are you saying?"

We continued walking, approaching the stairs leading down into the hall. The man kept his shoulder pressing into mine.

He spoke again, his words now in Arabic, clipped and low. "I disagree with everything you are saying. Everything you said is a lie."

I opened my mouth to speak, but he cut me off.

"You insult Islam and you mock Muhammad. You are the enemy of Islam."

Zak had already started down the stairs. I stopped and turned to this man, the crowd surging past us.

"Can I speak to you?" I asked him.

"No, you have already said enough," he replied in Arabic. Then he lowered his voice.

"People like you should be killed," he said.

America
1985–1991

1

In the Davids' living room, I began to accept that what I had learned about Christians and Americans was a lie. And if that was a lie, founded in the teachings of radical Islam, what else had I learned that was untrue? I had devoted my life to Allah, spilled my blood for him, killed for him.

After I left the Davids' house, a spiritual earthquake shook the depths of my soul. It was like the collapsing hotel roof times one thousand, the walls and ceilings of my faith crashing down on my head.

I wanted with every particle of my soul to believe Islam. I did not want to believe that I had committed my whole life to a lie. That I had *killed* for a lie.

In my apartment, there was a place I prayed, a window facing east. One morning not long after I moved out of the Davids' house, I fell on my knees there, the sun streaming onto my face.

My heart desperate within me, I raised my hands to heaven and cried out, "Allah, my Lord and my King! Why did you allow such a thing to happen to me? Why did you put me in the hands of those Christian people?" I do not remember the exact words of my prayer, but they poured out of me in a torrent of confusion. The Davids and their friends did not seem to be the evil people I had always hated. They were people who call on their God and received what they prayed for. They prayed for healing and received healing. They prayed for answers and received answers. "They hear their God speak," I cried. "I want to have a relationship like that with you."

But the room rang with silence.

Dimly, I was aware of the thick layer of dust that coated every surface of the apartment, the result of many weeks of neglect. The sun beat on me through the eastern window.

"I want to hear your voice!" I cried. "Allah, I want to hear that you *love* me. If you are real, *speak* to me."

I poured all my hope and faith into my prayer. But there was only silence. Stillness. Not one dust particle moved.

A deep sadness engulfed me. My whole life had been a vain masquerade, I decided. Empty and void.

There is no place for me to go. There is nothing left for me.

My mind skipped across the apartment to the laundry room. There, under the carpet near the washing machine, I kept several weapons. I stood and went to retrieve a 9 mm. What was left except to put it to my head and pull the trigger? An eye for an eye. My eye for many eyes.

But as I bent to lift the edge of the carpet, I heard a voice.

"Kamal, the Muslims believe in the God of Father Abraham, and so do the Jews and the Christians. Why don't you call on the God of Father Abraham, Isaac, and Jacob?"

The voice was so strong, so powerful, so *real*.

And I knew I would never have thought such thoughts on my own.

Terrified not to listen, I rushed back to the window and fell on my knees again. I cried out in a loud voice, with every fiber within me, "God of Father Abraham, Isaac, and Jacob, if you are real, *speak* to me! God of Father Abraham, Isaac, and Jacob, if you are real, I want to know you!"

Then, for the first time in my life, a miracle happened in front of me. The window brightened until its frame disappeared. The entire room was flooded with light. In this light, there was overwhelming peace and joy. My heart leapt within me because I knew it was the light of God.

"Who are you, my Lord?" I cried.

A voice spoke in my heart: "I am that I am."

"What does that mean?" I called out.

"I am the Alpha and the Omega," the voice said. "I have known you since before the foundation of the world."

"My Lord, I will live and die for you!" I said.

"Do not die for me," the voice said. "I died for you that you may live."

At that moment, I knew I met the Christian God. I knew I had met my Creator. There was no turning back.

Through the Christian Businessmen, I relearned what I knew about Jesus: that he was a Jew, not a Muslim, as I had been taught. That he really was the son of God, not merely a prophet or even merely the greatest prophet. That he died for the sins of the world and on the third day rose again. That he had made recompense before a holy God for every sin of every man who would simply declare faith in Him. Even *my* sins, which were worse than those of any man I knew.

Did that mean I might not someday have to pay an earthly price for the death and destruction I had caused? No. But I knew God had accepted me. Even if I someday reaped human consequences of my crimes, my soul was safe. That truth burned in the center of my soul like a sacred fire and rinsed my heart clean like a holy rain. I felt in my bones the words of King David: "In my anguish, I cried out to the LORD," he wrote in the Book of Psalms. "And he answered by setting me free."

About ten weeks after I rolled into the Davids' home in a wheelchair, I was able to walk out the front door on my own. To replace my totaled RX-7, the Christian Businessmen bought me a nearly-new used car, and I used it to explore a remarkable new freedom. Now I did not see the future through a narrow tunnel of hatred that would lead to many deaths including my own, but as broad and without limits, promising such simple joys as Abu Fox had offered me outside the cave in Afghanistan.

To enjoy this new freedom, I employed my old tricks, melting permanently into my identity as a Frenchman and moving only in the areas of the city where I knew my old network had not penetrated. We had targeted poor neighborhoods and prisons. My new friends were affluent Christians living and working on the opposite end of a sprawling major city. I quit my old life, as if cutting the chain to an anchor that had kept me stranded on treacherous rocks. I changed my phone number, bank accounts, everything. It was not difficult to avoid running into radical Muslims. But just to be sure, I got a job in a place where I knew no fundamentalist Muslim would ever set foot: a bar and grill that served alcohol and pork.

My new life was like a school where I learned about Americans. They were a rowdy, friendly group of many colors, I found. They loved to laugh. They embraced all faiths, and thought nothing of building a church, a synagogue, a temple, and a mosque on four corners of the same intersection. They respected their women, made them friends and partners. I remembered how my father and uncles treated their women as maids and incubators and contrasted that with American men, who did not merely *allow,* but expected their women to have their own wings.

Americans fought for their own country and for others, not to take them over, but to set them free. When disaster struck overseas, they sent aid to the hurting without asking first what gods that country worshipped. They griped noisily about their leaders and did not have to worry that they might be killed for it.

And where Americans had once seemed blind and foolish to trust someone like me, I began to appreciate their embrace of all cultures as a strength that had made this country great.

I fell in love with America. I fell in love with her people, who, I discovered, were mostly good-hearted, even when they were being blind and human.

After I left the Davids' house, I began visiting churches on Sundays and learned that in Christianity, houses of worship are as diverse and wonderfully messy as American life itself. At a Southern Baptist church, I heard the Bible preached, but to my Middle Eastern ears, it was as though the preacher was speaking Martian. At a different kind of Baptist church, I could understand the teaching better, but the people were so hoity-toity that I felt out of place. Then I went to an Eastern Orthodox church and found a worship style so similar to Islam that I ran for the hills.

Having lived for a lie all my life, I now thirsted for truth like a man emerging from the Sahara. At every church I visited, I asked the pastor a simple question: "Why should I worship here?" Many denominations gave me a troubling answer that went something like this: "Because we're not sure those other churches have their doctrine just right."

One Sunday, I was driving down the expressway and saw a huge white church with a tall steeple and a packed parking lot. I decided to pull in. As soon as I opened my car door, I heard music spilling from the building, not organs and choir voices as I had heard else-where, but drums and guitars. Inside, a man in his thirties dressed in blue jeans greeted me with a smile and handed me a program. Now I could hear rapturous singing, as though thousands of people sang with one voice.

I had never heard anything like it. "What's going on?" I asked the usher.

"They're celebrating God!"

I was astonished. "Where is He?"

"He's here!"

Entering the church sanctuary through wide double doors, I encountered a Sunday celebration such as I had never seen. In the cavernous, modern room, I saw thousands of people, smiling as they sang, some raising their hands to heaven. I sat down in a back row and watched, amazed.

They know *Him*, I thought. *They know God!*

After the service, I found the pastor, an athletic, well-spoken man in his fifties, talking with people near the pulpit. I waited in line for a chance to speak with him. When it was my turn, I introduced myself and told him I was a former Muslim.

"Why should I go to church here?" I asked.

The pastor put his hand on my shoulder and smiled. "It doesn't matter where you go to church. God is everywhere. All you need to do is find a church home where they teach the Word. You're welcome here while God helps you find your way."

He invited me up to his office and we chatted awhile about my spiritual journey. Of course, I left out the part about bombings and shootings and coming to America to destroy her. It would be nearly twenty years before I told another living soul about that.

2

It turned out I was a very good bartender. I could talk to anyone about anything for as long as they wanted to talk about it, all the while revealing very little about myself. Who could have known that all the years I spent finding common ground with people in order to manipulate them could be applied harmlessly in a real job?

In 1987, being a "Frenchman" helped me land a bartending job at a five-star European-style hotel, the city's finest, the destination of movie stars, politicians, and presidents. Very quickly, I was promoted to food and beverage manager of the property's fine dining restaurant, as well as every lounge, and even room service.

Two years into hiding, I still prayed daily that I would not cross paths with anyone from my old life. Meanwhile, I grew into myself, discovering a talent for management, dealing with the public, and smoothing the ruffled feathers of the wealthiest guests. After sweet-talking millions from Saudi sheikhs, I was not intimidated by American fat cats— though some of their wives, when displeased, were almost as scary as Saddam Hussein.

One Sunday morning, shortly after my promotion, I arrived early in the restaurant's kitchen to nurse along the hotel's Sunday brunch, a star attraction in the city. The brunch was so famous that even the famous would wait in line for hours to eat, so I was used to seeing "the beautiful people" line up at the restaurant's antique Austrian doors, peering in eagerly through the leaded glass. But I was unprepared for the beautiful blonde who appeared outside that day.

A cream-colored dress crocheted its way from her neck to her knees, and as she laughed and chatted with her brunch companions, her smile seemed to compete with the sun.

Mike, one of my waiters, saw me staring. "That's the D.O.M.," he said, meaning the hotel's director of marketing. "Her real name is Victoria-something, but everybody calls her the Velvet Hammer."

Her reputation preceded her. She was part of the Who's Who in the city, I had heard, lunching with dignitaries, sitting on all kinds of boards and committees. The rumor mill said she was tough and smart, with a Southern charm that blunted the pain when she bent you to her will.

But no one had told me about those green eyes. I was mesmerized.

Mike elbowed me in the side, then walked off to tend a table. "Don't even think about it, man," he said over his shoulder. "She eats people like you for breakfast."

I watched where the hostess seated Victoria-something and then, for show, made a round of the tables, chatting up my regular clientele. As soon as I thought I would not appear too eager, I sailed over to her table and extended my hand.

"You must be Miss Victoria," I said.

She shook my hand, and her smile sent electricity straight to my brain. "You must be Kamal, our new manager."

We talked for a few minutes and I felt an instant rapport, as if we had known each other for a very long time. Instantly, I wanted to know her more.

Despite the difference in our rank—she was an executive and I a low-level manager—we quickly became friends. I was drawn to her forthright honesty and regal style. It turned out we attended the same church, and so we began to go together some Sunday mornings. Since I was still a new Christian, I wanted to learn more about the faith quickly and sometimes felt like a starving man with a cracker—I could not fill up with knowledge quickly enough. But Victoria had just completed a series of courses at a Bible institute, so she poured her new knowledge into my mind as fast as I could receive it.

We shared casual dinners and movies—not dating, just spending time together, comfortable in each other's company. Over the weeks and months, we grew closer, our hearts knitting together in deep friendship as we shared trials and joys.

Victoria was a woman in charge of her environment, at the top of her field, respected even by her competitors. Politicians and corporate leaders sought her advice, and soon, so did I.

"You are constantly going out with all these bigwigs," I used to tease her. "Why do you keep wasting time with me?"

The truth was, I was jealous of the time she spent with "important" people. I thought no one was good enough for her, including me. At these times, Victoria would look at me very seriously and say, "There's something extraordinary about you, Kamal. I can't put my finger on it yet, but God has something special planned for your future."

At that time in my life, the most important part of my future involved becoming a true American. But that goal did not come easily; I had to fight. I applied for citizenship at the state immigration office and completed all the right classes. But just when I had only one more hoop to jump through, I ran into a 180-pound roadblock named Miss Pritchett.

Miss Pritchett worked at the state immigration office, and her manner said she had worked there since baby Moses floated down the Nile. Miss Pritchett did not like Middle Easterners, she thought we had all crossed the Atlantic with our pockets full of oil money and took unfair advantage of American opportunities and freedoms.

In my case, she was right, though not in the way she thought. But that Kamal Saleem was dead. I was a new man sitting across the desk from her, pleading to make America my home. Still, at every interview, Miss Pritchett was nasty and belligerent, and each time, she refused to forward my application.

But Miss Pritchett did not count on the Velvet Hammer.

Victoria, the big-city mover and shaker, had friends in high places who had gotten to know me, both at the hotel and at church. She made a few phone calls, and soon the state attorney general and a state Supreme Court justice provided character references that trumped Miss Pritchett's prejudice (which, even now, I admit was not entirely misplaced). Finally, at a ceremony in 1989, I raised my right hand and pledged my loyalty to America. Victoria and Dr. David were there. It was the proudest day of my life. Where I had once been ready to destroy America, now I vowed to watch over my adopted country like a father, serve her like a favorite son. When the immigration officer handed me a small American flag, I wept like a child.

But my joy that year did not last. Victoria was promoted to general manager, then transferred to Texas to manage another hotel. When she told me she was leaving, my heart broke, because I knew I was losing the best friend I had ever had. But when she actually left, I realized I was losing much more than that.

3

Like a schoolboy with a crush, I followed Victoria to Texas. I knew she was out of my league, a lioness when I was nothing but a goat. She had never hinted that our relationship would ever move to romance, and I could not dream that she would want someone like me. But I could not bear the loss of her friendship, so I quit my job, gave all my household goods to the church, and moved my clothes to Texas. We picked up where we left off. But I had only been there a few months when she told me the hotel chain was transferring her again, this time to New Orleans.

I knew I could not let her go. I could not afford to move again, and if I did not gather the courage to tell her how I felt, I might lose her forever.

It was after midnight when I knocked on her apartment door.

"Kamal?" she said, pulling a silk robe tight around her slender frame as she opened the door. "What are you doing here?"

She seemed surprised, but there was something else in her eyes, something I could not place. Before I could lose my nerve, I walked rapidly to the couch and sat down. "Come here, Victoria. I have something to tell you."

She sat down beside me, and I took both her soft hands in mine. "I love you," I said. "I have loved you for a long time. But I could not tell you because you are so much higher than me, too good for me. But now you are leaving me again, and I could not let you go without telling you."

When I stopped talking, I realized my heart was hammering inside my chest so hard I feared she would hear it. I looked down at my lap, holding her hands tight. I had seen her deliver bad news gently to other people many, many times. And now I braced myself, waiting to be let down easy. But when I raised my eyes to look at her, I was shocked to see joy on her face.

"I know you love me," she said through tears. "I love you, too. But I was waiting for you to tell me. I needed to hear it from you first."

4

In November 1990, the Velvet Hammer became Mrs. Victoria Saleem. She took the job in New Orleans, and we moved into a white gabled house with magnolia trees in the yard. I loved the historic feel of the city, the French Quarter's narrow streets, and the beignets—soft, light pastries that reminded me of Paris. But it did not take long before tragedy knocked on our door.

At home one weekend, the phone rang and Victoria answered. It was my youngest brother, Samir. Without any greeting or warm-up, he said, "Tell Kamal to call home. His brother Emad is dead." Then he hung up.

Shocked, Victoria ran to the bedroom and told me the news. I snatched up the bedroom extension and quickly dialed home, my hands shaking as the long distance connection sniffed its way across the world. Hassan answered.

"Samir, it's Kamal! What happened?"

"Emad is dead," my brother said quietly. "He broke up with that Christian girl he was dating. She came here with a gun and shot him in the chest, right on Mama's front step."

"When! When did this happen?"

"Two years ago."

Two years ago? Had I heard him correctly? I looked desperately at Victoria, grabbed her hand and squeezed. "Did you say two years ago? Two years?"

"Yes. Mama asked me to call and tell you now."

Anger consumed my brain, a cloud of orange fire. *"My brother died two years ago and you are just calling me now?* What kind of people are you? What kind of *family* are you?"

I slammed down the phone and fell to my knees, sobbing, keening. Victoria knelt to comfort me as great, heaving bursts of grief pealed from my throat. "It is my fault! It is my fault!" I cried. "If I had let him come to America, my brother would still be alive!"

Several times since I had moved to the United States, Emad had asked to come and join me. But I had not wanted him corrupted by infidels; I had seen so many young Muslim men lured by American lusts.

Now, my heart melted like wax. And for the next three weeks, I did not leave the house. Sometimes, I stalked from room to room, wailing as though Pain itself had invaded my body and was pulling my insides out through my mouth. Sometimes, I lay on the bed in utter, stony silence.

If I had not been so selfish, I thought, *my brother might not only be alive, but enjoying the freedom that is now mine.*

I passed twenty-one days pinned under crashing waves of blackest grief. I could not eat. I was as the psalmist, David, who wrote of anguish so great that he cried even when he drank, his tears rolling down his face into his cup. Then one night, Emad came to me in a dream, appearing the way I remembered him, smiling, strong, and full of youth.

"Why do you cry for me, my brother?" he said. "It was not your fault. And where I am, I am happy."

The dream released me from my guilt, but not from the pain of losing my brother whom I had not seen for more than ten years.

The following year, I was surprised when I opened my mailbox and found a letter from my father. While I lived in his house, he had gloried in my growing status with Fatah, then the PLO. But it was to me as if he was basking in a light not his own. He did not love *me*, but only the respect I earned him in the neighborhood. When I left Lebanon for Riyadh, I left him behind, cut him out of my life. No more stolen glory. Now after all these years, I held a letter written in his hand, black ink on air mail stationery, Arabic script flowing across the page like islands and streams.

I tore open the flap, pulse quickening as I shook out a single sheet. My eyes raced over the page. Routine family news, as though we had never lost touch. Some Islamic exhortations and quotes from the *ha-dith*. Then, on a line alone, two words: *I'm sorry*.

That was all. No explanation. The words pierced my heart like an arrow shot from halfway around the world. I knew my father was approaching the winter of his life. Perhaps he wanted to right old wrongs, knit together the torn pieces of our past. But I did not know, because he did not have the manhood to say *why* he was sorry.

Lebanon
1991

1

It was that letter and Emad's death that in 1991 propelled me back to Lebanon. I did not want to lose another member of my family to time and distance. Victoria flew with me as far as London, and I flew on to Lebanon alone in the dead of winter, hiring a car to carry me home.

The second phase of the fifteen-year civil war had ended only the year before, and as I had expected, the jewel city of my childhood still lay in ruins. Burned out, bullet-scarred buildings. Sidewalks heaped with rubble. The blackened shells of cars. Syrian army patrols lurked on every corner, providing "security." As my driver picked his way to my neighborhood, anticipation percolated in my belly. What would my parents look like? My sisters and brothers? How would my father receive me? The car dropped me at my parents' building, and I climbed the stairs.

"*Yah ibny!*" My mother stood at the door, tears streaming from her eyes.

I swept her into my arms. "Mama! I missed you so much!" My brothers and sisters streamed in from the living room and clustered around us.

My mother's face had aged, but she was slimmer than before and seemed vibrant, full of life. I held her for a long time, and her familiar gardenia scent whisked me back to boyhood. I made my way into the crowded entry, from brother to brother, sister to sister—laughter, hugs, a joyous homecoming.

Finally, I reached my father. "Welcome home, son," he said.

His appearance stunned me. His brilliant black hair had gone a dirty white, and his moustache was thin and yellow. Where one of his arms had once been bigger than both of my legs, now the power had fled his body, leaving behind frail limbs and mottled hands that clutched and worried at a string of Muslim prayer beads.

That evening passed in a flurry of food and catching up on old times. Mama had cooked *yaknah,* my favorite, and served it on a huge platter with stacks of pita. We sat around the table on *tesats,* now crowded shoulder to shoulder because we were all grown. Fouad worked as an engineer for a company that installed commercial kitchen equipment. The company operated out of an underground garage, since its three locations in the city had been destroyed in the war. Ibrahim, who had grown a huge beard down to his chest, owned an air-conditioning and refrigeration shop. Omer had become a renowned chef and was opening Planet Hollywood cafés all over the Middle East and Europe. My youngest brother, Samir, worked as a rich family's chauffeur. My sisters Amira and Sanaa were still married and busy having more children.

I shared about my career in the hospitality industry, how I had started as a bartender and worked my way into management. But I told my tale as one who shares his diary only after ripping out the incriminating pages. I explained my travels in Europe and the Middle East, but omitted Fatima, recruitment, and my fleecing of the sheikhs. I told of my settling in America, but left out my activities in *jihad.* I related the story of my accident, but kept dead quiet about my conversion to Christianity.

Throughout the chatter, I caught my father stealing glances at me. Where he had embraced me at the door, he now seemed cool and remote, sitting in his high place at the table, watching and smoking a cigarette. Finally, he spoke. "Why did you decide to go to America and never come back?"

"It was the war, Papa. Death. Oppression. It was no way to live," I said. I flashed back to the ride in from the airport and added, "It is still like that here. You can smell it in the air."

My father regarded me with hooded eyes. "If America is so great and you are doing so well, why did you not send any money?"

2

The next day, I went with my father to visit Emad's grave. We took a *serviz* to the cemetery, and I watched through the window as my old world flickered past. Women in black *abbayah* hurried from shop to shop, heads down, their coats pulled tight around them. I did not see klatches of old men smoking or children playing in the streets. Was it the chill wind that kept them inside or the palpable hatred I could feel in the streets?

The cemetery was a sprawling, unkempt collection of marble headstones that rambled over the hills uncomfortably close to Sabra. A concrete half-wall topped with spears of black iron hemmed in the dead. When the *serviz* dropped us there, I hurried through the wrought iron gates, praying I would not run into Abu Ibrahim or, worse, Abu Yousef. That chapter of my life was as dead as the occupants here. I wanted to keep it that way.

A sharp wind sang through the tall pines standing guard over the headstones, which huddled in family clusters. In life, Lebanese people gathered around kitchen tables. In death, they regathered here. The war had accelerated that process, and as we wound our way through the cemetery, I saw many fresh graves.

Finally, we came to Emad's, and when I saw his name etched in stone, black grief swept over me again, knocking me to my knees. I crawled to his headstone and clung to it, my tears tracing tracks down its front. In that moment, my grief swelled to encompass all things: a childhood lost, Mohammed and Yahya. A murderous faith, the blood on my hands. Half a life lived for the sake of death. Now my brother, half his life unlived, lying cold in the grave. Sobs tore from my lips, and in my heart I cried out to God for mercy and comfort.

Behind me, I heard the flick of a match. Lifting my head, I turned to see my father cupping a cigarette against the wind. When it was lit, he took a long draw and exhaled, regarding me with dry eyes as the smoke skated off into the trees. He did not say a word, but the look on his face spoke loudly: "It is all your fault."

I knew then that some things do not change. I knew it again the next day when I went for a walk with my mother on the *corniche,* a high concrete walkway overlooking the Mediterranean. It was a gray day, and I trailed my hand along the blue metal railing that separated us from the splashing sea.

"You were always my favorite," my mother said, smiling up at me over her *hijab.* "Many, many times over many years, I prayed for you, that Allah would keep you safe."

I put my arm around her shoulder, bent, and kissed her forehead. "Thank you, Mama. I prayed for you, too. I still pray for you."

"Why don't you come home, my son? Why don't you move back to Lebanon, make a life here?"

"I cannot, Mama. I have a life in America now. I have a wife."

My mother stopped walking and turned to me, her eyes suddenly dark. "Your wife is an infidel! Do not give her your seed. She will bear you a child that is impure."

Just then, two young girls in *abbayah* strolled past us on the *corniche,* and my mother suddenly softened, linked her arm through mine and began walking again. "See? There are plenty of girls here who would love to marry you. Why should you stay married to that infidel woman when there are so many virgins to serve you and give you good Muslim children?"

At that moment, my heart broke for my mother. Islam would always cause her to sort human beings into opposing categories: virgins and whores, clean and unclean, worthy of heaven and worthy of death. Islam would always keep my mother shackled, a slave to an ancient hatred.

Southwestern United States
1991–2004

1

I spent the next ten years looking over my shoulder while hiding in plain sight. No one in my new life, as I still considered it, knew about my old one. Not even my wife.

As the computer industry took hold in the early 1990s, I made a career transition from the hospitality industry to information technology. By 2001, I had climbed the corporate ladder to become IT department manager for an international telecom, overseeing the company's nerve center from an underground facility in the Southwest that we called the War Room. To gain access to the War Room required badging at laser-powered security boxes three times.

Beyond the final security checkpoint was a sprawling rectangular space divided into cubicles, with four enormous monitors hanging from the ceiling. Using them, we tracked the company's worldwide network, each monitor a blinking maze of nodes, ladders, servers, and load.

I was always one of the first people in each morning, usually there by 5 A.M. or earlier. Other diehards like my friend and coworker Christy Bonham trickled in with me to relieve the night crew. One morning in September 2001, Christy was sitting in her cubicle munching on breakfast, her tiny ten-inch television tuned into a local morning talk show.

The room was quiet; not many people in for the day shift yet, but I had let most of the overnight skeleton crew go home.

Suddenly, I heard a loud gasp. "Oh my God!"

It was Christy. She sounded so stricken, so terrified, that I jumped up and rushed to her cubicle. Was it something with her kids?

When I rounded the gray fabric partition, I saw her staring at the tiny television screen. One tower of the World Trade Center was burning. A local news anchor was saying, "Again, an American Airlines passenger jet has crashed into the north tower of the World Trade Center—"

An alarm sounded in my head, oddly like the air raid sirens I had heard in Lebanon.

"Those poor people!" Christy was saying, sounding near tears. "This has got to be the worst airplane accident I've ever heard of!"

I could not tell her what I instinctively knew: this was no accident.

Christy reached up and changed channels. The World Trade Center was burning there, too. She flipped to another channel and another. All the broadcast stations carried the footage.

I glanced up at our telecom monitors. Server load had soared dramatically and was still climbing. My mind flashed to the calendar. September.

Jordan, 1970. Vienna, 1683. Islamic defeats. Black Septembers.

I dashed to my desk and called Victoria. She had seen the news.

"Go to the store right now," I told her. "Buy water, groceries, flashlights, and a radio," I told her.

"What? Why?"

"This thing is not normal. Something is happening—" I could not tell her how I knew.

"Kamal, it's an *accident*. It's in New York City, two thousand miles away."

I tried to remain patient. "Baby, something is happening. The attack is on."

"Attack? What attack?"

"Victoria, I can't explain. It's some crazy people—"

"I think you might be the crazy one," she said, laughing gently.

"Victoria," I said, pouring as much urgency into my voice as I could,

"I do not want to argue with you about this. Just gather what I said. I'm getting Tamra and coming home."

I heard Christy behind me: "Oh my God!"

I whirled and ran back to her cubicle. A second jet had hit the south tower of the World Trade Center. This time the footage was live.

Mumbling something to Christy about Tamra, I grabbed my keys and within three minutes was in my car speeding toward my daughter's school. I flipped on the radio and listened as harried announcers improvised, delivering fresh news as it streamed off the wire: "The Federal Aviation Administration has grounded all flights into or out of New York Air Space . . . the Air Force has launched F-15s . . . possible terrorist attack."

As I barreled down the freeway, the blood in my veins turned to liquid fear.

The second strike! When will they launch the second strike?

When we planned attacks, we often created a diversion before the main event. Before we stole the Syrian rockets, for example, we planted bombs in Lebanon to lure Hafez al-Assad's secret service away from home.

What will be the second strike?

It took me twenty minutes to reach Tamra's school. I screamed into the parking lot, checked her out of class, and roared away again, her eight-year-old eyes wide at the look on my face.

Reports poured over the radio as I sped home. "Possible multiple hijackings . . . all U.S. airspace shut down." Ten minutes later, as I pulled into my driveway: ". . . a fire at the Pentagon . . . unconfirmed reports that another jet may have hit the Pentagon."

My stomach rolled in terror. *Is that it? The second strike? Is it over?*

As my family passed the day glued to CNN, we learned it was not. The Twin Towers would collapse. United Flight 93 would crash into a Pennsylvania field. The death toll would be 2,999, including rescue personnel and 19 young Middle Eastern men who had infiltrated America to destroy her.

Like me.

As my entire nation plunged into a pit of mourning wider and deeper than anything in her history, I plunged into an ocean of guilt more terrifying than the Bay of Haifa. Suddenly, I wished I had died there. Maybe the legend of the butterfly's wing was true: one missed beat could change history. If I had not lived to invade America, if I had not helped light the fuse, fan the flame, stir up *jihad* in the cities, perhaps Mohammed Atta and his eighteen accomplices would not have found America such fertile ground. Perhaps they would have had to build the Islamist network I built with my jihadist brothers, instead of going straight to flight school to learn how to pilot planes.

2

The whole country grieved, but my brand of grief shocked Victoria. Although no amount of mourning could seem out of proportion to such a tragedy, she still could not quite get over how much the September 11 attacks consumed my thinking in the weeks and months that followed. She chalked it up to a sensitive spirit and my ties to the Middle East. But as my spirit screamed inside me like a boiling cauldron with the lid on too tight, I could not tell her why.

I wanted to call the FBI, the CIA, even the White House, and tell them what I knew. Where to look for sleeper cells. How to spot a network. The conferences, the literature, the video boot camps. The money, the weapons, the training.

You are growing terrorists at home! I wanted to shout. *In your universities, your ghettos, your prisons!*

But I had kept quiet for so long, lulled into a false peace, like everyone else, by my comfortable American life. Now I had a wife, a child, a career. In the hot period following the September 11 attacks, I was afraid to step forward, terrified I would be stripped of my citizenship and thrown into prison. Or worse, packed onto the first plane bound for the Middle East.

I did not want to lose my family, but I also did not want to lose my country, my home. The tension between love and duty tore at me daily.

At one point, I actually filled out a civil service application, a stab at getting hired by federal law enforcement as a translator, a protocol officer, anything, so that I could share my knowledge, turn my former evil into good.

When America invaded Afghanistan in October 2001 to hunt down the Taliban, I cheered from the sidelines. While the talking news heads recalling the Soviet war of the 1980s mooed about the dangers of cave warfare and the wily *mujahadeen*, I laughed out loud. In the 1980s Afghanistan was a backward world of fragmented tribes that, when they were not killing Soviets, were robbing and killing each other. Had it not been for American assistance to Afghanistan, the Soviets would have destroyed the village-based *mujahadeen*, cut off the mountain supply routes, and left the remaining fighters to starve to death in their caves. Without the Americans, the *mujahadeen* and the Taliban were nothing.

Iraq was another matter. Still, when America invaded, I thought it was the right move. In league with other Middle Eastern leaders, Saddam had plotted for decades against America. To establish democracy there would drive a stake into the heart of a growing Islamist fanaticism that would end only one way: with more attacks on America. But as our casualties in Iraq mounted in 2004, and the media, then the public, began turning against the war, I grew frustrated.

When it comes to many things, Americans are mature in their thinking. But when it comes to war, many Americans see only the game that is being played in front of them, the battles that involve their soldiers. They don't understand the interconnections of the jihadist threat.

In 2002 alone, there were more than fifty jihadist attacks around the world. Most of them were in Israel. One of them was in the United States, when an Egyptian gunman opened fire in the Los Angeles airport, killing two Israelis. To the American mind, the airport attack was a blip. Here and gone. Forgotten. The other forty-nine attacks had nothing to do with them at all.

Wrong. To the Islamist, Israel is the hated bastard child and America is its evil mother, offering her breast. When jihadists bomb a train in Spain, an embassy in Pakistan, or a market in Israel, they are not just earning virgins. They have an end game in mind: *Umma*, one world under Islam. The jihadists' goal is to pull the West into a war not against a country, but against Islam. They hope to inflame Muslim moderates around the world with the battle cry that America, the Great Satan, is bent on destroying *all* Muslims. In many quarters, they have succeeded. When Danish cartoonists lampooned Muhammad, for example, Muslims rioted all over the world.

In May 2003, al-Qaeda bombers killed 26 people and injured 160 others at the American expatriate housing in Riyadh. In October 2003, a Palestinian bomber killed three Americans in a diplomatic convoy in the Gaza Strip. In August 2004, James Elshafay, a nineteen-year-old American high school dropout, planned to bomb New York's Penn Station during the Republican National Convention. He was recruited by Shahawar Matin Siraj, a twenty-two-year-old Pakistani national, who had been in the United States illegally for six years. A radical Muslim. A person like me.

In 2004, I considered the advance of *jihad* in the world. Europe had fallen. Canada was a eunuch. Only America was keeping the light of freedom burning for the entire world.

One afternoon late that year, I called my wife into our living room and asked her to take a seat on the couch. A war raged inside me, again the clash between heart and duty. I was terrified of losing my family, my home, my freedom. Of forfeiting this new life as payment for my old one. But I knew I could remain silent no longer.

My face crumbling, I sat down on the couch near my wife, then laid my head in her lap.

"Kamal, what's wrong?" she said.

Slowly, I turned over on my back and lay looking up at her, silent tears sliding down my cheeks. "Victoria," I said, "I have something to tell you."

Colorado Springs
2008

1

People like you must be killed.

The words of the young Palestinian at the Air Force Academy conference electrified me. Suddenly I realized why he had switched the conversation to Arabic. I was not afraid, but stunned. I was used to this kind of threat, this kind of anger. Over the course of years, I had been threatened by actual assassins rather than students with reckless mouths. Still, I was surprised that this man had the brazenness to say this thing in this place.

Now he brushed past me. I turned and followed him, watching as he threaded his way through the crowd and took a seat high in the auditorium near an exit. After getting a fix on him, I found my own seat next to Keith and settled in to listen to Walid, who was speaking next. I knew this: the tactic of radical Muslims was to disrupt, to throw events into chaos. I was not going to let that happen here.

The blue amphitheater hummed with muted conversation until Walid took the podium. My friend opened brilliantly. The war on terror, Walid said, was not a battle between Islam and Christianity, but instead a clash of civilizations. "Radical Islamists have their own government, and they are ready to put that government in place in the United States," he said.

About fifteen minutes into his talk, I leaned close to Keith. "You are not going to believe what just happened." I told him about the confrontation.

"Are you serious?"

"Zak heard it, too. By his accent, I think he was Palestinian."

Discreetly, Keith left his seat, and I watched him approach the major in charge.

The second Walid finished speaking, I found myself surrounded by a cluster of MPs, six or seven of them, all of them bigger than Dallas.

"Your manager told us what happened," said a uniformed man wearing an impressive stack of stripes on his sleeve. "Is this man still sitting in here?"

I turned and peered up to the exit-row seat where I had last seen the young student. It was empty.

"No," I said. "He left."

I was describing him when one of the MPs spoke up. "I remember that individual. He seemed agitated. Hostile. I was watching him."

The stripe-heavy MP said to me, "Could you identify this man if we took you around?"

"Absolutely," I said. "I will never forget the look in his eyes."

But it did not turn out to be so easy. By the time we began our search, the conference attendees had dispersed to breakout sessions in classrooms flung about the campus. We tramped from building to building, wing to wing, the MPs consulting a sheet to see which classrooms had been designated for the conference. At each, an MP would crack the door and I would peer in, scanning faces. Nothing.

Finally, at about the tenth room, I saw a man. *That's him,* I thought.

I paused in the doorway, the MP peering in behind me. As one, about thirty heads turned to look. I locked eyes with the student.

"I think that's him," I said.

The MP closed the door. "You have to be sure."

But I wasn't. The student who confronted me had been wearing a jacket. This man wore only a shirt. Also, sitting down, he seemed heavier.

Now the MP in charge caught up with us and pulled his men aside. He gestured urgently. I couldn't hear what he was saying, but it appeared to me he was upset that our search had not yielded fruit. The MPs clustered around me again and hustled me back to an area where Zak and Walid were waiting.

"I saw one man I thought might be the one, but I was not sure," I told them.

Walid looked at the MP in charge. "Do you have a list of the guests attending the conference?"

"Yes," the MP said.

"Show it to me and I will tell you who this person is."

Brilliant, I thought, and mentally slapped myself for not thinking of it. As in many eastern countries, a person's name reveals his origin. A note of irony sounded in my brain. It had been the Palestinians who taught me to differentiate between names: in Sabra, we learned how to use last names to identify Jews, in case we had a crowd of hostages and needed to know which ones to kill first.

An MP returned with a sheet of paper and handed it to Walid, who ran his finger down a neatly typed column of names. Midway down, his finger stopped.

"This man here," he said.

He was an exchange student. Based on his name, Walid knew instantly the man was Palestinian.

"How sure are you?" the MP asked.

"Ninety-five percent." Walid's finger brushed down the rest of the list until it found a second name. "Here's another possibility, but I would say it is only a 5 percent chance that this is the man."

Again, a knot of MPs rushed me across the campus. An MP went into the classroom and returned with the student, who glanced briefly my way. They stood a distance from me, and I could overhear snatches of the conversation.

"Did you speak to Mr. Saleem after lunch?" an MP asked the student.

"Yes."

"Did you say to him that he had insulted Islam?"

"Yes. I do not agree with his views. This is America. I have freedom of speech."

"Yes, you're right. This is America," the MP said. "But you're at the

Air Force Academy, not on the streets. Did you tell Mr. Saleem that people like him must be killed?"

"No."

2

An investigation revealed that the student was in America on an educational visa. But he had not threatened my life *directly,* I was told. He had not said *he* was going to kill me. The student completely denied my account, was not charged with any wrongdoing, and was free to go.

Do you think he is rare? If so, do not forget the taxi driver, the pizza boy, the roofer who planned to attack Fort Dix. Do not forget Syed Ahmed and Ehsanul Sadequee, the Georgia Tech students who collaborated with terrorists. Do not forget Hamid Hayat and his plan to "wage violent *jihad.*"

In March 2008, my nephew called me at home from Lebanon. I was just finishing lunch, a turkey sandwich.

"You have a new religion now," he said from miles away. It was more of an observation than an accusation.

"I am a Christian."

"There will be a war in the family. They will never talk to you again if they find out you are a Christian." I already knew that. For more than twenty years, I had hidden my faith from them—all except for my sisters, who loved me unconditionally.

You see, a Muslim who converts to Christianity is worse than an infidel, who, the theology goes, never experienced the glory and truth of Islam. An infidel is worthy of death—but it's not his fault. He is therefore given a chance: before they chop off his head, he is allowed an opportunity to convert.

But even if he converts, he will still have to pay the *jezyah,* the tax levied for having been an infidel. If he cannot pay it, he must, by law, teach ten Muslim men about the horrors of his old religion and why it is false.

In centuries past, when Muslims conquered a country, instead of taxing or killing, the conquerors lopped off infidels' right hands and left feet so that everyone would know they were vanquished infidels.

This is from Sura 5:33–34, the "Table Spread":

Those who wage war against God and His Messenger and strive to spread corruption in the land should be punished by death, crucifixion, the amputation of an alternate hand and foot or banishment from the land: a disgrace for them in this world, and then a terrible punishment in the Hereafter, unless they repent before you overpower them: In that case bear in mind that God is forgiving and merciful.

Merciful, indeed.

Those in America who defend Islam as if it were all of one cloth like to ignore these facts. Or pretend that *sura* like these are relics of an ancient era, like the New Testament admonition that women should not cut their hair. But only a couple of months before my nephew called, Islamists in Gaza murdered Rami Ayyad, the manager of the area's only Christian bookstore. Operated by the Palestinian Bible Society, the shop was located in a central part of Gaza City. Ayyad had received many death threats. Then one Saturday afternoon in October 2007, as he closed the Teacher's Bookshop, gunmen snatched him off the street. Two days later, Ayyad's captors dumped his body, bloody with knife and gunshot wounds, near the store. Ayyad was only twenty-six. He left behind two young children and a pregnant wife, Pauline.

His crime: he helped lead Gaza Baptist Church's AWANA group, a kids' Scripture memory club, and he directed the church's summer children's camp.

Sadly, Rami Ayyad is just one of hundreds martyred every year by Islamists whose white-hot hatred fires their killing. In July 2008 near Mogadishu, Somalia, two Muslim men approached Sayid Ali Sheikh Luqman Hussein, a twenty-eight-year-old convert to Christianity.

"Do you face Mecca when you pray?" the men asked Hussein.

"I am a Christian," Hussein said. "I do not have to face a specific direction to pray because God is everywhere."

A few days later, the men returned with an AK–47 and a handgun and shot Hussein to death. When his pregnant wife heard of her husband's murder, the shock triggered premature labor, and she delivered the new child dead.

When I have pointed out incidents like these, groups like CAIR have accused me of promoting "fear."

Am I afraid of Islam? No: I killed for it. Am I afraid of what radical Islamists will do if they continue their successful advance in America? Yes. And those who believe that America is so powerful that she is immune to such killing within her own borders are fools. It is already happening to Muslim women. And since 9/11, American authorities have exposed and halted no fewer than fourteen domestic attacks.

My nephew is among the blind. "Those things you are saying about what the Muslims do, their terrorism, is not real," he told me on the phone. "Those who do that are *muttarafeen*; they are not even Muslim."

I knew what he was saying: that moderate Muslims view groups such as the Muslim Brotherhood and al-Qaeda the way Christians view the Ku Klux Klan—as a radical splinter group that has laid claim to the teachings of a faith, but perverted them. Whether jihadists are a perverted splinter group or part of the true Muslim faith is a debatable *idea*. Their violence and its consequences are real.

Some moderate Muslims disagree with the jihadist and only wish to be left to live out their faith in Allah peacefully, treating the Koranic call to *jihad* as a throwback to a more barbaric time. In many cases, the moderates know the ruthlessness of the jihadists and are afraid to speak out against them. It is one thing to know that radicals consider you a neutered Muslim, an impotent pretender; it is another thing entirely to speak out against them and thereby mark yourself for death.

But there is still another group of moderate Muslims and many in this group have infiltrated the United States. These moderates have lives and jobs and families, but they secretly cheer on the jihadists as they do the dirty work. For example, the Holy Land Foundation was the largest charity delivering material aid to Islamic countries from America. In November 2008, five of its leaders were convicted of 108 charges of illegally funding the Palestinian terrorist group Hamas.[17]

In the days following September 11, 2001, the streets of countries where Muslims live should have been filled with "moderates" crying out against the atrocities done in their name, protesting, "What you have done is not godly!" Instead, all over the world—including New York, Chicago, Houston, and Michigan—so-called moderate Muslims celebrated what happened to America. They reacted with joy to the news that the sword of Islam had cut down the Great Satan.

Moderate or *muttarafeen,* they celebrated the same, with dancing in the streets. People have forgotten that. Americans have forgotten.

Some Americans also believe that our jihadist enemy consists mainly of unsophisticated Third World savages who could never truly threaten such a technologically advanced nation as the United States. That is not true. In November 2008, six months after my nephew called, Pakistani terrorists invaded Mumbai, India, targeting tourists carrying Western passports and ultimately killing 179 people including six Americans. Before they landed in Mumbai, authorities learned, the terrorists studied satellite images of the city, carried handheld global-positioning sets, and kept in touch with their handlers via Internet, cell-, and satellite-phones. Meanwhile, Iranian President Mahmoud Ahmadinejad, a fiery Shia radical, is leading his country toward becoming the first nuclear jihadist state. Ahmadinejad believes he has been chosen by Allah to usher in worldwide Islamic rule. But in a 2005 speech in Tehran to leaders of the terror groups Hamas and Islamic Jihad, the Iranian president did not ask his audience to imagine a Muslim-*ruled* America, but a world *without* America.

As I wrote this book, there were days when I wished I had never gone down this road. Often, I would open up Google News or some other Internet feed and find that I had once again been branded a fraud or a mercenary.

"Terrorism pays," one writer quipped, accusing me of being in this for the money. I wish I could have shown her my bank account.

People who had never met me, never bothered to hear my story from my own lips, were ready to say that not only had I never been a terrorist, but that I had never even been a Muslim. And that was when I was only doing a few speaking engagements.

What will happen when the book comes out? I asked myself.

The answer: *Professors, theologians, and historians will come out in force to try and discredit me.*

For example, my *real* name is not Kamal Saleem. When I began speaking out against radical Islam, a number of professors and journalists began speculating on my real name, thoughtless of the fact they were endangering my family in Lebanon. Apparently, when you make your living destroying reputations with unresearched words, it is not of concern whether your words will endanger real people living in places where murder in the name of religion is tolerated.

This is another reason I did not speak out the instant the World Trade Center towers crumbled: because I feared for my family, still living in Lebanon. I am not just an infidel, but an ultimate infidel. Not just a former Muslim, but a former terrorist, too. I must be killed. And whoever kills me gets a prize.

Perhaps that means that something my father told me as a boy has become in some small way prophetic: "I wish you were a girl," he spat, glowering over me in my mother's kitchen. "That way I could get rid of you, because I know you are going to be a thorn in my side."

I am not a particularly well-educated man, but I have a story.

I am not one of America's great patriots, scientists, innovators, or soldiers. I did not invent an alternative energy source or discover a cure for cancer. But I can tell my story. It includes a lot of my failures, a lot of my wickedness. But when bin Laden hit the World Trade Center, it turned out that my story also had a purpose: To say, "Wake up, America! You have a good heart toward foreigners, but it will be your death if you do not recognize your enemies and face them head-on."

My story has proven itself a thorn in the side of many who like to pretend that all Muslims are good Muslims and that anyone who warns against radical Islam is a radical himself.

Let us stop pretending: Many Muslims are kind and gentle people, but about one in ten, according to scholars who study *jihad*, have declared war on our way of life, and it is not a war that we can watch on CNN. As Americans, we must examine the patterns of *jihad* and be constantly on our guard at home and abroad.

Beware of attempts to establish Sharia law in your town, such as happened in Minneapolis. There, in response to Muslim cab drivers who did not want to transport Orthodox Jews or people carrying alcohol, the airport authority suggested that some taxis be marked as "Sharia" cabs so that passengers fitting the "no ride" profile would not have to face rejection. The idea did not catch on. Yet.

Beware of attempts to establish Muslim prayer rituals in public schools, such as happened at Carver Elementary School in Oak Park, California. There, Muslim students were allowed fifteen minutes of daily prayer, led by a staff member, a practice not allowed for other religions in public schools.

In warning Americans about such things, there is no gain for me personally. I had a good career in information technology that I quit to write this book. I will not be famous, but infamous. Whether you become infamous by speaking out, like Ayaan Hirsi Ali, author of *Infidel*, or famous, like Sir Salman Rushdie, author of *The Satanic Verses*, the Islamist sentence is the same: death by *fatwa*. Ali, and Theo Van Gogh, who teamed up to make a ten-minute film documenting the abuse of women in Muslim societies, were both targets of the same death threats. Van Gogh is already dead, shot eight times in 2004 on an Amsterdam street by an Islamist zealot who then nearly cut Van Gogh's head off with a knife.

People who are like I used to be do not get tired. They do not give up. They do not run out of money. And they do not run out of hate.

I am fifty-one years old, living the back stretch of my life. I am not the young man I used to be, shouting and screaming and waving a gun, attempting to change the world on the strength of my hatred.

But that young Beiruti boy who gazed through his dreaming window at the spot where the moon kissed the sea still lives inside me. That rooftop boy who cried out to his god under the shimmering stars grew into a man who still prays—not to a god of war, but to a God of peace.

I pray for my family's safety. I pray for this great country. And I pray for you, that you would never meet a man like me.

Appendixes

People

Abdel. The owner of the Beirut gift shop where Kamal worked.

Adnan. Kamal's neighbor and childhood friend.

Ahmad, Omar. The founder of CAIR (Council on American-Islamic Relations), which claims to be the largest Muslim civil liberties organization in the United States.

Ahmed, Syed Haris. Georgia Tech Student who cased and videotaped the Capitol and World Bank for a terrorist organization in 2006.

Ahmed. One of two adult *fedayeen* (Palestinian freedom fighters) who escorted Kamal and other recruits on a mission to transport weapons to the Palestinians.

Ali ibn Abi Talib. The cousin and son-in-law of the prophet Muhammad. Ali is regarded as the first imam and the rightful successor to Muhammad. The disagreement about Ali's place in the Muslim landscape split the Muslim community into the Sunni and Shia.

Ali, Abu. A Shia convert to Sunni and the leader of Kamal's first mission.

Amal. A young boy who went to school with Kamal and his siblings. Kamal watched as he was subjected to physical torture for stealing.

Amira, *See* Saleem, Amira.

Anani, Zakariah (or Zak). A student of the Koran, Zak traveled with

Kamal and another Muslim recruit named Walid on speaking assignments to recruit other young Muslims.

Arafat, Yasser. Chairman of the Palestine Liberation Organization and president of the Palestinian National Authority, he was the leader of the Fatah political party, which he founded in 1959. He died in 2004.

Assad, Hafez al-. President of Syria from 1971 until his death in 2000. Strongly anti-Zionist and a major supporter of Palestinian guerrilla organizations, he came into power after leading a coup in late 1970.

Azziz, Abu. An imam (religious leader) Kamal met when he took refuge in the mosque in Beirut. Member of the Muslim Brotherhood.

Bakr, Abu. An early convert to Islam and senior companion to the prophet Muhammad. After Muhammad died, Bakr became the first Muslim ruler.

Banna, Hassan al-. A schoolteacher and the founder of the Muslim Brotherhood.

Barak, Ehud. An Israeli politician, former prime minister and the current minister of defense, deputy prime minister, and leader of Israel's Labor Party.

Basha, Omar Al-. Plumber who worked high-rise buildings. Kamal went to work for him as an errand and clean-up boy.

Bobby and Patrick. Two IRA (Irish Republican Army) soldiers who trained at the camp with Kamal. After carrying out terrorist acts from England to Italy, Omar and Kamal killed them on orders from Abu Mustafa.

Eli. Kamal's best childhood friend (a Christian).

Elshafay, James. American high-school dropout recruited into *jihad* and arrested in the United States for planning to bomb New York's Penn Station during the 2004 Republican National Convention.

Emad. Kamal's uncle, whom the imam from the neighborhood mosque knew.

Faisel. A Palestinian driver who took Kamal to the training camp in the Sahara.

Farouge. An Armenian shop keeper in Kamal's Beirut neighborhood.

Fatima. The prophet Muhammad's daughter by his first wife. She was the wife of Ali.

Fatima. Kamal's grandmother.

Fouad. (See Saleem, Fouad)

Gaddafi, Muammar. The de facto leader of Libya since a 1969 coup. Although Gaddafi holds no public office or title, he is accorded broad honorifics in government statements and the official press.

Gemayel, Pierre Abdel. Founder of the Lebanese Phalanges, a political and military force which he led for almost fifty years. The Phalangist Party, geared toward Lebanese Maronite Christians, focused on the need for a strong Lebanese state. Harsh opponent of Palestinian refugees. He died in 1984.

Habbal, Sarri. A Muslim man who often drove Kamal to the training camp. He arranged for Kamal's job at the gift shop. He was also a thief and a gigolo.

Haroon. One of two *fedayeen* who rode in the Zodiac with Kamal on the mission to Haifa. He was half-Palestinian and half-Lebanese.

Hasson, Adham Amin. A man illegally in the United States, charged with providing material support to terrorists in 2002.

Hayat, Hamid. Resident of Lodi, California, convicted of attending a terrorist training camp in Pakistan in 2006.

Hayat, Umer. Resident of Lodi, California, charged with providing material support to terrorists. After his trial ended in a deadlock, he pleaded guilty to making false statements to the FBI. His son, Hamid, was convicted of attending a terrorist training camp in Pakistan in 2006.

Hussein. Son of Ali ibn Abi Talib. He was killed in a battle for power of the fifth Calipha.

Hussein, ibn-Talal. King of Jordan from 1952 until his death in 1999. Pious Muslims considered him to be a direct descendant of the prophet Muhammad.

Ibrahim, Abu. A Palestinian *fida'i* (*fedayeen* soldier) and leader of Kamal's Fatah/PLO cell.

Ibrahim. (See Saleem, Ibrahim)

Iskendar. One of the Shia Kurd boys who bullied and harrassed Kamal in Beirut.

Issa. A Lebanese *fedayeen* who challenged Kamal at the training camp and spoke to him disrespectfully.

James, Kevin. A U.S. national and founder of Jam'iyyat Ul-Islam Is-Sa-heeh, a radical Islamic organization that identifies the U.S. government and Jews as major targets. He recruited co-conspirators Levar Washington, Gregory Patterson, and Hammad Riaz Samana to carry out attacks on the National Guard, Los Angeles International Airport, two synagogues, and the Israeli consulate in Los Angeles.

Jihad, Abu. A Sunni Palestinian who visited the mosque in Beirut and recruited Kamal for Fatah (Arafat's armed force).

Karim, Abdul al-. Kamal's uncle for whom Kamal worked as a child.

Khalid. Kamal's uncle.

Mahmoud. One of Kamal's uncles.

Marie. One of Kamal's Christian childhood friends from the Beirut neighborhood.

Marwan. The concierge of the Baath party office, he and his wife were taken hostage by Kamal and his fellow terrorists in order to obtain access to the Baath headquarters.

Mezin. Baathist leader on Kamal's first mission.

Mohammed. One of Kamal's childhood friends from the Beirut neighborhood.

Mu'awiyah. An early Islamic leader and founder of the great Umayyad Dynasty of caliphs. He fought against the fourth caliph, 'Ali (Muhammad's son-in-law), seized Egypt, and assumed the caliphate after 'Ali's assassination in 661. He restored unity to the Muslim empire and made Damascus its capital. He reigned from 661 to 680.

Mughrabi, Dalal. A female Palestinian terrorist who participated in the Coastal Road Massacre in 1978. In all, she and her companions killed thirty-five civilians including several Americans and thirteen children and wounded seventy-one others along Israel's coastal highway. Along with the other terrorists, she was killed when she blew up a hijacked bus on Israel's coastal highway. Many Muslims now consider her a martyr.

Muhammad, Prophet. Considered the central human figure of the religion of Islam, Muhammad, born in the year 570, is regarded by Muslims as a messenger and prophet of God, the last and greatest law-bearer in a series of prophets.

Mukhtar. A young boy who went to school with Kamal and his siblings.

Mustafa, Abu. Palestinian leader and the secretary general of the Popular Front of the Liberation of Palestine from July 2000 until he was killed by Israeli forces in 2001.

Nabil. A young boy who went to school with Kamal and his siblings.

Nasser, Gamal Abdel. Second president of Egypt from 1956 until his death in 1970. He led the Egyptian Revolution in 1952 and was a co-founder of the Palestinian Liberation Organization.

Nizhar. The Lebanese leader of the mission against Haifa.

Omar. Father of Mohammed, Kamal's childhood friend.

Omer. (See Saleem, Omer.)

Padilla, Jose. An American citizen convicted of conspiracy in the United States in May of 2002.

Patterson, Gregory Vernon. A U.S. national, he joined co-conspirators Levar Washington and Hammad Riaz Samana and Kevin James to plan attacks on the National Guard, Los Angeles International Airport, two synagogues, and the Israeli consulate in Los Angeles.

Qaffin. One of two adult *fedayeen* (Palestinian freedom fighters) who escorted Kamal and other recruits on a mission to transport weapons to the Palestinians.

Rabin, Yitzhak. An Israeli politician and general. He was the fifth prime minister of Israel, serving two terms in office: 1974–1977 and 1992 until his assassination in 1995.

Rahman, Abdul. A Sunni imam (religious leader) in Beirut who rescued Kamal from a gang of Shia bullies and gave him refuge in the mosque. He later introduced Kamal to extreme Islam and the Muslim Brotherhood.

Royer, Randall Todd. A communications expert and civil rights director of the Council on American Islamic Relations (CAIR). He was indicted in 2003 for terrorist activities in connection with the Virginia Jihad Network.

Sadat, Anwar. Third president of Egypt, serving from 1970 until his assassination in 1981. He succeeded Gamal Abdel Nasser and brought much political reform to Egypt.

Sadequee, Ehsanul Islam. Georgia Tech student who cased and video-taped the Capitol and World Bank for a terrorist organization in 2006.

Sadr, Musa as-. An Iranian-born Lebanese philosopher and prominent Shia religious leader who spent many years of his life in Lebanon as a religious and political leader.

Salam, Saeb. A Lebanese politician, who served as prime minister four times between 1952 and 1973. He was well connected with the Saudis and led one of the factions after Black Saturday (*See* Events).

Saleem, Amira. Kamal's oldest sister.

Saleem, Fouad. Kamal's oldest brother.

Saleem, Ibrahim. Kamal's older brother.

Saleem, Omer. Kamal's younger brother.

Saleem, Sayed Mohammed. Kamal's father.

Samana, Hammad Riaz. A permanent U.S. resident from Pakistan, he joined co-conspirators Levar Washington and Gregory Patterson and Kevin James to plan attacks on the National Guard, Los Angeles International Airport, two synagogues, and the Israeli consulate in Los Angeles.

Samra. The wife of Baath party office concierge Marwan. She was taken hostage by Kamal and his fellow terrorists in a raid against the Baath party headquarters.

Shafiq. Kamal's uncle.

Shoebat, Walid. One of the two Muslim men who traveled with Kamal on speaking engagements. The grandson of a Muslim chieftain, he became an advocate for Judaism after reading the Jewish Bible and was marked for death by the *jihadists*.

Siraj, Shahawar Martin. A Pakistani national in league with James Elshafay in a plot to bomb New York's Penn Station during the Republican National Convention in 2004.

Tahsein. One of two *fedayeen* who rode in the Zodiac with Kamal on the mission to Haifa.

Tawfiq, Abu. An imam (religious leader) Kamal met when he took refuge in the mosque in Beirut. Member of the Muslim Brotherhood.

Washington, Levar Haley. A U.S. national, he joined co-conspirators Gregory Patterson and Hammad Riaz Samana and Kevin James to plan attacks on the National Guard, Los Angeles International Airport, two synagogues, and the Israeli consulate in Los Angeles.

Yahya. A friend of Kamal's from the training camp. He was killed during an early mission.

Yassin, Sheikh Ahmed. An Islamic cleric from Gaza and the founder of Hamas, the Islamic Resistance Movement.

Yazid. The son of Syrian governor Mu'awiyah.

Yousef, Abu. Leader of the camp where Kamal was trained as a terrorist, and Kamal's main mentor in Fatah and the PLO.

Zachariah (or Zak). *See* Anani.

Places

Abu Dhabi. The capital and second most populous city in the UAE (United Arab Emirates) and the seat of government for the emirate of Abu Dhabi.

Aleppo (or Halab). One of the oldest inhabited cities in the world, located in northern Syria. The largest governorate in Syria, it serves as the capital of the Aleppo Governorate.

Avivim. An Israeli *moshav* (a type of cooperative agricultural community) located in far northern Israel in Upper Galilee less than 3,000 feet from the Lebanese border. Founded in 1958, it was abandoned soon after and resettled in 1963 by immigrants from North Africa— mostly Moroccan Jews.

Chad. Officially known as the Republic of Chad, a landlocked country in central Africa. Chad is bordered by Libya to the north, Sudan to the east, the Central African Republic to the south, Cameroon and, across Lake Chad, Nigeria to the southwest, and Niger to the west.

Dubai. One of the seven emirates in the UAE (United Arab Emirates).

Fort Dix. A U.S. Army installation and basic training center in New Jersey named for Major General John Adams Dix, a veteran of the War of 1812 and the Civil War.

Gaza Strip. A long, narrow coastal strip of land along the Mediterranean Sea, bordering Egypt on the southwest and Israel on the north and east. The approximately 1.4 million Gazan residents are Palestinian Arabs. The Gaza Strip is not recognized internationally as part of any sovereign country, but it is claimed by the Palestinian National Authority as part of the Palestinian territories.

Golan Heights. A strategic plateau and mountainous region at the southern end of the Anti-Lebanon Mountains. The geographic area lies within, or borders, the countries of Israel, Syria, Lebanon, and Jordan.

Green Line. The 1949 Armistice lines established between Israel and its neighbors (Egypt, Jordan, Lebanon, and Syria) after the 1948 Arab-Israel War. The Green Line separates Israel not only from these countries but also from the territories Israel captured during the 1967 Six-Day War (West Bank, Gaza Strip, Golan Heights, and Sinai Peninsula). Its name is derived from the green ink used to draw the line on the map during the talks.

Haifa. The largest city in northern Israel and the third largest in the country. Haifa has a mixed population of Jews and Arabs.

Hamra District. A shopping district in Beirut, Lebanon. It hosts a good number of hotels, furnished apartments, and coffee shops that cater to visitors and students from the American University of Beirut and the Lebanese American University located nearby.

Herat (or Aria). The third largest city in Afghanistan, located in the western province of Herat, a fertile area known for its wine production.

Kandahar (or Qandahar). The capital of Kandahar Province in southern Afghanistan, it is the country's second-largest city and the religious headquarters of the Taliban, an Islamic, fundamentalist movement.

Karantina. A strategically situated slum district in Beirut, Lebanon, controlled by forces from the PLO (Palestine Liberation Organization). It is inhabited mainly by Kurds and Armenians, along with some Lebanese and Palestinian Muslims.

Karbala. A city in Iraq considered by Shia Muslims to be one of the holiest cities in the world after Mecca, Medina, Jerusalem, and Najaf. Located southwest of Baghdad, it is best known for the battle of Karbala in October of the year 680.

Kuwait. A sovereign Arab emirate on the coast of the Persian Gulf enclosed by Saudi Arabia to the south and Iraq to the north and west. A constitutional monarchy with a parliamentary system of government. Kuwait City serves as its political and economic capital. The name is a diminutive of an Arabic word meaning "fortress built near water."

Marroush. A chain of Moroccan restaurants owned by Marouf Abouzaki. Primarily located in London, where it has eleven restaurants, it has expanded to Beirut, Lebanon, as the Beirut Express.

Masjid al-Bakar. A mosque in Beirut, Lebanon, located in the center of the populous Sunni Muslim territory.

Mogadishu. An important regional seaport located in the Benadir region of Somalia on the Indian Ocean. Since the collapse of Somalia's central government in 1991, Mogadishu has endured seventeen years of fighting between rival militias. It is considered one of the most dangerous and lawless cities in the world.

Nablus. A Palestinian city in the northern West Bank, about 39 miles north of Jerusalem. Located in a strategic area between Mount Ebal and Mount Gerizim, it is the capital of the Nablus Governorate and a Palestinian commercial and cultural center.

Niger. A landlocked country in western Africa, named for the Niger River. It is one of the poorest and least developed countries in the world. More than 80 percent of its territory is covered by the Sahara Desert.

Ribiana Sand Sea. Located in Africa's Libyan Desert, these dune fields, created by the wind, rise up to 110 meters and cover 25 percent of the Libyan Desert.

Riyadh. The capital and largest city in Saudi Arabia, it is also the capital of the Riyadh Province in the center of the Arabian Peninsula.

River Litani. An important waterway in southern Lebanon, rising west of Baalbek in the fertile Bekaa Valley and emptying into the Mediterranean Sea north of Tyre (one of Lebanon's largest cities). It is the longest river that originates and flows entirely within the borders of Lebanon.

Raouché. A residential and commercial area located at Beirut's westernmost tip, known for its upscale apartment buildings, restaurants, and seaside sidewalk. Just off the coast of Raouché is a natural landmark called the Pigeons' Rock, two massive rock formations that stand like silent sentinels. The name derives either from the Aramaic word *rosh*, meaning head, or the French word *roche* (*rocher*), meaning rock.

Sabra-Shatila. The site of a 1982 massacre carried out by the Lebanese Forces militia group. It is alleged that Israeli Defense Forces allowed Lebanese Christian Phalangist militiamen to enter two Palestinian refugee camps, where they massacred civilians.

Sahara Desert. The world's largest hot desert. The Sahara covers most of northern Africa, an area stretching from the Red Sea and including parts of the Mediterranean coasts, to the outskirts of the Atlantic Ocean.

Sidon. A city located in the South Governorate of Lebanon on the Mediterranean coast, about 25 miles south of the capital. Its inhabitants are primarily Muslim (both Sunni and Shiite), Greek Catholic, and Maronite Christians. The name means "fishery."

Souq al Motaa (or Souk Shramit). A notorious area in downtown Beirut, known as the "Market of Whores."

Syria. An Arab country in southwest Asia, which borders Lebanon and the Mediterranean Sea to the west, Israel to the southwest, Jordan to the south, Iraq to the east, and Turkey to the north.

Tartuse. A Syrian port city.

Tripoli. The capital and largest city in Libya, located in the northwest part of the country on the edge of the Sahara Desert on a point of rocky land projecting into the Mediterranean Sea and forming a bay. The name means "three cities."

Turbat. A town situated on the left bank of the Kech River, a tributary of the Dasht River, southwest of the Balochistan Province in Pakistan.

U.A.E. (United Arab Emirates). A constitutional federation of seven emirates, it was formally established in 1971. UAE is located on the southeastern end of the Arabian Peninsula and is governed by a confederate of absolute monarchies. UAE is funded by MB Petroleum Services, a multinational drilling and well-services corporation.

Valley of the Jews (or Wadi Abu Jamil). A district in the heart of Beirut, Lebanon, which once had the largest Jewish population in

Lebanon, known for money-brokering and the establishment of banks. Most of the Jewish residents left after the onset of the war in Lebanon.

Verdan Street. A shopping district in Beirut, Lebanon.

Zaidaniah District. A district of Beirut, Lebanon, located in the Aisha Bakkar area.

Groups

Al-Assifah. The mainstream armed wing of the Palestinian party and militant group Fatah. It was established in 1964 to protect the political wing of Fatah from reprisals.

Al-Ikhwan. *See* Muslim Brotherhood.

Al-morabitun (or al-moravids). A dynasty of Berbers (the indigenous peoples of North Africa west of the Nile Valley). The al-Moravids were founded by Yusuf Ibn Tashfin in the Sahara and preached a strict respect for Koranic instruction. In Arabic, the group's name means "brotherhood of warrior monks."

Al Muhajiroun. Thought by many to be the most extreme Islamist group operating in the West, Al-Muhajiroun, which is Arabic for "the emigrants," was established in 1996 and based in England. Because the group was banned in England, it may be operating as The Savior Sect.

al-Qaida (or al-Qaeda). An international Sunni Islamist movement founded in 1988. Under the leadership of Osama bin Laden, the group seeks to replace Western-influenced governments with Islamic regimes under the rule of Islamic law. In Arabic, the group's name literally means "database," referring to the computer file of thousands of *mujahadeen* (various loosely aligned Afghan opposition groups) who were recruited and trained with help from the CIA to defeat the Russians.

Amnesty International. A human-rights organization founded in 1961 by Englishman Peter Benenson. It campaigns internationally against the detention of prisoners of conscience, for the fair trial of political prisoners, to abolish the death penalty and torture of prisoners, and to end extrajudicial executions and disappearances throughout the world.

Baathist. A member of the Arab Socialist Ba'th Party (also spelled Baath or Ba'ath), founded in the 1940s in Damascus. It is the original secular Arab nationalist movement intended to combat Western colonial rule. In Arabic, *ba'ath* means renaissance or resurrection.

Bedouin. The primarily nomadic Arab peoples of the Middle East. They form about 10 percent of the population and are of the same Semitic stock as their sedentary neighbors (the fellahin), with whom they share a devout belief in Islam and a distrust of any but their own local traditions and way of life.

Black September. A militant Palestinian group, Black September is infamous for the kidnap and murder of eleven Israeli athletes and officials and a German police officer during the 1972 Olympic Games in Munich, Germany. The name is taken from a conflict that occurred on September 16, 1970, in Jordan. The *fedayeen* had attempted to seize power from King Hussein which caused him to declare military rule. Thousands of Palestinians were killed or expelled as a result.

CAIR (Council on American-Islamic Relations). A civil liberties and advocacy group for Muslims in North America created in June 1994. Its professed goals are to enhance understanding of Islam, promote justice, and empower American Muslims.

Fatah. The Movement for the National Liberation of Palestine, this organization was founded in the 1960s by Yasser Arafat and is the largest faction of the Palestine Liberation Organization (PLO), which is a multi-party confederation.

Gaza Baptist Church AWANA group. In the Gaza Strip's only evangelical church, planted about fifty years ago by Southern Baptist missionaries, almost all AWANA (an organization that helps churches and parents worldwide to teach children Christian service) members are Greek Orthodox or Roman Catholic and continue to successfully reach their parents, friends, and neighbors with the gospel.

Hamas. An Arabic acronym for the Islamic Resistance Movement, a Palestinian Islamic fundamentalist organization founded in 1987. It seeks to establish an Islamic state in Israel, the West Bank, and the Gaza Strip.

Hezb-e-Islamie-i-Gulbuddin. One of the major *mujahadeen* (loosely aligned Afghan opposition groups) in the war against the Soviets. The group, founded in 1974 to fight the government of Mohammed Daoud Khan (the first president of Afghanistan), has long-standing ties to Osama bin Laden. The group has staged small attacks in its attempt to force U.S. troops to withdraw from Afghanistan, overthrow the Afghan Transitional Administration, and establish a fundamentalist state.

Islamic Thinkers Society. A Muslim group based in New York City that seeks to restore the Islamic Caliphate (the rulership of Islam) and create "an ideal Islamic society."

Islamic Union for the Liberation of Afghanistan. A political party in Afghanistan led by Abdul Rasul Sayyaf. Founded in the late 1970s, it was originally an attempt to bring unity among Islamist opposition forces in Afghanistan. The new umbrella organization, however, effectively created a split and IULA became a political party of its own.

Israeli Defense Force (IDF). Israel's military forces (ground, air, and navy), the IDF is commonly known in Israel as the *tzahal.*

Jamiat-i-Islami. One of the original Islamist parties in Afghanistan established in the 1970s by students at Kabul University. Its leader, Burhanuddin Rabbani, was a lecturer for the Islamic Law Faculty.

Kataeb. A Lebanese political party founded in 1936 as a national movement to secure Lebanon's independence and advance the social rights of the Lebanese. Officially a secular group, it is primarily supported by Maronite Christians. The name is an Arabic translation of the Greek word *phalanx* or *battalion.*

Lebanese Army. The military forces of the Republic of Lebanon. They are aligned with the Phalangist Maronite Christians.

Maronite Christians. A Christian denomination found mainly in Lebanon. It is currently the largest Christian community in the country. Inside the denomination, religion and politics are inextricably mixed, explaining why the group has played a central role in Lebanon's frequent struggles over political power.

MAYA (Muslim Arab Youth Association). Until it became inactive in early 2004, MAYA was listed on various Islamic reference websites as an organization set up to sponsor Muslim youth conferences and matrimonial services. In the aftermath of 9/11, the U.S. government placed MAYA on its list of the many organizations to be investigated as to whether they "finance terrorism and perpetuate violence." MAYA was established in the 1970s and incorporated in Plainfield, Indiana, in 1989.

Mossad. Headquartered in Tel Aviv, the Mossad, which is Hebrew for *institute,* is responsible for human intelligence collection, covert action, and counterterrorism, as well as the clandestine movement of Jewish refugees out of Syria, Iran, and Ethiopia.

MSA (Muslim Students' Association or Muslim Student Union, also known as MSA National). A religious organization dedicated to establishing and maintaining Islamic societies on college campuses in Canada and the United States. Established in 1963, it was the precursor of the Islamic Society of North America and several other Islamic organizations.

mujahadeen. A military force of Muslim guerrilla warriors engaged in a *jihad.* The CIA secretly sent billions of dollars of military aid to the *mujahadeen* in Afghanistan in a United States-supported *jihad* against the Soviet Union.

Muslim Brotherhood. Muslim Brotherhood organization established in Egypt in 1928 for the purpose of spreading the principal Islamic idea that Islam is "creed and state, book and sword, and a way of life." Its first leader, Hassan Al-Banna, purposed to give the organization strong internal rules so that it could carry on independent of any particular leader. It now has branches in more than seventy countries around the world.

Nasseriyeen. A group of fighters loyal to former Egyptian president and PLO (Palestinian Liberation Organization) cofounder Gamal Abdel Nasser.

Nuristani tribes. Located mostly in Laghman Province and the Nurestan Province of Afghanistan, the Nuristanis are Muslims whose ancestors practiced an ancient Indo-European polytheistic religion until they were forcibly converted to Islam around the year 1895. The Nuristanis were the first citizens in Afghanistan to successfully revolt against the communist overthrow of their government in 1978.

Pashtuns. The Sunni tribe of Afghanistan, which forms the dominant ethnic and linguistic community. It accounts for just over half the population.

PFLP (Popular Front for the Liberation of Palestine). A violent Marxist faction within the Palestinian national movement. The group conducted a series of plane hijackings for ransom and political extortion during the 1970s.

People's Democratic Party of Afghanistan. A communist party founded in 1965. In 1978, the PDPA overthrew the government of Mohammed Daoud Khan in the so-called Saur Revolution and founded the Democratic Republic of Afghanistan. During its years of governance (1978–1992), Soviet troops combated insurgent groups in the country.

Phalangist Party. Led by Maronite Christians, the Phalangist party is primarily pro-Western and opposes pan-Arabism.

Saudis. Citizens of the Kingdom of Saudi Arabia (KSA), the largest country on the Arabian Peninsula. The Saudis remain the world's leading source of money for al-Qaeda and other extremist networks and has failed to take key steps requested by United States officials to stem the flow.

Shia. The second largest denomination of Islam. Though a minority in the Muslim world, Shias make up the majority of the population of Iran and Iraq.

Sunni. Sunni Islam is the largest denomination of Islam. The word *Sunni* comes from the word *Sunnah*, which means the words and actions of the prophet Muhammad.

Syrians. Citizens of the Syrian Arab Republic in southwest Asia. The population is primarily Muslim but with a significant Christian minority.

Taliban. A Sunni Islamic group that ruled Afghanistan from 1996–2001, when it was removed from power by the Northern Alliance and NATO forces. The group re-formed in 2004 as an insurgency movement and has been staging a protracted guerrilla war against the current government. Literally translated, *Taliban*, also anglicized as *Taleban*, means "students."

Wahhabi Muslims. Saudi Arabia's dominant faith for more than two centuries, Wahhabism is an austere form of Islam that insists on a literal interpretation of the Qur'an. Strict Wahhabis believe that all those who don't practice their form of Islam are heathens and enemies. Critics say that Wahhabism's rigidity has led it to misinterpret and distort Islam, pointing to extremists such as Osama bin Laden and the Taliban.

Zionists. An international political movement that originally supported the reestablishment of a homeland for the Jewish people in Palestine, it now provides support for the modern state of Israel.

Events

1967, June. *The Six-Day War.* Also known as the 1967 Arab-Israeli War, the Third Arab-Israeli War, Six Days' War, an-Naksah (The Setback), or the June War. It was fought between Israel and Arab neighbors Egypt, Jordan, and Syria. The nations of Iraq, Saudi Arabia, Sudan, Tunisia, Morocco, and Algeria also contributed troops and arms to the Arab forces. At the war's end, Israel had gained control of the Sinai Peninsula, the Gaza Strip, the West Bank, East Jerusalem, and the Golan Heights, affecting the geopolitics of the region to this day.

1969, November. *Signing of the Cairo Agreement.* During talks brokered by Egyptian President Gamal Abdel Nasser, PLO (Palestinian Liberation Army) leader Yasser Arafat and General Emile Bustani of the Lebanese Army reach an agreement, establishing principles under which the presence and activities of Palestinian guerrillas in southeast Lebanon will be tolerated and regulated by the Lebanese authorities.

1972, May. *Hijacking at Lod Airport in Tel Aviv.* Five gunmen belonging to the Black September Organization of Palestine guerrillas (a splinter group of the PLO) hijack a Sabena aircraft at Lod airport in Tel

Aviv. Twelve Israeli soldiers disguised as maintenance staff storm the plane and release the one hundred people on board.

1972, September. *The Munich Massacre.* During the Summer Olympics in Munich, West Germany, eleven members of the Israeli Olympic Team are taken hostage and eventually murdered by members of the Black September Organization of Palestine.

1973, March. *The Khartoum Assassinations.* Members of the Black September Organization of Palestine kidnap and assassinate three Western diplomats in the Saudi Embassy in Khartoum, the capital city of Sudan.

1973, May. *The Omagh Car Bombing.* Five British soldiers are killed by a car bomb planted by the IRA (Irish Republican Army) at Knockna-Moe Castle Hotel in Omagh, Ireland.

1973, September. *Hijacking of Jewish Immigrants.* Three Jewish immigrants from Russia are taken hostage by Arab terrorists aboard a train bound for Vienna, Austria. They are later released after the Austrian government agrees to close a transit camp for Russian immigrants en route to Israel.

1974, October. *The Guildford Pub Bombing.* Five people are killed and sixty-five seriously injured by bombs planted by the IRA at the Horse and Groom and Seven Stars Pubs (both popular with military personnel) in Guildford, UK.

1975, December. *Palestinian Refugees Killed.* In retaliation for an earlier attack on Maronite leader Pierre Gemayel, Maronite Christians, members of the Lebanese Phalange militia, ambush a bus carrying Palestinian refugees. Thirty Palestinians are killed.

1975, December. *Black Saturday.* A series of massacres and armed clashes in Beirut kill as many as one thousand people and spark a Lebanese Civil War.

1975–1990. *Lebanese Civil War.*

1987, December. *The First Intifada.* A collective Palestinian popular uprising erupts against Israel in the West Bank and Gaza, now known as the *Intifada* or "shaking off."

2001, October. *United States Invasion of Afghanistan.* In response to the terrorist events of 9/11, the United States invaded Afghanistan with the stated purpose of capturing Osama bin Laden, destroying al-Qaeda, and removing the Taliban.

2003, May. *Riyadh Bombing.* Twenty-six people are killed at American expatriate housing in Riyadh. The Arab press reports bomb attacks targeting American, Jewish, and Belgian interests in Riyadh and Casablanca.

2003, October. *U.S. Convoy Bombing in Gaza.* Three American security guards traveling in a U.S. convoy in the Gaza Strip are killed by a bomb detonated by Palestinian terrorists.

2004, November. *Van Gogh Murder.* Theo van Gogh, descendant of the brother of Vincent van Gogh, is murdered by a Muslim extremist after making a film condemning violence against women in Islamic societies.

2004, August. *Attempted Bombing at New York's Penn Station.* A plan to bomb New York's Penn Station during the Republican National Convention is foiled by police and military personnel during a random search.

2007, October. *Palestinian Christian Bookstore Owner Murdered.* The Palestinian Baptist manager of a well-known Christian bookstore in Gaza City is kidnapped and murdered by Islamic gunmen for spreading Christianity.

2008, July. *Murder of Christian Convert.* Twenty-eight-year-old Sayid Ali Sheik Luqman Hussein converts from Islam to Christianity and begins to actively evangelize in the community in which he is working as a teacher. On July 8, near Mogadishu, Somalia, he is gunned down by two Muslim men.

Foreign Words and Weapons

155 mm shell. Standard explosive projectile used by the U.S. Army and Marines.

abbayah (or abayah). A long, robe-like garment with a hood that covers from head to toe except for the eyes. Muslim women often wear a traditional dress, casual clothes, or even a business suit underneath.

abu. An Arabic word literally meaning "father of." The father automatically takes the name of the oldest son prefaced with *abu*. If the oldest son is Mike, the father becomes "*Abu* Mike" or "Father of Mike."

Adha (*or* Eid al-Adha). Known as the Feast of Sacrifice, Adha is the most important feast of the Muslim calendar and concludes the pilgrimage to Mecca. The celebration lasts for three days and commemorates Ibraham's (Abraham's) willingness to sacrifice his son in obedience to God. Muslims believe the story is about Ishmael rather than Isaac.

AK–47. A clip-fed, gas-operated, 7.62 mm assault rifle of Soviet design, used throughout the world by armed forces and paramilitary organizations.

al ashat (or Isha). The fifth of the five daily prayers recited by Muslims. It is also called the evening prayer.

al shayeed (or shaheed). Muslims who die in a legitimate struggle with the sword or Islamic holy war are considered *shaheed* or martyrs. The word literally means "witness."

Al-Toquah (or Al-Taqiyah). Refers to a Muslim military doctrine, which advocates the use of deception to infiltrate the enemy and spread internal strife (working undercover).

al wodoug. An area of a mosque where worshippers cleanse themselves before prayers.

al wudu. The Islamic act of washing parts of the body with water in preparation for ritual prayers and the handling of the Qur'an. *Wudu* often refers to "partial ablution" while *ghusl* refers to full ablution.

Allahu akbar. The *takbīr* or *takbeer* is the act of saying the phrase Allāhu akbar, which translated as "God is great." The expression is used as both an informal expression of faith and a formal declaration or exclamation.

al-mani. A term Lebanese Muslim Sunnis use to refer to an unbeliever.

amin. The Islamic and Arabic word for "amen."

Ashura. Meaning "tenth" in Arabic, the Day of Ashura is the tenth day of Muharram, an Islamic day of mourning for the martyrdom of Husayn ibn Ali, the grandson of Muhammad on A.D. October 10, 680.

balaclava. A form of headgear covering the whole head, exposing only the face and often only the eyes; also known as a "balaclava helmet" and "ski mask."

Bata. Chain of shoe stores.

Beluchi (or Belochi). A western Iranian language closely related to Kurdish.

C-4 (or Composition C-4). A common variety of military plastic explosive.

cadeau (or cadout). Borrowed from the French, *cadeau* means "gift, present or treat."

calipha (or caliph). Used as a title, *calipha* refers to a successor to Muhammad as temporal and spiritual head of Islam.

caliphate. The office or dominion of a caliph.

corniche. Borrowed from the French, a corniche is a road built along a coast and especially along the face of a cliff.

dish-dash. Typically worn by men in the Arabian Peninsula and surrounding countries, this is an ankle-length garment, usually with long sleeves, similar to a robe. It is most often made of cotton for warmer climates and wool for cooler climates.

Dushka (or DShK). A Soviet heavy anti-aircraft machine gun, frequently deployed with a two-wheeled mounting and a single-sheet armor-plate shield.

em. The equivalent of the male term *abu*, this is an Arabic word literally meaning "mother of." The mother automatically takes the name of the oldest son prefaced with *em*. If the oldest son is Mike, the mother becomes "Em Mike" or "Mother of Mike."

Enta majnoon. An Arabic term meaning "you are crazy." *Enta* means "you" and *majnoon* means "crazy."

fatire (or fatayer). Small triangular spinach pies.

fatwa. A religious opinion on Islamic law issued by an Islamic scholar.

fedayeen. Several distinct, militant groups and individuals in Armenia, Lebanon, Iran, and the Arab world. The term means "freedom fighters."

fez. A red felt hat in the shape of a truncated cone. The *fez* is of Turkish origin.

fida'i. A single soldier in the *fedayeen*.

hadith. Oral traditions relating to the words and deeds of the prophet Muhammad.

hijab. The Arabic word for "cover." In most Arabic-speaking and Western countries, the common meaning is "modest dress for women." Most Islamic legal systems define modest as covering everything in public except the face and hands.

Hind helicopters. The Russian Mil Mi-24 Hind is the helicopter most identified with the war in Afghanistan.

hudna (or hudibiyya, khudaibiya). An Arabic word often translated as "cease-fire." Historically used as a tactic aimed at allowing the party declaring the *hudna* to regroup while tricking an enemy into lowering its guard.

hūrīyah (or hur). Arabic word used to refer to a "pure virgin being" or "pure companions" of paradise to be awarded to Muslims who die for the sake of the Islamic *jihad.*

imam. In Islam, a recognized leader or religious teacher.

Jabal Sunnin (*or* Jabal Sannine). Also known as Mount Lebanon, near Beirut.

jannah. A place of eternal bliss in the afterlife for believing Muslims.

jezyah (or jizyah). A nominal annual protection tax levied on non-Muslims under the protection of Muslim rule. It is one dinar (about four grams of gold) per person per year. The elderly, women, children, and the poor are exempt.

jihad. Holy war or any combat for the sake of Allah.

jinn (also djinn). The equivalent of a genie, in Islam they are believed to be unseen supernatural creatures that possess free will and inhabit the earth along with mankind. They can be both good and evil, but are most often associated with ghosts or demons. According to pre-Islamic Arabian folklore, jinn were created by Allah. The iconic genie or jinn is Iblis or Satan.

Kalashnikovs. *See* AK–47.

kanafa. A pastry made with shredded wheat and walnuts and covered with a cold lemon sauce.

Katyusha. A type of Russian rocket launcher originally built and used in the field during World War II.

keffiyeh (also keffiyah). An Arab headdress consisting of a square of cloth folded to form a triangle and held on by a cord.

khefir. The Arabic word for "infidel."

khefir kabier. This term refers to the ultimate infidel, *khefir* meaning "infidel" and *kabier* meaning "great, large, or big."

Koran (also sometimes transliterated as Qur'an, Al-Coran or Al-Qur'ān) The central religious text of Islam. Muslims believe the Koran to be the book of divine guidance and direction for mankind, dictated by God to Muhammad, and consider the original Arabic text to be the final revelation of God.

kursi. An Arabic word meaning "chair." It refers specifically to a unique chair in the mosque on which the Koran is placed when it is being read.

lamajoun. Baked Armenian thin-crust pizza made with ground lamb, onions, tomatoes, peppers, and spices.

Ma sha'a allah (or mashalla). A common Muslim declaration meaning "until the time the God wants, forever."

madrassa *(or* madrasah, madrash, medresa, madreseh, or madressa) The Arabic word for school, most often used to refer to an Islamic religious school.

Mafia. A group of criminals (*mafiosi*) organized into so-called families and operating in many parts of the world.

Makarov PM. A 9x18mm semi-automatic pistol designed in the late 1940s by Russian Nikolai Fyodorovich Makarov. This was the standard pistol used by military and police in Russia until the end of the twentieth century. Large numbers of these firearms are still in use in Russia.

manara. The Arabic word for "lighthouse."

Masjid al Bakar. *Masjid* is the Arabic word for "mosque." *Al Bakar* refers to the specific mosque being mentioned.

MiG-29 (or Mikoyan MiG-29). A fourth-generation, Russian-built, jet fighter aircraft developed in the 1970s. It has been used by the Russian Air Force, as well as many other nations, since it entered service in 1983.

mufti. An Islamic scholar who is an interpreter or expounder of Shari'ah or Islamic law. A *muftiat* or *diyanet* is a council of *muftis*.

mukhtar. The head of a village or neighborhood in many Arab countries. The word means "chosen" in Arabic and refers to the fact that *mukhtars* are often chosen in some type of election.

mullah. A Muslim schooled in Islamic theology and sacred law. The title is derived from the Arabic word *mawla*, which means "vicar" or "guardian." In large parts of the Muslim world it is simply the title given to local clerics and mosque leaders.

muttarafeen. Radical Muslims.

niqab. A veil covering the face. It was worn by some Muslim women starting at puberty. The terms *niqab* and *burqa* are often used interchangeably.

nuniah. An Arabic/Lebanese word for potty chair or potty trainer.

Quad .50. An anti-aircraft artillery gun.

qurush. The *riyal* is the basic monetary unit in Saudi Arabia. Twenty *qurush* equal one riyal.

Ramadan. The ninth month of the Muslim year, during which all Muslims must fast during the daylight hours. Indulgence of any sort is forbidden during the fast. Only soldiers, the sick, and the young are exempt. Because of the purely lunar calendar, Ramadan falls in different seasons.

RPG-7. A shoulder-fired, muzzle-loaded, recoilless antitank and antipersonnel rocket-propelled grenade launcher that launches fin-stabilized, oversized rocket-assisted heat grenades.

SA-7 or SAM (or Surface to Air Missile). The SA-7 is a Soviet-built, shoulder-launched, surface-to-air missile developed in 1959 and first used in combat in 1968. The SA-7 is intended to force low-flying enemy aircraft into higher altitudes where they can be detected by radar.

sajada. The Arabic word for "a prayer rug."

salat. The five daily Muslim prayers.

Schweizerische Industrie Gesellschaft (SIG), German for "Swiss Industrial Company" produced one of the finest semi-automatic pistols—the SIG 210 series. However, the pistol was not affordable until SIG entered a business collaboration with the German gunmaker J. P. Sauer & Sons, creating the SIG SAUER line of handguns in the 1970s.

Seminov. A 7.52mm semi-automatic rifle.

serviz. A chauffeur-driven shuttle.

shahada. The Muslim declaration of belief in the oneness of God and the acceptance of Muhammad as his prophet.

Sharia (or Shariah). The body of Islamic religious law. The term means "way" or "path."

sharmouta. A loose woman or a prostitute.

Sheikh Ahmed Yassin. The co-founder with Abdel Aziz al-Rantissi of Hamas, a Palestinian paramilitary organization and political party. Yassin served as the spiritual leader of the organization, which has been characterized by many western nations as terrorist in nature.

sheikh (also sheik, cheikh, shaikh). An Arabic term literally meaning "elder," and used to designate an elder of a tribe, a lord, a revered wise man, or an Islamic scholar. The term usually refers to a man, but in a few cases a woman.

shiska. A hamburger cooked with mint and red onion and served in pita bread.

Sikhoi. A Russian bomber.

souk (also sook, souq, or suq). A commercial quarter in an Arab or Berber city. The term is often used to designate the market in any Arabized or Muslim city.

sunnah. In Sunni Islam, those religious achievements that were instituted by the Prophet Muhammad during the twenty-three years of his ministry. The word literally means "trodden path," and therefore the sunna of the Prophet means, "the way and the manners of the prophet."

sura. A term commonly used to mean a chapter of the Koran. The Arabic word literally means "something enclosed or surrounded by a fence or wall."

Sura al Anfal. The eighth chapter of the Koran. In Arabic, it literally means "the spoils of war."

Tanakh (also Tanach, Tenakh, or Tenak). The Bible used in Judaism. The elements of the Tanakh are incorporated in various forms in Christian Bibles, in which, with some variations, it is called the Old Testament.

Tesat (or besat). A rug that is homemade, using old cloth no longer needed by the family.

Umma. One Muslim nation. The Arabic word *umm* means "mother," and from that is derived "mother nation."

yah habebe. *Yah* in Arabic is always followed by a descriptive word. *Habibi* is an Arabic word that translates "my baby" or "my darling" or "my love" or "my boy."

yah ibny (or yah waldie). An Arabic term of endearment meaning "my son."

Notes

1. "Egypt Makes Muslim Brotherhood Arrests," Associated Press Online, August 23, 2007.
2. Steven Emerson, *American Jihad* (New York: The Free Press, 2003), 172.
3. Ibid.
4. Emerson, *American Jihad*, Appendix A.
5. Joseph Abrams, "List of Thwarted Terror Attacks Since Sept. 11." Fox News. Online at; http://www.foxnews.com/printer_friendly_story/0,3566,335500,00.html]
6. Hanan Greenberg, "IDF arrests Palestinian boy carrying explosives," August 30, 2007. Online at: http://www.ynetnews.com/articles/0.7340.L-3443790.00.html.
7. Yaakov Lappin, "Egypt primes children for jihad," July 5, 2006. Online at: http://www.ynetnews.com/articles/0,7340,L-3271274,00.html.
8. "The Military Use of Children." Online at: http://en.wikipedia.org/wiki/Military_use_of_children#Middle_East:_Palestine.
9. John Burns, "Palestinian Summer Camp Offers the Games of War," *New York Times,* Aug. 3, 2000.
10. Howard M. Sachar, *A History of Israel: From the Rise of Zionism to Our Time* (New York: 1976), 660.

11. Adnan Mijad, "Pleasantly surprised by 'Three Ex-Terrorists' event," *The Stanford Daily*, April 18, 2007.

12. Amnesty International, "Violence against women in Pakistan." Online at http://www.amnesty.org/en/library/asset/ASA33/010/2002/en/dom-ASA330102002en.html.

13. Austin Fenner and Hasani Gittens, " 'Honor' killing for God—Dad's 'sick confession,' " *New York Post*, August 6, 2008, p. 15.

14. Pam Zubeck, "Factious choice in public speakers," *The Gazette*, February 5, 2008.

15. Neil MacFarquhar, "Speakers at Academy said to make false claims," *New York Times*, February 7, 2008.

16. Steven Emerson, "Paper of CAIR," National Review Online, February 8, 2007. Online at http://www.investigativeproject.org/article/600.Notes

17. "Islamic Charity Convicted in Retrial," Facts on File World News Digest, December 23, 2008.

Acknowledgments

It is with great shame that I acknowledge my terrible past.

But it is with great joy that I acknowledge those who brought me out of it and those who made this book possible:

My Lord Jesus—whose unconditional love completely disarmed the hate that guns and bombs could not.

My best friend and wife, Victoria, and my children and grandchildren, who stood with me. I love you more than you'll ever know.

My literary agent, Lee Hough, who listened, believed, and championed my story through every stage. My trust is sacred; you've earned it, friend.

My cowriter, Lynn Vincent, was simply incredible. Your tireless efforts at interviewing and your wordsmithing were a godsend. We both got a little bloody accomplishing this mission. You know what I mean. But you never quit. Victoria and I cannot thank you enough.

My editor, Philis Boultinghouse, who caught the vision when no else did and worked tirelessly with more than just expertise—but also with love.

And this book would not have come about without all the hours and hours invested in me by my pastor, Mark C.

Finally, I must acknowledge the love and support of our close friends—they kept me, my family, Lee, Lynn, and the publisher in constant prayer as we all worked together. They pray even now, dear reader, for you.

I humbly thank you all.